Fashion Buying and Merchandising

T0384023

Fashion buying and merchandising has changed dramatically over the last 20 years. Aspects such as the advent of new technologies and the changing nature of the industry into one that is faster paced than ever before, as well as the shift towards more ethical and sustainable practices have resulted in a dramatic change of the roles. As a result, contemporary fast fashion retailers do not follow the traditional buying cycle processes step by step, critical paths are wildly different, and there has been a huge increase in 'in-season buying' as a response to heightened consumer demand.

This textbook is a comprehensive guide to 21st-century fashion buying and merchandising, considering fast fashion, sustainability, ethical issues, omnichannel retailing, and computer-aided design. It presents an up-to-date buying cycle that reflects key aspects of fashion buying and merchandising, as well as in-depth explanations of fashion product development, trend translation, and sourcing. It applies theoretical and strategic business models to buying and merchandising that have traditionally been used in marketing and management.

This book is ideal for all fashion buying and merchandising students, specifically second- and final-year undergraduate as well as MA/MSc fashion students. It will also be useful to academics and practitioners who wish to gain a greater understanding of the industry today.

Rosy Boardman is a Lecturer in Fashion Business at the University of Manchester, teaching on both the Fashion Buying & Merchandising and Fashion Marketing programmes. Her research focuses on digital strategy and innovation in the retail industry. Rosy worked as both a fashion buyer and marketing assistant prior to her career as a lecturer.

Rachel Parker-Strak is Academic Lead and a Lecturer in Fashion Buying & Merchandising at the University of Manchester. Her teaching and research focus on fashion product development and buying and merchandising. Prior to joining academia, Rachel's industry career was in product development positions for a UK-based womenswear brand.

Claudia E. Henninger is a Lecturer in Fashion Marketing & Management at the University of Manchester with a research interest in sustainable fashion and the circular economy. Her research is published in internationally renowned journals.

Mastering Fashion Management

The fashion industry is dynamic, constantly evolving and worth billions worldwide: it is no wonder that Fashion Business Management has come to occupy a central position within the business school globally. This series meets the need for rigorous yet practical and accessible textbooks that cover the full spectrum of the fashion industry and its management.

Collectively, *Mastering Fashion Management* is a valuable resource for advanced undergraduate and postgraduate students of Fashion Management, helping them gain an in-depth understanding of contemporary concepts and the realities of practice across the entire fashion chain – from design development and product sourcing to buying and merchandising, sustainability, and sales and marketing. Individually, each text provides essential reading for a core topic. A range of consistent pedagogical features are used throughout the texts, including international case studies, highlighting the practical importance of theoretical concepts.

Postgraduate students studying for a Master's in Fashion Management in particular will find each text invaluable reading, providing the knowledge and tools to approach a future career in fashion with confidence.

Fashion Buying and Merchandising
The Fashion Buyer in a Digital Society
Rosy Boardman, Rachel Parker-Strak and Claudia E. Henninger

For more information about the series, please visit www.routledge.com/Mastering-Fashion-Management/book-series/FM.

Fashion Buying and Merchandising

The Fashion Buyer in a Digital Society

Rosy Boardman, Rachel Parker-Strak and Claudia E. Henninger

Routledge
Taylor & Francis Group

LONDON AND NEW YORK

First published 2020
by Routledge
2 Park Square, Milton Park, Abingdon, Oxon OX14 4RN

and by Routledge
52 Vanderbilt Avenue, New York, NY 10017

Routledge is an imprint of the Taylor & Francis Group, an informa business

©2020 Rosy Boardman, Rachel Parker-Strak and Claudia E. Henninger

British Library Cataloguing-in-Publication Data
A catalogue record for this book is available from the British Library

Library of Congress Cataloging-in-Publication Data
Names: Boardman, Rosy, author. | Parker-Strak, Rachel, 1978- author. |
    Henninger, Claudia E., 1985- author.
Title: Fashion buying and merchandising: the fashion buyer in a digital
    society / Rosy Boardman, Rachel Parker-Strak and Claudia E. Henninger.
Description: New York : Routledge, 2020. | Series: Mastering fashion
    management | Includes bibliographical references and index.
Identifiers: LCCN 2019059187 (print) | LCCN 2019059188 (ebook) |
    ISBN 9781138616318 (hardback) | ISBN 9781138616325 (paperback) |
    ISBN 9780429462207 (ebook)
Subjects: LCSH: Fashion merchandising. | Clothing trade. | Purchasing. |
    Internet marketing. | Consumer satisfaction.
Classification: LCC HD9940.A2 B63 2020 (print) | LCC HD9940.A2
    (ebook) | DDC 746.9/20688—dc23
LC record available at https://lccn.loc.gov/2019059187
LC ebook record available at https://lccn.loc.gov/2019059188

ISBN: 978-1-138-61631-8 (hbk)
ISBN: 978-1-138-61632-5 (pbk)
ISBN: 978-0-429-46220-7 (ebk)

Typeset in ITC Giovanni Std
by Swales & Willis Exeter, Devon, UK

Contents

Figures

CHAPTER 1

The evolution of fashion buying and merchandising

Introduction

Fashion buying and merchandising has changed dramatically over the last 30 years, resulting in an evolution in roles and responsibilities for people working in this industry. The advent of the internet and new technologies, coupled with the new concept of fast fashion (and now super-fast fashion!), plus the reactive shift towards more sustainable and ethical practices has resulted in a fast-paced and ever-changing industry that buyers and merchandisers have had to adapt to. The primary aim of this book is to explain, analyse, and discuss the roles and responsibilities of fashion buyers and merchandisers in the 21st century. With such monumental changes occurring in the industry, there is a paucity of work detailing how these roles have evolved and what careers in these areas look like today. After working in the industry and lecturing in fashion business, buying and merchandising and sustainability for a number of years we felt compelled to write this book in order to update the current literature based on our experience and insights from our own academic research. Building on previous bodies of work that have provided a valuable and detailed insight into buying and merchandising from the early 2000s–2010s, our contribution to the literature resides in the additional analysis and discussions of new issues and developments, such as technology, sustainability, and the changing nature of sourcing, and how buying and merchandising has evolved as a result. Furthermore, this book brings together aspects that have not previously been detailed in the literature, such as in-depth explanations of fashion product development and trend translation.

Overall, this book has been written in order to provide an insight into fashion buying and merchandising today in order to help prepare people for their career in these areas and for students and academics who wish to gain a greater understanding in these areas. As such, we envision this book to be helpful for students, academics, and practitioners. It covers three main themes interwoven throughout: the digital transformation of buying and merchandising, (super-)fast fashion and the need for speed, and the rise in importance of sustainability and ethical issues as a consequence.

This chapter focuses on providing a brief introduction of the evolution of buying and merchandising and defining key terms. It outlines the challenges that are faced in the industry and how the 21st century provides exciting opportunities for the buyer and merchandiser in terms of utilising 'channel' strategies to their advantage.

After reading this chapter, you should be able to:

- Discuss the '7Rs' (Figure 1.1) that form a crucial part within the role of the buyer and merchandiser;
- Outline key changes in the fashion environment in terms of
  - Seasonality;

- Sales channel transformation;
- Internationalisation.

The evolution of fashion buying and merchandising

Fashion buying and merchandising roles will vary from company to company depending on the type of retailer that it is (e.g. luxury, fast fashion) and the specific processes and systems that it has in place. Nevertheless, the principal roles and their objectives are broadly the same throughout the industry. Thus, literature surmises that fashion buying and merchandising is about *'getting the right product at the right price, at the right time, to the right place'* and additionally that it needs to be delivered in the *'right quantity'* and to the *'right customer'* (Shaw, 2006, p. 139; Stone, 2012, p. 7).

The *right product* means the product is 'right' in terms of the trend for that season, ascertained through extensive trend forecasting, and 'right' for the overall business strategy. For instance, if the brand's mission is to be at the forefront of the latest fashion trends then it needs to ensure that the items that it sells incorporate the key trends of that season.

The *right price* means the buyer negotiates an attractive cost price to produce the garment. This usually involves the buyer negotiating a price that is acceptable to both the company and the supplier. The buyer needs to maximise profits for the retailer and also ensure that the selling price is realistic and in line with their brand.

The *right time* means launching the product to market at the correct time to meet consumer demand. Market research is conducted in order to determine this time and the product released early enough so that demand is only just being generated so that the brand can offer the product to customers when this trend gathers momentum during the peak selling period.

The *right place* means launching the product on the correct channels (online, in-store, via mobile, on social media) and allocating it to the right stores (out-of-town, concession, flagship) to meet consumer demand and maximise its availability for purchase in the market.

The *right quantity* means that the right order quantity is placed for each product. This is difficult for buyers and merchandisers to gauge: order too much and there will be excess stock left at the end of the selling period, which will have to go into markdown, losing profitability for the company, and sometimes then even landfill, which has a terrible impact on the environment. However, order too little and the retailer may sell out before consumer demand has been fulfilled, meaning that consumers will have to turn to their competitors to buy the product, again impacting on profitability. This also involves skilful negotiation with the supplier in order to meet their minimum or maximum order quantities.

The *right customer* means that the product range has to be tailored to meet the demands of the target market. The product needs to be 'right' for the customer in terms of their demand for that type of product in terms of style, fashionability, and quality level. Extensive research is conducted in order to ensure that buyers develop the range in order to appeal to their customers. This is discussed in detail in Chapter 6.

In today's society, we argue that another 'R' needs to also be considered by buyers and merchandisers: that the product range is delivered *'in the right way'*. With the increased

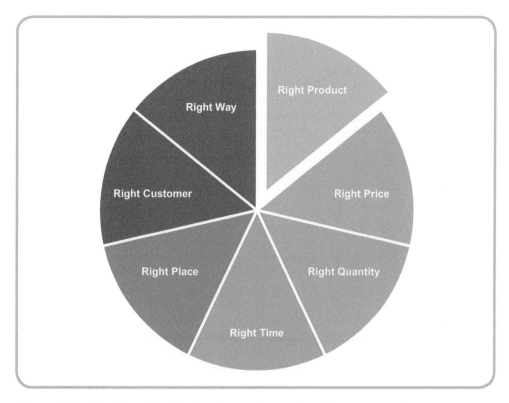

Figure 1.1   The 7Rs of fashion buying and merchandising

awareness of ethical issues and sustainability, this now plays an important part in the production and delivery of a range.

To be successful, retailers must bring new products to the market which can completely satisfy customers' expectations, as well as the business desire to increase profitability. Yet in today's market, consumers have more choice, and at cheaper prices than ever before. In summary, *fashion buying and merchandising focuses on getting the right product at the right price and right quantity, at the right time to the right place and to the right customer* in the right way.

Fashion

Fashion has been defined in numerous ways, but is generally considered to refer to 'a contemporary style that has traditionally been reflected through individuals' clothing, accessories, hair styling and cosmetics' as they make up a person's appearance (Jackson & Shaw, 2001, p. 2). Fashion has always been an important part of human society as throughout history it has enabled people to show their belonging to certain groups or classes and express their status and identity through what they wear. Today, fashion is still embedded in culture and society and represents an important way in which people can express themselves as well as helping them to either integrate with or disassociate themselves from others through their clothes. Indeed, Kang et al. (2013) found that clothing is a tool that assists consumers in achieving an ideal appearance and has the ability to alter one's mood, enabling them to either camouflage or bolster their self-confidence. Further research shows that clothing is used as a vehicle of self-presentation whereby an individual can defend, maintain, and create identities in an attempt to align oneself with perceived social norms (Baumeister, 1982; McNeill, 2017). As such, fashion is a complex art and one that, when got right by businesses, can be very profitable, but understanding this fast-paced and ever-changing industry is never easy!

Fast fashion and super-fast fashion

Fast fashion can be defined as a business model that provides the perception of fashionable clothing at affordable prices via operating through a highly responsive supply chain that can adapt to a product assortment that is constantly changing (Caro & Martínez-de-Albéniz, 2015). Thus, the goal of fast-fashion retailers is to get products into stores as quick as possible (Bruce & Daly, 2006). The advent of fast fashion has resulted in trends rising and falling quicker than ever before, a phenomenon that makes it difficult for trend and sales forecasting and for buyers and merchandisers to keep up!

Initially discussed as a new concept over 30 years ago, fast fashion has now evolved past just being a buzzword to being a product strategy to achieve a competitive advantage (Varley & Clark, 2019). Fashion consumers expect and thrive on constant change and so retailers are under pressure to provide new products on a frequent basis (Bruce & Daly, 2006). This need for instant gratification has increased over time, and where buyers would have previously had one year to work on a product range from concept to customer, they now can have as little as three to six weeks, or even one week in the case of some pureplay (online-only) retailers! Indeed, fast fashion itself has now evolved and can be divided into the iconic pioneering fast-fashion brands, namely Zara, but also H&M and Topshop to name a few, and the 'new kids on the block', pureplay retailers that have sped this process up even further to make a super-fast-fashion business model, such as Boohoo, Pretty Little Thing, Missguided, and In the Style. As a result, there has been a huge increase in 'in-season' buying for all fast and super-fast-fashion retailers, completely changing the traditional nature of buying and merchandising and leading us to question whether the traditional fashion seasons are now no longer relevant.

Death of the seasons?

Traditionally there have been two seasons that structure the fashion calendar: spring/summer and autumn/winter. Fashion items are traditionally sold during these specific seasons in order to maximise saleability. For example, maxi dresses are usually sold between April and August when the weather is warmer and people are more likely to go on holiday. However, the unpredictability of the weather, and the fact that travel is easier, cheaper, and therefore done all year round, as well as the advent of online and mobile stores (which do not have constraints of space like physical stores) has meant that maxi dresses, for instance, are now sold throughout the year. Furthermore, with central heating and air conditioning available all year round to maintain moderate temperatures, consumers now have more transitional wardrobes in general (Varley & Clark, 2019). For instance, in the past people went out to the shops at the start of autumn to buy jumpers and a winter coat. Nowadays, if the weather is unseasonably cold in June, they may buy jumpers then; or, if it is equally unseasonably hot in September, people may still be buying T-shirts and summer dresses as opposed to autumn/winter clothes. This makes the ability to buy the right products in at the right time more difficult due to the unpredictability of consumer demand, their lifestyle, and the weather. The roles of fashion buying and merchandising are therefore more challenging than ever before. Furthermore, with the advent of fast fashion and now super-fast fashion, consumers are constantly demanding newness, so there is a pressure on retailers to refresh their ranges much more frequently. Online and mobile retailing means that people are shopping more often, on a daily basis in some cases, rather than solely at the weekend as in the past. This has led to retailers providing faster and faster turnovers with their ranges in order to retain customers and keep them interested, an aspect that has had a profoundly negative impact on the environment.

Thus, in retail terms there are now multiple 'seasons' per year called 'microseasons'. In some cases fast-fashion retailers have as many as 50–100 'microseasons' per year (*The True Cost*, 2015). This has resulted in an added pressure on buyers and merchandisers to ensure that they get the right product to the right place at the right time, and moreover, in the right way so that they do not push their suppliers to result to unethical practices to fulfil this strategy.

New sales channels: e-commerce, m-commerce, and s-commerce

Traditional buying and merchandising texts discuss the roles and responsibilities in, as well as processes involved for, physical store retailing. With the advent of the internet, *e-commerce* was born in the mid 1990s, creating a whole new set of challenges for buyers and merchandisers. Electronic commerce, or e-commerce, is defined as 'all electronically mediated information exchanges between an organisation and its external stakeholders' (Chaffey, 2015, p. 13). The advent of e-commerce exposed consumers to lower prices and a larger product selection, as well as the ability to shop anytime, anywhere based on convenience. Consumers now have access to global brands at their fingertips, extending the traditional market competition exponentially for retailers. Mobile commerce, or *m-commerce*, is an extension of e-commerce and as consumers have their mobiles on them at all times, this has increased the amount of times that they can interact with a brand. This combination of portability and ubiquity has disrupted the traditional nature of the fashion industry by giving consumers the power to buy and search for products immediately. Consumers can scroll through brands' apps or mobile sites, save their favourite products, add them to wish lists, and indulge further in a see-now-buy-now shopping culture (Bürklin et al., 2019).

Social commerce, or *s-commerce*, can be defined as a component of e-commerce, which employs social media to facilitate buying and selling activities of products/services (Marsden, 2010). Social media has facilitated a more direct relationship between brands and consumers. Brands can share videos, blogs, and product information, or even pose questions to encourage responses to get feedback in an effective and efficient way, reaching a global audience, whilst consumers have the opportunity to share this content or create their own, like and comment on pictures, or share their concerns instantaneously and in real time (Bürklin et al., 2019). S-commerce has even had implications in the manufacturing process, as some brands use their social media platform to get consumers involved in their design and range planning, for example, asking them which products they prefer. Thus, e-commerce, m-commerce, and s-commerce all enable brands to provide added features and value to the consumer shopping journey, such as personalisation or further product details like catwalk videos or 'street style' pictures, all showing how the product can be worn and styled and how it fits.

On the other hand, physical stores are becoming increasingly challenged, with consumers focusing on discount pricing and the perceived ease of online shopping (Middleton, 2018). Indeed, the 'death of the high street' has been well documented in recent years, with major store closures occurring on an almost weekly basis. High-street stalwarts and household names such as BhS, House of Fraser, Debenhams, Karen Millen, Marks & Spencer, and LK Bennett have all gone into administration or had major store closures recently. Online sales are forecast to continue to grow in double digits until 2023, which will certainly impact physical stores further (Mintel, 2018a). Additionally, it is reported that only 59 per cent of consumers under 25 agree that shopping is an enjoyable experience (Mintel, 2018b) and Boardman and McCormick (2018) found that the popularity of shopping in stores decreases with age, with consumers in their twenties much less inclined to shop in stores than consumers in their sixties. This suggests an uncertain future for physical stores. Retailers must innovate, providing store experiences that create a point of difference for the brand to re-engage a disenchanted consumer, and re-invigorate a tired transactional service industry (Drapers, 2018; Mintel, 2018b). Going forward, in order to bring people back into stores retailers must create compelling store designs and visual merchandising to provide an engaging and enjoyable experience for customers.

There are further implications of the rise of e-commerce, m-commerce, and s-commerce for buyers and merchandisers. The scale of product that can be accessed by consumers is incredible, meaning that buyers must ensure that their product stands out in such a crowded market. Consumers now have unlimited access to information on the latest market trends, the newest product innovations and styles, and the launch of new brands and product concepts. No longer are the biannual fashion shows exclusively seen by buyers; consumers can stream the shows live on their phones and watch their favourite influencers' vlog the whole of 'fashion month', providing an almost equal footing between buyers and consumers in terms of trend-forecasting information. This increased access to brand and product knowledge has influenced and driven a change of roles and responsibilities for buyers and merchandisers.

On the positive side, the ability to sell online has eliminated the traditional problems of space on the shop floor. When designing a range for an online store the buyer has fewer restrictions in terms of the size of the range and so can ensure that all predicted 'hero' products can be included. New products can be added throughout the season to refresh the range, keeping the retailer's offering exciting and 'new'. Furthermore, e-commerce has revolutionised the distribution system, making it much clearer in terms of communication and leaner in terms of timings, and, as a result, can be considered one of the greatest achievements of the 20th century (Qin et al., 2014). Indeed, the development of e-commerce as a new distribution system has benefited not only large corporations, but also small-to-medium enterprises, allowing them to effectively compete in international markets against their larger counterparts (Cavusgil & Knight, 1997).

In some cases, having no physical store changes the analysis process for the buying and merchandising team as there is no need to analyse store performance when considering range-planning decisions. In such a volatile and unpredictable high street with very high business rates, this is certainly an advantage. However, extra analysis is needed to identify which products have good or bad returns rates, the cost of those returns, and the impact of returns on average stock levels and stock turn. Having a much wider customer base extends the trends and product types that are relevant for the retailer's customer base, resulting in expanding product assortments and portfolios in order to provide a wider choice to suit a broader customer demographic than an average high-street shop. This larger multi-market consumer base means that seasons, range planning or the 'open to buy' budget (used for in-season buying) becomes questionable. Thus, stock availability, speed of purchase, and an efficient order delivery and returns process at the customer's convenience are all important and new considerations when we think about the buying and merchandising role. Furthermore, the management of stock during its pre-process, purchase, and returns journey needs to be as transparent as possible. With no constraints of space, any products can be sold within the considerations of the retailer's strategic plan in order to satisfy consumer demand. However, the negative implications that this strategy has for the environment and the high number of items that could end up in landfill begs us to ask the question: how many products does the business need?

Multichannel to omnichannel retailing

The growth of new technologies and new sales channels has forced the majority of retailers to adopt a multichannel strategy in order to stay competitive in the current retail climate. Multichannel involves a retailer selling its products across more than one channel, such as in physical stores and online through its website. As technology has evolved, so has multichannel retailing, with consumers demanding faster and superior devices to stay connected (Boardman & McCormick, 2018). Thus, multichannel retailing has transformed into a more complex concept: omnichannel retailing. Whereas multichannel focuses on the sales per channel, omnichannel retailing looks at the total sales (Park & Lee, 2017). Omnichannel involves the idea that consumers can interact with the brand from a number of different touch points, starting anywhere and continuing throughout the whole customer journey, and that these interactions and interchanges are seamless (Varley & Roncha, 2019). The shift from multichannel to omnichannel is challenging, requiring retailers to create a seamless and cohesive cross-channel retail experience (McCormick et al., 2014).

The growth in omnichannel retailing has led to empowered customers, who seek channel advantages throughout their shopping journey and shop in the way that is most convenient for them at all times (Boardman & McCormick, 2018). For instance, omnichannel retailing has encouraged cross-channel behaviour by customers, whereby they start a purchase in one channel, such as browsing on their mobile, then complete it later on another channel, such as going into the store to purchase it. Cross-channel shopping behaviour has led to a discussion concerning show-rooming, which involves consumers browsing in-store and moving to virtual channels to purchase (Schiffman & Wisenblit, 2015), and web-rooming, whereby consumers browse online, but purchase in physical stores (Arora & Sahney, 2017). This is challenging for merchandisers as it is hard to track where the sales originate and where the optimum places to allocate product lines are. This is also challenging for analysing sales figures and returns, a key part of the research and planning process for the next product range.

Omnichannel retailing also enables consumers to check prices and compare quality and durability through online product reviews whilst shopping. This puts more pressure than ever on buyers to ensure that quality standards on all products are upheld, an aspect that is not easy when working with multiple suppliers on a tight deadline, and on merchandisers to ensure prices are competitive but profits still high.

International fashion retailing

The fashion sector is one of the most prolific sectors in terms of internationalisation strategies with fashion retailers expanding continuously into foreign markets (Moore et al., 2010). From the highest to the lowest degree of control and risk, Alexander and Doherty (2009) summarise the nine market entry methods: flagship stores, organic growth, merger and acquisition, joint ventures, franchising, licensing, concession, exporting and wholesaling, and internet sales. The classification based on the risk/control continuum implies that entry methods that grant the retailer with a higher level of control also tend to be riskier. However, this notion is challenged by the emergence of more unconventional entry modes in recent years, such as pop-up stores and e-commerce, which enable retailers to exercise a high level of control with lower resource commitment (Alexander & Doherty, 2009; Picot-Coupey, 2014).

Entering new international markets is no simple matter and requires a great deal of strategic planning. Retailers initially enter overseas markets through a few locations and then progressively build their retail networks; thus, alterations or combinations of operational modes at later stages should be reasonable (Picot-Coupey et al., 2014). Retailers must familiarise themselves with the laws and regulations of the country they wish to enter, as well as conducting extensive consumer and market research on preferences, competition, and retailing infrastructure (Varley & Pickard, 2019). For instance, UK retailers wishing to enter the Chinese market would have a better chance of success if they collaborated with the Chinese e-commerce platforms such as Alibaba, Taobao, and JD.com due to their dominance in the market and Chinese consumers' reluctance to shop on own-brand websites.

Selling products internationally can be financially lucrative if got right, but it can be very costly if it is not done effectively, and very high risk. Consumers in different countries and cultures may not have the same taste as consumers in a retailer's home country and climates may be vastly different. As a result, ranges may need to be adapted in order to make them more appropriate and suitable for that market (this is discussed in detail in Chapter 6). On the other hand, the influence of social media has helped to create a more global style norm for the followers of brands, bringing different countries' styles closer than ever, making this slightly easier for brands in some cases now than it was previously (Roncha & Gee, 2019).

Expanding internationally has added further complexity to retailers' supply chains. Retailers need to work with factories on the other side of the world and may have to set up warehouses and distribution centres across continents in order to ensure that their products can be delivered to customers worldwide. This requires careful critical path monitoring to ensure that product ranges are delivered on time and are consistent for the brand in all the countries that it is operating in.

CHAPTER SUMMARY

This chapter emphasises the importance of the '7Rs', thereby highlighting what a crucial and challenging role buyers and merchandiser face in terms of *getting the right product at the right price and right quantity, at the right time to the right place and to the right customer* in the right way. We have further provided a brief outline of the evolution of fashion and its associated seasonality, or the lack thereof, which is continuously being challenged.

The 21st century has already brought forward a lot of changes in terms of innovations and technology moving from e-, to m-, to s-commerce, whilst at the same time transitioning from a multichannel to an omnichannel experience. As such, brands now have to adapt to this new world of e-commerce, mobile commerce, and social commerce, competing on an international scale with more competitors than ever before, whilst all the time trying to maintain a consistent brand image and product offering across all channels. Buyers and merchandisers are facing exciting times that continue to be dominated by change, new opportunities, and problem solving. Whether retailers and brands stay in their home market or dare to internationalise, they are working in an ever-evolving, volatile market environment, in which they now have a global audience.

References

Alexander, N., & Doherty, A. (2009). *International Retailing*. Oxford: Oxford University Press.

Arora, S., & Sahney, S. (2017). 'Webrooming behaviour: A conceptual framework', *International Journal of Retail & Distribution Management*, 45(7/8): 762–781.

Baumeister, R.F. (1982). 'A self-presentational view of social phenomena', *Psychological Bulletin*, 91(1): 3–26.

Boardman, R., & McCormick, H. (2018). 'Shopping channel preferences and usage motivations: Exploring differences amongst a 50-year age span', *Journal of Fashion Marketing and Management: An International Journal*, 22(2): 270–284.

Bruce, M., & Daly, L. (2006). 'Buyer behaviour for fast fashion', *Journal of Fashion Marketing & Management*, 10(3): 329–344.

Bürklin, N., Henninger, C.E., & Boardman, R. (2019). 'The Historical Development of Social Commerce', in Boardman, R., Blazquez, M., Henninger, C.E., & Ryding, D. (eds), *Social Commerce: Consumer Behaviour in Online Environments*. London: Palgrave Macmillan, pp. 1–16.

Caro, F., & Martínez-de-Albéniz, V. (2015). 'Fast Fashion: Business Model Overview and Research Opportunities', in Agrawal, N., & Smith, S.A. (eds), *Retail Supply Chain Management*. Boston, MA: Springer US, pp. 237–264.

Cavusgil, S.T., & Knight, G.A. (1997). *Explaining an Emerging Phenomenon for International*

Marketing: Global Orientation and the Born Global Firm. East Lansing, MI: Michigan State University.

Chaffey, D. (2015). *Digital Business and E-commerce Management: Strategy. Implementation and Practice.* 6th ed. Harlow: Pearson Education.

Drapers. (2018). 'Drapers fashion forum 2018', n.d., available at: https://blog.mercaux.com/drapers-fashion-forum-2018-highlights.

Jackson, T., & Shaw, D. (2001). *Mastering Fashion Buying and Merchandising Management.* London: Palgrave.

Kang, J.Y., Johnson, K.K.P., & Kim, J. (2013). 'Clothing functions and use of clothing to alter mood', *International Journal of Fashion Design, Technology and Education*, 6(1): 43–52.

Marsden, P. (2010). 'Social commerce: Monetizing social media', 17 February, Syzygy Group White Paper, available at: https://digitalwellbeing.org/social-commerce-monetizing-social-media-syzygy-group-whitepaper/.

McCormick, H., Cartwright, J., Perry, P., Barnes, L., Lynch, S., & Ball, G. (2014). 'Fashion retailing, past, present and future', *Textile Progress*, 46(3): 227–321.

McNeill, L.S. (2017). 'Fashion and women's self-concept: A typology for self-fashioning using clothing', *Journal of Fashion Marketing and Management: An International Journal*, 22(1): 82–98.

Middleton, I. (2018). 'Opinion: How to survive the crisis on the high street', n.d., Retail Week, available at: www.retail-week.com/innovation/opinion-how-to-survive-the-crisis-on-the-high-street/7029373.article.

Mintel. (2018a). *Executive Summary – Online Retailing UK.* London: Author.

Mintel. (2018b). *How Can Retail Venue Catering Facilities Embrace the Changing Retail Landscape?* London: Author.

Moore, C.M., Doherty, A.M., & Doyle, S.A. (2010). 'Flagship stores as a market entry method: The perspective of luxury fashion retailing', *European Journal of Marketing*, 44(1/2): 139–161.

Park, S., & Lee, D. (2017). 'An empirical study on consumer online shopping channel choice

behaviour in omni-channel environment', *Telematics and Informatics*, 34(8): 1398–1407.

Picot-Coupey, K. (2014). 'The pop-up store as a foreign operation mode (FOM) for retailer', *International Journal of Retail Distribution Management*, 42(7): 643–670.

Picot-Coupey, K., Burt, S., & Cliquet, G. (2014). 'Retailers' expansion mode choice in foreign markets: Antecedents for expansion mode choice in the light of internationalisation theories', *Journal of Retailing and Consumer Services*, 21(6): 976–991.

Qin, Z., Chang, Y., Li, S., & Li, F. (2014). *E-commerce Strategy.* Heidelberg: Springer.

Roncha, A., & Gee, L. (2019). 'International Growth Strategy in Fashion Markets', in Varley, R., Roncha, A., Radclyffe-Thomas, N., & Gee, L. (eds), *Fashion Management: A Strategic Approach.* New York, NY: Red Globe Press, pp. 59–78.

Schiffman, L.G., & Wisenblit, J.L. (2015). *Consumer Behaviour.* 11th ed. London: Pearson Education.

Shaw, D. (2006). 'Fashion Buying and Merchandising', in Jackson, T., & Shaw, D. (eds), *The Fashion Handbook.* New York, NY: Routledge, pp. 132–153.

Stone, E. (2012). *In Fashion.* 2nd ed. New York, NY: Fairchild Books.

The True Cost. (2015). Film. Directed by Andrew Morgan. Untold Creative/Life Is My Movie Entertainment, distributed by Life Is My Movie Entertainment/Bullfrog Films.

Varley, R., & Clark, J. (2019). 'Fashion Merchandise Management', in Varley, R., Roncha, A., Radclyffe-Thomas, N., & Gee, L. (eds), *Fashion Management: A Strategic Approach.* New York, NY: Red Globe Press, pp. 155–173.

Varley, R., & Pickard, H. (2019). 'Fashion Supply Chain Management', in Varley, R., Roncha, A., Radclyffe-Thomas, N., & Gee, L. (eds), *Fashion Management: A Strategic Approach.* New York, NY: Red Globe Press, pp. 175–193.

Varley, R., & Roncha, A. (2019). 'Introducing a Strategic Approach to Fashion Management', in Varley, R., Roncha, A., Radclyffe-Thomas, N., & Gee, L. (eds), *Fashion Management: A Strategic Approach.* New York, NY: Red Globe Press, pp. 3–17.

CHAPTER 2

Fashion buying and merchandising roles and responsibilities in the 21st century

Introduction

This chapter will discuss the role and responsibilities of fashion buyers and merchandisers in industry today. A discussion of how these positions have and will further change as contemporary retailing continues to evolve will also be addressed. Whilst the buying and merchandising jobs are connected and complementary they are also extremely different. Fundamentally, for both positions the end goal is to deliver a producible, saleable, and profitable garment range. One of the biggest challenges for people at the beginning of their career is determining if they are a buyer or a merchandiser and recognising where their strengths lie within the skill sets for each of the positions. This chapter will outline the different skills needed for buyers and merchandisers and also the differences between own-label and branded buyers in order to make them clear and aid in this decision.

Learning outcomes

By the end of this chapter you will be able to:

- Explain the role and responsibilities of a fashion buyer as well as the typical career path;
- Identify the differences between an own-label buyer and a branded buyer;
- Explain the role and responsibilities of a fashion merchandiser as well as the typical career path;
- Identify the skills needed to work as a fashion buyer and fashion merchandiser;
- Identify how buyers and merchandisers collaborate with other departments;
- Discuss how the roles have evolved over time and how they may change in the future.

Structure of a buying and merchandising office

Fashion retailers' head offices are busy, open-plan spaces where category or product teams generally sit together. It is not uncommon for design, buying and merchandising teams to all sit and work collectively in order to facilitate quick and easy communication about different products and product ranges. As the product-development process is a range of activities carried out by this multidisciplinary team, as well as other internal and external partners, it is essential that the office design enhances effective collaboration for the process to run smoothly within the challenging time frames and lead times.

The buying and merchandising teams

The buying and merchandising teams vary depending on the size and type of the retailer. However, there is a general hierarchy of different positions that mark progression during a career in the buying and merchandising field, outlined in Figure 2.1.

The specific job roles vary from company to company and in reality, many companies will have their own unique structure and it is not as formulaic. However, this structure

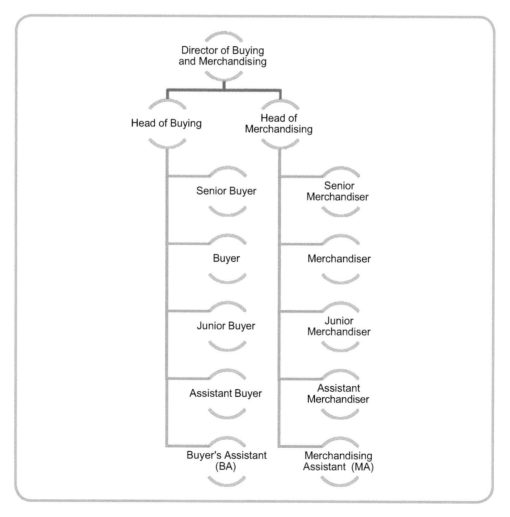

Figure 2.1   **Hierarchy of buying and merchandising roles**

provides a general overview, which still holds true for traditional high-street retailers. The main differences between the roles are summarised below.

Director of buying and merchandising

In some instances, this role may be split into a director of buying and a director of merchandising depending on the business size, structure, and strategy. The buying director is responsible for designing the strategy of the buying direction and communicating this to the buying teams. The merchandising director is responsible for implementing the merchandising direction of the fashion brand to the merchandising teams. Both roles are responsible for delivering balanced, commercial, and financially viable fashion product ranges.

Head of buying or buying manager

The role of the head of buying is ultimately to lead, support, manage, and motivate individual buying teams. The size or variety of buying teams varies across businesses and the head of buying's responsibility may stretch across full departments, such as womenswear or menswear, or combinations of these. The head of buying ensures that commercial yet profitable product ranges are developed in order to achieve maximum profit and sales.

Senior buyer

In large businesses with multiple departments and product lines, a senior buyer will support and bridge the gap between the buyer and the head of buying/buying manager. Having vast experience and responsibility at the buyer level, the role is business-dependent and involves whatever is necessary to ensure a smooth-running operation. The senior buyer holds a leadership role, overseeing and supporting buyers and their teams within each of their categories. The senior buyer ensures that the strategic buying direction is maintained and implemented appropriately.

Buyer

The buyer is responsible for managing the product assortment in terms of sales and profitability within a specific category, such as dresses or outerwear (Jackson & Shaw, 2001). Buyers are expected to lead a team of junior buyers, buying assistants, and buying admin assistants in order to achieve their goal. They also have line management responsibilities, which includes guiding individuals' career development within their team (Jackson & Shaw, 2001).

Junior buyer

The junior buyer is solely responsible for their own range within a product category. As such, they are heavily involved in the product development and the financial negotiation of the range. The junior buyer is expected to contribute to buying meetings alongside the buyer and may visit suppliers and participate in inspiration visits to support future range developments.

Assistant buyer

The assistant buyer supports the buyer by selecting the right product mix, managing purchase orders, monitoring inventory, preparing budgets, and completing other administrative tasks. Assistant buyers work closely with suppliers, analyse market trends, and observe competitors' product assortments for comparisons. They are expected to deputise for the junior buyer in their absence, a task that can range from simple decision-making or taking on full responsibility for product ranges (Jackson & Shaw, 2001).

Buyer's admin assistant

The role of the buyer's admin assistant, sometimes referred to as the BAA, is a highly administrative role within the fashion buying team. The role is usually the starting point for a career in buying, providing essential support to the buyers at different levels in their team. Principal tasks include organising and controlling the distribution of samples, including colour and fabric swatches, and the monitoring of stock orders and deliveries (Jackson & Shaw, 2001).

Head of merchandising or merchandising manager

Depending on the size and structure of the business, the head of merchandising is responsible for merchandising teams across a department such as womenswear, menswear, footwear, or accessories. The head of merchandising ensures that commercial, yet profitable product ranges are developed in order to achieve maximum profits and sales.

Senior merchandiser

In large businesses with multiple departments and product lines, a senior merchandiser will support and bridge the gap between the merchandiser and the head of merchandising. Senior merchandisers will oversee, support, and lead merchandisers and their teams within their categories (e.g. womenswear, menswear, footwear). Ultimately the senior merchandiser is responsible for ensuring that the strategic merchandising direction is maintained and implemented appropriately.

Merchandiser

The merchandiser is responsible for managing the product assortment and its sales and profitability within a specific category, such as dresses or outerwear (Jackson & Shaw, 2001). They are expected to lead a team of junior merchandisers, merchandising assistants, and merchandising admin assistants/allocators in order to achieve their goal. They also have line management responsibilities and are responsible for guiding their teams' career development, just as the buyer does at the same level.

Junior merchandiser

The junior merchandiser will often be solely responsible for their own fashion range within the merchandising department. The junior merchandiser will report to the merchandiser and/or more senior members of the fashion merchandising team. They will be involved in the sales and stock for the current season, but also start to plan future fashion seasons by setting out how much stock should be bought for the ranges that they are responsible for. A junior fashion merchandiser will play a large part in the Monday morning trading meetings, where they will review the previous week's sales, as well as the best and worst sellers for the department. They will also manage the workloads of the assistant merchandiser and the merchandising admin assistant.

Assistant merchandiser

The assistant merchandiser is responsible for particular planning and distribution activities (Jackson & Shaw, 2001). Similar to the assistant buyer, they may have to deputise for the junior merchandiser at times. However, they are primarily responsible for analysing sales and suggesting any rebuys or promotional activity needed. They will work closely with the assistant buyer, monitoring the budget carefully.

Merchandising admin assistant or allocator

The job role of a merchandising admin assistant (MAA), sometimes referred to as an allocator, is to assist with the administrative tasks within the team. The role is usually the starting point for a career in merchandising and primarily focuses on the allocation of stock within a business. Merchandising admin assistants will analyse the weekly sales reports and monitor sales and stock figures; however, this can vary dependent on business type and size. When studying the sales inventory reports they will analyse the needs of each type of retail store to determine the correct quantities of merchandise to send to them (Granger, 2015). They may also plan and manage merchandise deliveries received from suppliers to the retail stores.

It is important to remember that different retailers have their own ways of organising teams and, in some cases, some of the earlier positions may not be necessary; thus, graduates will start in more senior positions. Ultimately the role of the buying and merchandising teams is to connect the creative and financial product requirements of a fashion brand through range planning and operational trading to optimises a fashion business opportunity (Clark, 2015). Retailers and brands will use a variety of different structural ways to organise and manage this process.

It is also important to remember that, as contemporary fashion retailing evolves with the continued development of technological enhancements, and the way in which we shop changes, so will the buying and merchandising roles. Development of further skills, new structures, and positions, as well as internal and external inputs and outputs, will all influence the hierarchy of positions within buying and merchandising and the traditional career progression route. Indeed, the roles and responsibilities of buyers and merchandisers have already become more blurred in recent years. For instance, H&M does not have merchandiser roles per se, but rather their responsibilities are incorporated into the buyer's job description. Gone are the days when buyers were 'all creative' and merchandisers 'all numbers'. These stereotypes are no longer accurate and representative of contemporary buyers and merchandisers. Nowadays, buyers must be analytical, good with numbers, and work in tandem with the merchandisers. Merchandisers, on the other hand, must now be creative, have a solid understanding of patterns in both trends as well as sales, and be expansive in terms of explaining what the numbers mean. Hence, the roles of buyers and merchandisers are more fluid than they used to be, and vary across retailers. Despite the increasing overlap of roles, and the differences between companies, the key roles and responsibilities of buyers and merchandisers are loosely the same throughout the industry and are outlined in more detail throughout the rest of this chapter.

Role of a buyer

The primary role of a buyer is to purchase a range of products that epitomises the brand's identity and corporate strategy, appeals to the brand's target consumer and ultimately makes a profit. Buyers are responsible for all of the product purchases for a company, or for a particular section of that company, working within a set budget (Granger, 2015). The buying role will differ between companies, but ultimately all fashion buyers are responsible for overseeing the development of a range of products aimed at a specific type of customer and within a set price bracket. It is the buyer's job to transform the brand's corporate strategy and values into the products that it sells in order to make the company a success.

Larger retailers usually have separate buying departments for menswear, womenswear, childrenswear, etc. Buyers usually purchase products for a specific product area or category, making them focused and specialist. Ultimately, for all product decisions, buyers must consider if there is sufficient customer demand, and if the price, quality, and availability of the product is appropriate for the customer. They must also research fashion trends, which will determine the colours, fabrics, and styles for each season. They also need to be aware of social, political, economic, and cultural occurrences in the wider market and how it may affect their target consumer. Understanding the customer and brand is extremely important in terms of ensuring product success. Thus, buyers work hard to research fashion trends, their core customers, and the wider market, and then source materials and products from suppliers in order to produce a range for the brand to sell (Shaw & Koumbis, 2014).

Responsibilities of a buyer

The primary responsibility of a buyer is to develop a range of products that achieves the profit margin and is consistent with the retailer's buying strategy. These products must be sufficiently researched to ensure that they are relevant to the customer, brand or retailer, and the market. By monitoring consumer behaviour, buyers can determine, to a certain extent, what consumers want to buy and when and then meet that need/want with their product. Buyers can analyse previous sales data to help forecast how well a product will sell and try to minimise the risks involved in selling a new item. Trend forecasting also ensures that buyers can prepare by choosing which of the latest trends to buy into and how to translate them to suit their brand identity. Fashion trends and the fashion industry change constantly and rapidly, so buyers need to be reactive and proactive in order to ensure that the brand is contemporary and appealing. Furthermore, buyers will conduct comp (comparative) shops and directional shops (see below and Chapter 6 for further information) as well as visiting trade shows when designing a product range in order to gain inspiration and information. Using previous sales data, market information, and trend and fashion knowledge they will develop a range of products that are appropriate in price, quality, and style for a season. Buyers work collectively with teams internally, such as designers, merchandisers, garment technologists, and marketers, as well as senior management. Each of these areas inform and support the buyer to help develop a profitable range that can be manufactured effectively and meet the needs of the customer.

One of the main responsibilities of a buyer is to source and develop products from an effective supplier base. The buyer will be given a set budget to work with in order to produce the range and they are responsible for the negotiating the best deals with the supplier in terms of cost and delivery. It is, therefore, important that buyers communicate effectively with suppliers and build up an effective relationship with them in order to enable both businesses to flourish.

Buyers are also responsible for effectively managing and developing the buying team to not only make sure that the correct information is communicated throughout the team, but also in developing the skills of the individuals to support them in their career development.

Skills and competencies

To succeed in this career, buyers need to have foresight and develop skills in people management and time management. Their skill set centres on their knowledge and understanding of products and creativity; however, they must also be analytical in order to understand the impact of their decisions on the commercial strength of a business, and possess unlimited enthusiasm and passion for their industry (Clark, 2015). They must understand the fashion industry with its past and present fashion trends, coupled with commercial awareness when it comes to product decision-making. Furthermore, buyers must have a good understanding of their customers and the level of the market that they retail within in order to assess how they will react to the latest trends.

Fashion buyers need to be creative and have an appreciation of aesthetics, a technical appreciation of garments and fabrics, and an understanding of the supply chain (Varley & Clark, 2019). Buyers should have effective negotiation skills when they are dealing with suppliers to ensure that they can achieve a deal that is mutually acceptable to both parties and in order to accomplish the business objectives as well as the aesthetic goals. Thus, buyers must possess excellent communication skills and be detail-oriented and able to deal with deadlines and stress (Granger, 2015). As such, buyers need to be able to adapt to unexpected situations. Aspects such as the weather, the economy, new trends, and transport issues may disrupt plans and schedules; thus, the buyer must always be prepared to have a contingency plan.

Ultimately buyers must be the following:

- Good at multitasking;
- Good communicators;
- Flexible;
- Self-motivated;
- Task-oriented;
- Good at time management;

- Skilled in IT;
- Analytical;
- Organised;
- Creative;
- Good negotiators;
- Good at budgeting;
- Team players.

Different types of buyers

Depending on the retailer or brand that the buyer works for, their role will have a vast variety of different responsibilities. The different types of buyer can be split into the following;

- Own-label buyer – also known as own-brand buyer, private-label buyer, or retail high-street buyer;
- Branded buyer:
  - Department store buyer;
  - Wholesale buyer.

Own-label buyer

An own-label buyer works for a retailer that only sells its own products and not those of any other brand. Thus, the majority of high-street fashion retailers employ own-label buyers. This type of buyer is involved in the whole product-development process, from idea right through to manufacturing and distribution. Own-label buyers, therefore, have an influence on the design of a product, such as the colour, fabric, and style details. The relationships with their suppliers are key to the success of the business as they liaise with these manufacturers to create their own items from scratch. They have to negotiate a desirable cost, price, and quantity for each of the products in order to make profits. Own-label buyers will discuss product trims, fabric quality, lead times, sampling, and additional orders with suppliers in order to get the best deal. This negotiation with the supplier is essential to maintaining a profitable business; thus, there is quite a lot of pressure on the buyer.

As own-label buyers are heavily involved within the whole product-development process they work with many other internal and external departments, such as designers, merchandisers, and garment technologists. However, as this is both labour- and time-intensive they will only usually work on one category, such as dresses or jersey tops. Some of the key activities that own-label buyers participate in are:

- Consult merchandisers and analyse the sales history of certain products to determine the best and worst sellers, as this will provide an idea of what will work well in the future;
- Analyse the current wider marketplace and consumer behaviour within their target market, including social media trends;

- Consult trend-forecasting information and take inspiration from design teams on future trends to look out for;
- Consult with garment technologists on issues with products from previous seasons in order to avoid repeating mistakes;
- Attend branded trade shows and fashion weeks for inspiration, and textile trade shows for ordering fabrics;
- Complete comp shops to see what their competitors are doing, analysing their ranges to see if there are any key items missing from their own range that need to be included;
- Complete directional shops to look at inspirational brands and see what key trends will be filtering down to their level of the market.

These activities support the creation of the range so that the buyer has an insight into what key ideas, styles, and looks should be included. An own-label buyer will conduct trend-forecasting research and work alongside the design team, who will inform them of the key trends, fabrics, colours, and prints that will need to be translated for that season. They will then work with several suppliers to ensure that they get the best manufacturers to develop the product successfully. Once the prices, lead times, and orders have been negotiated and confirmed, the buyer will authorise them with the merchandisers and book the orders. Conducting the research and development processes, followed by the negotiation with suppliers and subsequent manufacturing, delivery, and distribution, results in long lead times for each item, an aspect that fast-fashion and super-fast-fashion companies are always aiming to speed up. Yet, taking time to complete each of the stages of the buying cycle thoroughly means that the buyer is more likely to get the key decisions right.

Figure 2.2 shows the different stages and activities that are more dominant for a retail buyer. These stages and activities will be discussed in more detail in later chapters, but below is a short summary.

- *Product development* – at this stage the buyer's role is concerned with the research, planning, and development of ideas, followed by the trend and market translation of those ideas to sampling, fitting, and costing. Thus, the product-development stage involves getting the product from the idea stage to an accurate sample ready for manufacturing by a supplier.
- *Manufacturing* – at this stage the buyer's role is concerned with the manufacturing of the products and tracking them using the critical path. Buyers constantly monitor products as they need to be created and transported within the correct time frames and delivered to retail stores or put on the website ready for trading.
- *Trading* – at this stage the buyer's role is concerned with the performance of the products that have been created and developed. Buyers will monitor how they sell and if they meet the expected sales targets. If the items perform better than expected, then this can help inform the products that are still in development as well as plans for the next season and any rebuys for the current trading season.

Branded buyer

A branded buyer purchases products from a variety of different brands. They purchase stock that has been designed and developed by other brands or labels and, therefore, have no control over the design and product development of these items, such as style

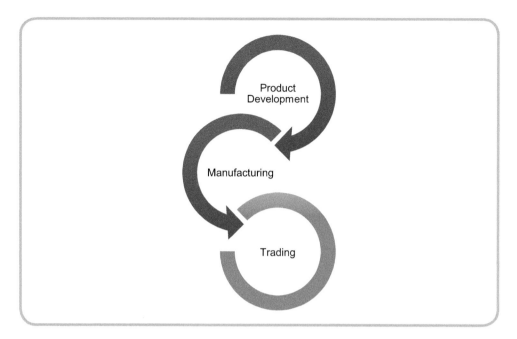

Figure 2.2 **Stages of the product-development process for an own-label buyer**

details, colours, and/or fabrics used. As a result, branded buyers are able to work much closer to the season than own-label buyers can. The buying seasons are very important to branded buyers as they are the dedicated times and places for them to make their orders and develop supplier relationships. Similarly to own-label buying, the best and worst sellers, customer demand, and the individual aspects of the stores are still very influential to the buyer's decision-making. However, unlike in own-label buying, they will purchase directly from brands via an agent or showroom, trade show, or wholesaler, or sometimes a mixture of the three.

Figure 2.3 shows the different stages and activities that a branded buyer is generally concerned with, summarised below:

- *Research and planning* – at this stage the branded buyer's role is concerned with research, planning, and development of ideas for the coming season. They focus on analysing historical sales, product and brand performance, consumer demand, and what the brand strategy for future buying may be. From this, the buyer will create a plan consisting of the product assortments, brands, and designers that they want for the upcoming range. The range plan will detail a breakdown of the budget available and the specific product quantities that they want.
- *Buying season* – the buying season is the specific time slot when the brands and designers that sell to branded buyers are available to take orders. Buyers will visit garment trade shows, showrooms, and head offices to view the available collections and place orders. Branded buyers must make sure that the brands and labels that they choose to purchase work well as a collective for their store, and that the products that they buy complement each other as well as the overall brand strategy.

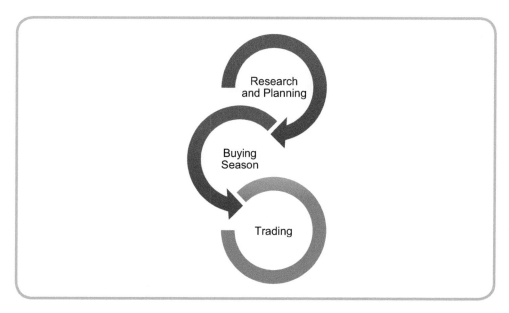

Figure 2.3   **Stages of the buying season for a branded buyer**

- *Trading* – at this stage the branded buyer's role is concerned with the performance of the products that have been bought. Branded buyers will monitor how they sell and if they meet the expected sales targets. If the items perform better than expected, then this can help inform the products that they purchase the next season as well as any rebuys for the current trading season.

Retailers' businesses can vary in size; thus, the branded buyer can often have a variety of other roles specific to that company. The size of the retailer will also dictate what the buyer may be responsible for, such as full departments (e.g. womenswear or accessories) or specific brands. For example, smaller businesses, such as one-store independents, will appoint buyers to be responsible for the entire product mix in store, and junior and assistant buyers to help with the admin, etc. There are no fixed rules on the job roles and responsibilities except to work in a way that is best for the retailer. Branded buyers will also use some of their budget each season for in-season buying to make sure they have fresh stock at all times, an aspect that is very important in terms of meeting customer demand and maintaining an up-to-date range.

Department store buyer

The department store buyer will have a category that they will buy for, such as men's fashion shoes or women's branded fashion. They will have in-depth discussions with sales managers for each individual store, a responsibility that is very important as it ensures that the correct stock is purchased and distributed to the correct locations. Department store buyers have great power as they have the ability to bring in lesser-known brands, which can increase brand awareness for that brand on the high street. The larger the size of the department store and the more premium the location that it resides in, the larger the budget and spending power that the buyer has.

Visits to trade shows and fashion shows are key for the role of the department store buyer as it is important that they are aware of what is current in their specific area. Comp shops and directional shops are also essential in determining which are the right products to sell. Despite department store buyers having no control over the product, some brands create ranges just for specific department stores, making the items exclusive. As department store buyers order larger volumes, this is economically viable for the brand and it gives the department store the edge over its competition. As with all other types of buyer, department store buyers will use a portion of their budget to purchase items within the trading season and for repeat orders of bestsellers.

Wholesalers and wholesale buyers

Wholesalers are the people in the middle of the retailer and the manufacturer. Wholesalers purchase directly from brands or manufacturers and then sell the items to retailers at a small profit. They occasionally take end-of-lines or cancelled orders from large manufacturers. Once the wholesaler receives the stock they display their products in large units that are similar to shops, but not open to the public (they only sell to businesses). Wholesalers' customer base is small boutiques, independent stores (either online or physical stores), and market traders who sometimes do not have the buying power to order in large quantities or those that want fast fashion to sell instantly that day or week. Wholesalers need to be aware of market trends and consumer demand in order to stock the products that high-street fashion retailers will want to purchase. Wholesalers may visit trade shows themselves to showcase their collections to retail buyers or to meet manufacturers to purchase from.

Wholesale buyers visit these wholesale stores and purchase the stock to take away that day, or later in the week if the order is large. Wholesale buyers tend to operate in the lower and middle end of the market. The main advantage of a buyer purchasing stock from a wholesaler is the lack of lead times. Wholesale buyers need to be aware of what sold well last season, or whether that wholesaler's stock received many returns, and the reasons for these, in order to inform their future purchasing decisions. Similar to other forms of buyers, they also need to be aware of wider market trends to spot opportunities for their business. Wholesale buyers will have good relationships with the wholesalers that they purchase from as they are in a supply-and-demand relationship, and the wholesaler will, in turn, have a good relationship with the manufacturers that they purchase from in order for all parties to get the best deals available. Wholesale buyers may visit trade shows as part of their responsibilities as this may be where their wholesale suppliers showcase their items. For both wholesalers and wholesale buyers, building up strong relationships with the people that they purchase from and sell to are crucial to the success of their business.

Role of a merchandiser

Fashion merchandisers are responsible for the development of a balanced, marketable, profitable, and timely product range (Granger, 2015). The role of a fashion merchandiser is one that is glamourised less often and is less renowned than that of a fashion buyer (Varley & Clark, 2019), yet the two roles run parallel to each other, possessing a symbiotic relationship in order to achieve the best product range for the business. Fashion merchandising is a multidisciplinary function involved in the planning, management, and control of products with an emphasis on maximising profits and reducing risks. Merchandisers oversee the creation of a product range from a financial and analytical point of view coupled with an understanding of fashion trends and influences (Clark, 2015). Ultimately, merchandising involves the analysis of what is selling and using this information to develop profitability; thus, merchandisers rely heavily upon sales data to make decisions. Managing risk is another of the fundamental roles of a merchandiser as they need to ensure that the business has as much profitable stock as possible, which is achieved through the management and control of products from their development through to their delivery to stores. Merchandisers also need to ensure that product ranges are well balanced in terms of the high- and low-risk items in order to meet financial targets.

The advent of new sales channels and international fashion retailing has resulted in the role of a merchandiser being even more strategic, as all the different selling options need to be carefully considered alongside new market developments (Varley & Clark, 2019). Furthermore, today the merchandising role is more valuable than ever with more in-season buying taking place in response to high consumer demand.

Responsibilities of a merchandiser

When planning a new product range, fashion merchandisers will calculate cost estimates for new products, choosing and quantifying which styles should be produced (product authorisation) (Granger, 2015). They will also analyse and assess the performance of product ranges throughout a fashion season (Clark, 2015). They do this by comparing and reviewing the performances of the best, average, and worst sales using key-performance-indicator calculations in order to ensure that decisions are accurate and non-judgemental.

Thus, like buyers, merchandisers will work on several seasons at once:

- *Last season* – clearing and marking-down products;
- *Current season* – delivering, monitoring, and reacting to sales by buying more or less stock;
- *Future season* – planning samples, writing orders, and planning delivery phasing.

Merchandisers work closely with buyers to create the initial range plan, analysing sales figures from previous seasons, fashion trends, and consumer demand (Granger, 2015). The merchandiser's main input to the range-planning stage is to maximise the commercial opportunities for products. Merchandisers also work closely with designers on the development of cost-effective and marketable styles (Granger, 2015). When presenting the upcoming ranges at the pre-selection and final selection meetings, merchandisers are responsible for providing the *'so what?'* to the figures so that staff know exactly what they mean and what to do about them. They will estimate a sales plan using historical sales and market information and plan stock levels to achieve a high gross margin for departments and products. Merchandisers play a significant part in the retailer's performance: they are responsible for managing the process that enables the products selected by the buying teams to arrive on time in the right quantities to the correct locations (Goworek & McGoldrick, 2015).

Merchandisers are also responsible for effectively managing the merchandising and distribution team to ensure that the correct information is communicated throughout the team. They will manage product stock distributions and allocate product ranges to specific stores based on customer demand, available selling space, and seasonal selling opportunities.

During the season they will provide regular analysis and progress reports referring to stock levels, sales performance, and stock purchases to senior management. It is essential that the merchandiser reacts effectively to the information as it arrives. For example, fast sellers need to be re-purchased quickly; poor sellers may need to be marked down to lower the price and increase consumer demand (Jackson & Shaw, 2001). Throughout the season they manage stock intake and commitment to accommodate stock requirements using the open-to-buy budget.

Skills and competencies

Merchandisers need to understand consumer sales patterns, the wider market, and fashion trends, and have a sense of commercial awareness. To succeed in this career merchandisers have to develop key skills in terms of people and time management. They should be skilled with numbers and possess an analytical mind. Merchandisers need to be able to spot trends and relationships in sales and stock figures and work in a reactive manner during a season to reach the most profitable outcome for the business.

Ultimately merchandisers must be the following:

- Logical and rational;
- Able to multitask;
- IT-oriented;
- Skilled with numbers;
- Analytical;
- Creative;
- Good at paying attention to details;
- Assertive;
- Good at retaining information and recollecting it;
- Excellent communicators – orally, visually, and in writing;
- Team players.

Different types of merchandiser

Dependent on the retailer or brand that the merchandiser works for, their role will have a vast variety of different responsibilities specific to that business. However, unlike the buyer's role there is not a great deal of difference if a merchandiser is dealing with

own-label products or branded products. The amount and type of products and categories and how a business retails will determine the different levels of importance for the
activities.

The main difference between the own-label and branded merchandiser is the influence that they have during the range-planning and development stages. An own-label
merchandiser will inform the buyer of the historical sales information pertaining to the
best- and worst-selling products in order to help with the planning of size ratios, colourways, and style quantities, as well as determining the product margins. Therefore, the
own-label merchandiser heavily impacts the product-development processes of product ranges. A branded merchandiser, on the other hand, would not participate in these
activities as the products are already creatively developed when the buyer purchases
them. They, therefore, like the buyer, work much closer to the season. Nevertheless, they
will still use historical sales data to inform the buyer about which brands and types of
products to purchase.

Branded buying and merchandising vs own-label buying and merchandising

There are some great differences as well as similarities between branded vs own-label
buying and merchandising. The lead times between the two differ significantly as the
product ranges that they deal with are at different stages within the buying cycle; one
participates during the whole process whilst the other participates in only certain sections. Figure 2.4 illustrates the different buying cycles for branded and own-label types
of buying and merchandising.

Figure 2.4 shows that there are some identical stages and activities and some that are
completely different. It also illustrates the timings when each of the stages generally take
place for both types. However, it is important to note that the illustrations do not indicate the lead times for each of the buying cycles or how long each of the stages takes for
products to move through them. This is something that is specific to each type of retailer
and the market level that it trades in. For example, this will be different if it is a fast-
fashion pureplay retailer or if it is a high-street retailer with a large portfolio of stores,
and in some cases depends on the type of products that are sold.

Figure 2.5 shows a breakdown of the different responsibilities and roles for branded
vs own-label buyers and merchandisers.

As Figure 2.5 illustrates, there are some similarities and differences between the roles
and responsibilities. Again, the type of retailer or brand that they are working for, and the
market level that they trade in will determine the key roles and responsibilities.

Buyer and merchandiser partnership

The relationship between the buyer and merchandiser is often likened to a marriage in
which the two work together to create saleable, profitable, and producible product ranges.
They will not always agree, but a good buyer and merchandiser will listen and influence
each other to get the best possible result (Clark, 2015). They must work together closely

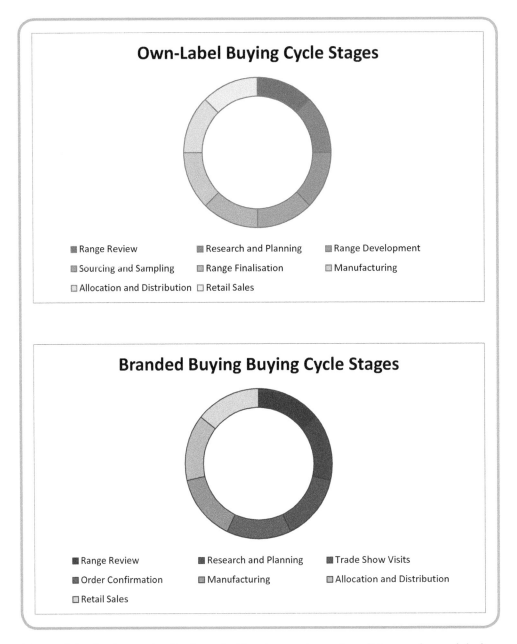

Figure 2.4   Buying cycles for branded buying and merchandising and own-label buying and merchandising

during the range-planning stage to maximise opportunities for products to sell at the best possible price and time. Thus, both roles are of equal importance during this stage; buying is an imperfect science, so merchandising helps the difficult decision-making. Whereas the buyer is generally more concerned with the qualitative aspects of range planning, merchandisers focus more on the quantitative side, dealing with the numbers

	Branded	Own-Label
Buyer	Historical Sales Analysis/ Customer Demand	Most complex and demanding type of buying.
	Select ranges from fashion brands or manufacture brands (via agent or show room, trade show or wholesalers)	One category only
		Works on the design development in conjunction with design team.
	Buying seasons and trade shows	More creative role
		Historical Sales Analysis/ Customer Demand
	No control over the product design	Attend trade shows (e.g. Premiere Vision)
	Negotiation skills	Comp shops/ Directional shops
	Supplier Relationships	Source products from international
	Shorter lead times/purchase in season	manufacturers (suppliers) and create products from scratch with them
	Low volume of order	Negotiation skills
	Have much higher involvement with how product will appear in store than own-label buyers	Build and maintain good relationships with suppliers
		Long lead-times
		High volume of orders
Merchandiser	Manage the minimum orders, order quantities, markdowns, and delivery dates for a variety of brands	Participate in range planning with sales information on size, colour, fabric, and best and worst information
	Manage the open-to-buy budget and the challenges with external brands	Maintain order quantities
		Develop order quantities, markdowns, and delivery dates and budgets
	Manage relationships with external brands to support successful delivery and rebuys if needed	Only contact with own supplier base

Figure 2.5   Breakdown of key responsibilities for branded buyer and merchandiser and own-label buying and merchandising

and financial aspects, both roles working in collaboration and supporting each other (Varley & Clark, 2019).

No two days are the same for fashion buyers and merchandisers. The fashion industry is very fast-paced and, as a result, the roles require lots of flexibility and quick reactions. It is also important to note that not every range will be successful, and that trade varies. Analysis is always key and needs to be ongoing regardless of whether the range is successful or not. For instance, if the range is not selling well then buyers and merchandisers should be asking 'Why are we not selling enough?', 'Should we mark down, and if so by how much?', and 'What can we learn from this mistake?' On the other hand, if the range is selling well, buyers and merchandisers should be asking: 'Will we run out of stock?', 'How can we capitalise on this further and maximise profits?', 'When/how much should we reorder?', and 'Can this be carried forward to future seasons or is it a fad/season-specific?'

How buyers and merchandisers work with other departments

Buyers and merchandisers have to develop and maintain relationships with other internal departments. The product-development process is complex and challenging, and thus requires a multidisciplinary team of highly skilled people. The relationships with the key departments are discussed below.

- *Design* – designers turn trend concepts and ideas into actual garment designs that the buying team can choose from to develop further. This process begins with trend research regarding colour, styles, and fabrics that is then translated into ideas and trend boards and then into product-specific designs relating to the brand's signature style. Designers need to consider the material and the cost of materials as well as the practicalities in making the garment when conceptualising their designs. The buyer will work with the designer to match trends and moods to the product concept that has been devised in tandem with the merchandiser (Clark, 2015). The designs will be created by the designer as CAD (computer-aided design) drawings to illustrate product ideas, which enables buyers to have a starting point for product development, sampling and costing, and accurate communication with suppliers. Many designs will be discarded at this point and only the most suitable (in terms of price, quality, and practicality for production) and those that meet the customer needs/trends will be carried forward to the next stage.
- *Garment technologists* – the relationship between the buyer and the garment technologist is crucial. Buyers rarely have a technological background or training, so they tend to rely heavily on their technologist to give guidance and advice on a wide variety of product suitability, durability, and reliability issues (Shaw & Koumbis, 2014). Garment technologists work with the buying team regarding the fit and quality of the samples that are being considered for the following season. They will also advise on and provide support with any fault issues that may have occurred with products that are currently for sale. Once a new product has been sampled by a supplier, it is important that the cost and aesthetics meet the buying team's objectives. Once this is achieved it is vital that the fit of the product is also measured to ensure that it is appropriate and meets the customer's expected size requirements of the brand. The fit of the product is also checked to ensure that it can be worn appropriately by the consumer; for instance, it is not too baggy and there is no excess fabric anywhere. Thus, checks are made by the garment technologist on how the garment fits, feels, and wears, as well as the quality of the fabric, linings, and fastening, and washing suitability. The more attention to detail paid at this stage, the less likely it is there will be returns based on sizing and fit issues later on.
- *Marketing* – buyers and merchandisers need to work with the marketing team in order to ensure that promotional campaigns are appropriate in terms of the range identity and availability. Whilst marketing primarily focuses on the external communication

for brands, the department will work closely with the buyer to understand the products in terms of their strengths and values to the business as well as how the customer is responding to it (Clark, 2015). Buyers will liaise with marketing to provide the key looks and styles (hero products) to be featured in marketing campaigns, social media dialogue, and promotional activities. It is important that any products featured are presented appropriately and have enough available stock to support an increase in sales, making the merchandiser's knowledge in this area essential to the marketing team. They also need to work in the reverse, so if products are not performing as planned the buying and merchandising team need to work with marketing to develop reactive promotional activities to increase sales and product attention.

- *Studio* – the studio team photograph all finalised products and develop the images and information ready to be uploaded to websites so that the items can be sold. The team will consist of photographers, stylists, and post-production support. It is important that buyers deliver the approved sample to the studio team at the correct time and hand over the key information about styling ideas in order to present the product in the most appealing way. This key communication and hand-over must take place on time in order to ensure that there are no additional delays in the holistic process, which could then delay the uploading of the product to the website and miss the peak selling period.

- *Retail staff* – sales data is sent straight to head office from all sales channels for the buying and merchandising teams to analyse through a centralised computer system, an aspect that will be discussed in more detail in Chapter 3. It is essential that buyers and merchandisers are still in communication with the retail staff personally in order to obtain key qualitative information about the product range. Buyers and merchandisers need to hear how customers are reacting to the stock, which items they are trying on, which items cause excitement, and whether any comments are made about items regarding the fit or the material. Having a good rapport with store management is key to successful sell-through (Shaw & Koumbis, 2014) as buyers and merchandisers can discuss with retail staff which items should be put at the front of the store or on mannequins, such as the hero pieces of the range. This communication with retail stores enables buyers and merchandisers to have a good indication and understanding of the range and what is working and not working. Customer feedback is extremely valuable for developing ranges going forward as this is the best way to inform on customer demand. Strong communication between the buying teams and the retail store management teams will foster an environment that simultaneously works to drive sales; it is a group collaboration that has one goal: profit (Shaw & Koumbis, 2014).

CHAPTER SUMMARY

A very important message that is conveyed in this chapter is that although there are generic 'job descriptions' available highlighting what individual buying and merchandising roles entail, it is essential to keep in mind that these may differ depending on: (1) the fashion retailer itself, in terms of type (e.g. own-label, wholesaler) and the size of the business; (2) the ever-changing fashion environment, such as technological development and new business models. As such, the job roles and responsibilities of fashion buyers and merchandisers, as well as the skill sets needed for these careers, should be used as guiding principles, rather than considered as set in stone. Nevertheless, the hierarchies depicted for both the fashion buyer and fashion merchandiser provide an insight into career progressions and responsibilities. The chapter draws on the differences between branded and own-label buyers and merchandisers, in that branded buyers are not responsible for finding garment manufacturers to produce their product range, but rather they have to select items to sell directly from different brands. Contrarily, own-label buyers and merchandisers are more heavily involved in the product-development stages. As such, the chapter further alludes to the key relationships that need to be built between the buyer and the merchandiser, as well as between these two key roles and other departments and external suppliers. Without these solid relationships, the roles of the buyer and merchandiser may potentially not be able to fulfil their purpose.

References

Clark, J. (2015). *Fashion Merchandising; Principles and Practices*. Basingstoke: Palgrave.

Goworek, H., & McGoldrick, P. (2015). *Retail Marketing and Management: Principles and Practice*. Harlow: Pearson.

Granger, M.M. (2015). *The Fashion Industry and its Careers*. 3rd ed. New York, NY: Bloomsbury.

Jackson, T., & Shaw, D. (2001). *Mastering Fashion Buying and Merchandising Management*. London: Palgrave.

Shaw, D., & Koumbis, D. (2014). *Fashion Buying*. New York, NY: Fairchild.

Varley, R., & Clark, J. (2019). 'Fashion Merchandise Management', in Varley, R., Roncha, A., Radclyffe-Thomas, N., & Gee, L. (eds), *Fashion Management: A Strategic Approach*. New York, NY: Red Globe Press, pp. 155–173.

3 The influence of technology on fashion buying and merchandising

Introduction

The vast amount of change that has occurred in the fashion buying and merchandising roles over the last few decades is all due to the rapid development of new technologies. Technology has proven to be an indispensable tool in making the process of design creation, development, and management more agile (Guerrero, 2009). This chapter outlines the key digital advances that have influenced fashion buying and merchandising this century.

Learning outcomes

By the end of this chapter you will be able to:

- Explain how technology has changed the fashion industry over time;
- Discuss the importance of technology and how it underpins the roles of a fashion buyer and fashion merchandiser today;
- Outline the use of computer-aided design in the fashion industry and its importance in fashion buying and merchandising;
- Discuss the use of technology in the production of a fashion garment.

The influence of technology on the fashion industry

The development of new technologies has had a huge influence on the fashion industry throughout its history, from the development of looms to the move towards electronic till systems. However, the last three decades have seen technological advancements speed up with the advent of the internet in 1989, completely changing the way that businesses run and how retailing is conducted, from an employer, employee, and consumer perspective. In contemporary society, technology has enabled consumers to purchase products and engage with retailers and brands anywhere and at any time. Technology has increased the availability of products for consumers, providing them with exposure to more brands, retailers, and product lines as well as facilitating a more efficient and streamlined transactional process. On the other hand, technology has enabled retailers to digitise their operations, monitor sales and stock more accurately than ever before, create compelling customer experiences, sell across many different sales channels, and even change their production processes. However, technology is delivered in so many formats that it is important for retailers to quickly adapt to changing market trends and understand consumer behaviour in both brick-and-mortar locations and e-commerce sites (Shaw, 2017). In particularly, for buyers and merchandisers, technology can be used to enhance communications and reduce any issues with timescales, speed, and time differences. Having everything digitised enables buyers and merchandisers to behave in a more reactive manner in terms of product development in order to meet consumer demand, maintain accurate and appealing stock levels, and ensure effective allocation to stores.

Social media

With the advancement of Web 2.0 technologies, social media has developed and grown its user base at a phenomenal pace over the last two decades. Indeed, the number of social media users worldwide reached 3.484 billion in 2019, which is an increase of 9 per cent year-on-year (Chaffey, 2019). The streaming of the fashion-week shows on social media has made them more accessible to consumers, thus creating further challenges for buyers. Unlike in previous years where buyers would attend the fashion-week shows in person and translate the trends into their product range, dictating what consumers would buy, the fact that consumers can see the trends themselves gives them more power and influence over the creation of the product range. Now, the promotion of brands' collections on social media during and directly after fashion shows has led to a desire of fashion immediacy amongst consumers (Mountney & Murphy, 2017). Buyers and merchandisers must monitor this demand and ensure that they meet it accordingly in their product range in order to maximise profits. Social media channels also enable a dialogue to develop between the consumer and the brand that can be used to inform the design and development of products during the early stages in order to review consumer interest and anticipate potential product popularity. Thus, social media supports co-creation, and can be used by companies as a never-ending focus group (Fenton et al., 2019). Buyers and merchandisers also review social media for missed product opportunities and use it as another avenue to monitor their competitors. As such, it is fast becoming a channel to utilise as a form of product introduction for uncertain styles that brands want consumer input on. Hence, for buyers and merchandisers, social media platforms are valuable forms of collecting research and monitoring reactions to inform product assortment, pricing, and missed opportunities.

Social media also influences the sales and performance of products in the current trading range. Word-of-mouth (WoM), or electronic word-of-mouth as it is on social media (eWoM), has the ability to alter the information processing of consumers (Kozinets et al., 2010). A distinctive feature of eWoM is its higher levels of credibility and its ability to better convince consumers in comparison with information sent straight from the brand (Sivadas & Jindal, 2017). Research shows that consumers perceive social media sites to be more trustworthy sources of information than traditional advertising channels (Mangold & Faulds, 2009; Christodoulides et al., 2013). As a result, consumers are now using social media channels to search for products and source information about brands in place of traditional media (Mangold & Faulds, 2009; Bambauer-Sachse & Mangold, 2011; Christodoulides et al., 2013). Consumers share their experiences of items as well as photos of themselves wearing garments, which is very influential in terms of decision-making for other consumers. People share their reviews of products, and feedback on the delivery of items, their packaging, and the general features of the item, which becomes a motivating factor for individuals to browse for information on social media and influences online purchase intentions (Blazquez et al., 2019). Furthermore, the invention of social commerce now enables consumers to actually buy products directly through social media platforms such as Instagram and Facebook. This new transactional format is proving very popular, especially amongst younger consumers, with 44 per cent of 18- to 24-year-olds having purchased through Instagram and 40 per cent through Facebook in the last year (Drapers, 2019). This means merchandisers must carefully monitor yet another sales channel when assessing the performance of their product range.

Communication between buyers and suppliers

Technology has been instrumental in facilitating and improving the buyer–supplier relationship. In the past buyers communicated with various departments, store managers, and suppliers by fax, post, or phone calls, which was a laborious and rather restricted process. Buyers had to visit suppliers multiple times to discuss various stages of the production process, which was very time-consuming. The advent of the internet has changed the nature of communication completely, resulting in a plethora of tools that can be used to contact suppliers, other departments, and store managers, such as Facetime/Skype, WhatsApp, and email. This has resulted in a constant connection between buyers and suppliers and the ability to speak 24/7 from anywhere in the world.

Computer-aided design

Computer-aided design (CAD) has given designers the freedom to easily change and edit their sketches in a quick and inexpensive way (Stone, 2012). CAD enables designers to experiment more with colour combinations and styles without having to worry about mistakes and it being too time-consuming. As technology has advanced, CAD has become increasingly sophisticated, allowing designers to add folds, creases, and work on 3D images of garments. This enables designers to show the drapes and texture or garments accurately, which helps with the range-planning process as the buyers can see a realistic version of the garment without the expense of having a sample created. This is further advantageous for retailers as not having to get a sample created saves on the time and expense that this would involve and is more environmentally friendly. Furthermore, CAD also has the facility to aid the creation of the initial sample, as the darts, seams, and tailors' markings can be added to the image, which will result in fewer samples having to be made as the initial one will be more accurate, which again saves on time and expense and is better for the environment.

CAD techniques have many advantages; however, there are some key aspects of them that make the product-development process a much simpler, streamlined, and speedier process, as summarised by Guerrero (2009):

- Ability to modify or alter the image without changing its presentation;
- Able to develop designs using different elements and apply a uniform shape and colour;
- Ability to work in layers and handle each element separately, which gives more control over the image outcome;
- Convenient for storing images, enhancing communication between different departments and suppliers as they can easily be shown to them.

The CAD images are now commonly shown at pre-selection meetings in order to save on the cost of creating samples and minimise the negative environmental impact of having a sample shipped over by a manufacturer or wasting fabric. With the development and advances in a global and digital community that are part of the product-development process, it is more important than ever that the sharing of information is done in a recognisable and standardised format. The ease of sending and showing the CAD images (Figure 3.1) of products reduces misunderstandings between designers, buyers, and

Figure 3.1   **Example of a CAD product image**

suppliers, streamlining and simplifying communication as well as enhancing accurate product orders and requirements. This supports a much more sustainable approach to responsible sampling, an area that is a particular challenge for fashion retailers.

Digital printing

The computer design of fabrics has changed the nature of production in the fashion industry. New powerful computers will mean that fashion companies will be able to set the cost price of fabrics and garments before they are knitted or woven (Stone, 2012). This is a very positive move in terms of reducing garment waste and making businesses more sustainable. It is also good for the retailer in terms of sales and stock management, as it will only need to produce enough to meet the exact demand and not be left with surplus stock that has to go to markdown or eventually be destroyed.

There are many advantages of using digital printing (Guerrero, 2009):

- It can be applied to many different kinds of fabrics;
- Ability to instantly change designs;
- Samples and production use the same techniques, therefore ensuring accuracy and consistency between samples and mass production;
- Reduction of dyes and chemicals and labour, therefore making it a more sustainable option;
- Minimises excess stock of products and delivery time;
- More precision and finer details within imagery.

3D printing

3D printing, also known as additive manufacturing, is 'an automated additive manufacturing process that builds a product by depositing material into successive layers until it is complete' (Vanderploeg et al., 2017, p. 170). 3D printing is used in the fashion industry by numerous fashion retailers and designers for prototypes, customised made-to-order products, and artistic pieces. Furthermore, haute couture designers are now showing intricate, 3D printed dresses and accessories on the runway (Vanderploeg et al., 2017), and the technique has been used to make jewellery (Shapeways, 2018), bikinis (aRks, 2016), and shoes (Heater, 2018), thus making items available for a wider audience (McCormick et al., 2019).

The predominant use for 3D printing technologies is to produce prototypes of new garments and/or accessories (Yap & Yeong, 2014). Using 3D printing allows for objects to be printed in layers, from the ground up, based on digital designs, making the production cost per item the same as the cost of producing 10,000 items, thus radically lowering barriers to entry for start-ups that manufacture in small quantities and making customised products more cost-effective to produce (Abnett, 2016). Hence, 3D printing technology has revolutionised the supply chain by reducing the number of steps necessary to create a finished garment as well as the waste created when manufacturing a garment and/or a collection (McCormick et al., 2019). Therefore, 3D printing provides a cost-effective and fast way of producing low-volume, customised products (Huang et al., 2015). It is a more sustainable method of production as rather than producing off-cuts (surplus material) through traditional manufacturing, 3D printing uses only the necessary amount of raw materials to produce an item, totalling zero waste (Bak, 2003; Vanderploeg et al., 2017). However, a key disadvantage of using 3D printing is the time and energy it takes to create an item, meaning that only low volumes can be produced, thus making 3D printing more relevant for the luxury market as opposed to fast fashion (McCormick et al., 2019).

Moreover, 3D printing increases the availability and accessibility of personalised products for consumers. This idea of manufacturing within a range of products can not only give retailers a point of difference in a saturated market, but also if consumers are involved within the development of their own product there is much less chance of returns. However, McCormick et al. (2019) found that consumers do not associate any benefits with 3D printing, despite the fact that they found it to be novel and interesting and that only one one of 15 participants had actually purchased a 3D-printed item. This suggests that 3D printing is not yet mainstream in the mass market and so will be an area to watch for change over the next few years, and a potential opportunity for growth.

Measuring technologies

Body scanning

Body scanning captures the 3D form of a body using laser light sources in order to analyse individual measurement points (Gill, 2015). Body-scanned images can provide a realistic view of the body as it is generated from point cloud data taken from the participant's outline (Brownbridge et al., 2016). This method is advantageous for gaining a better understanding of the human body and its proportions, making it a more effective way of analysing body shape than manual measurement, photographs, or videotapes (Ashdown et al., 2004; Bye & LaBat, 2005). Once set up, body scanning is quite a quick process to use and the company can scan many people in one day, thus generating quite a large set of data in a reasonable timeframe. This makes body scanning a worthwhile investment by retailers/brands as it will aid garment technologists and buyers to ensure that the fit of garments is more accurate, thus reducing the number of potential returns.

Consumer measuring technologies are also being introduced in order to aid consumers in their decision-making process. Measuring technologies can be used to advise customers on the most suitable size for them to purchase. Consumers can simply use their own smartphone to measure their precise body and fit, which creates a unique sizing ID that can be accessed on retailers' websites and apps to easily figure out which size is best for them. This facilitates a much more efficient online experience and also reduces size-related returns (Imms, 2019).

Computer-aided manufacturing

Computer-aided manufacturing (CAM) involves the use of computers and new technologies to assist in all phases of product development, including planning, production, mechanisation, timing, administration, and quality control (Guerrero, 2009).

CAM is now common in most garment-producing factories and involves the use of computerised, programmable sewing machines, patternmaking machines, and cutting machines. This is so revolutionary as, previously, cutting garments by hand was very time-consuming. In textile mills, new machines combine higher production speeds with lower energy consumption; automated knitting and weaving machines produce more items with fewer operators than ever before (Stone, 2012). Thus, automation technology has seen the replacement of humans on the factory floor with robots and is fuelling a move away from the sourcing model of low-cost-labour countries to those that have these technologies in place and are closer to home (geographically) in order to minimise lead times (Twigg, 2017). In an industry plagued by ethical issues such as poor working conditions and low wages in factories, without the over-reliance on people working on the machines going forward, this could result in fundamental change. Furthermore, with CAM, data from many of the computers in the factory is linked during all stages. This enables suppliers to see what stage the garment is up to at any given time in the production process and ensure that it is progressing at optimum speed. This also minimises the capacity for errors as data is automatically inputted into the system.

Product life-cycle management systems

Product life-cycle management (PLM) systems are IT-based organisational software that help to manage the processes and information relating to product development, manufacturing, and distribution (Varley, 2019). As PLM platforms are 100 per cent IT-based they can be used anywhere in the world, enabling visibility, control, collaboration, and assistance in decision-making throughout the product's life cycle (Guerrero, 2009). This enables all the key information about products and the important decisions to happen and be stored on one key platform. The platform is visible to buyers, merchandisers, and suppliers across the product's whole life cycle, with each able to edit it and consult it at any time.

As the complexity and variety of products increases, so does the need for knowledge and expertise for developing products in order to avoid lengthy product-development cycles, higher development costs, and quality problems (Ameri & Dutta, 2005). By aiding and supporting quicker and more accurate communication across global networks and supply chains as well as the data collection of product histories, PLM systems facilitate a much more effective process. The technology promises quicker innovation in terms of creativity and technical design and can be seen both as a business strategy and also as a specialised information system, supporting all the product-related processes from development to disposal (d'Avolio et al., 2015). The information is externally stored so it is not specific to a set location. This integrated approach to product development has many benefits, including (PLM, n.d.):

- Products have a faster time to market;
- There are fewer errors and fewer re-works of products;
- Improved and better product quality;
- A greater insight into the process with better reporting and analytics;
- Improved communication and integration, including throughout the extended supply chain;
- Standardisation across all of the supply-chain network.

PLM systems have become a valuable tool for retailers and are increasingly being used throughout the fashion industry. However, there are also risks to be aware of when implementing a PLM system. It can be a challenging responsibility to learn and use new, complex technology platforms and software systems on top of an existing job role, placing extra stress and pressure on certain individuals. Furthermore, there can be issues that occur with learning and updating a system that can distract from the real job. Whilst technological advancements show positive results in terms of stock control and management, they can also create disruption. To fully benefit from a PLM system, all the key players in the supply-chain process, from design through to manufacturer, need to engage with the software and have the infrastructure to support it. PLM software packages need product data management (PDM) systems, as well as synchronous and asynchronous local and remote collaboration tools and a digital infrastructure allowing exchanges between software programmes (Segonds et al., 2014). It involves great commitment from top management, super-users, key-users, and consultants in order to achieve both the tactical and the strategic goals (d'Avolio et al., 2015). It is also important to note that in order for the PLM process to be accurate and effective it must be updated and used in a timely and correct manner. However, PLM implementation within fashion companies will address specific business needs; thus, opportunities and issues may vary from one company to another (d'Avolio et al., 2015).

Electronic data exchange and radio frequency identification

Every product contains a barcode, which, when scanned, logs information into a computer system, called an electronic point of sale (ePoS). Electronic data exchange (EDI) is the transfer of data electronically between different areas of the supply chain, compiled using ePoS equipment. This enables the merchandising team to see the sales data at each store on a daily basis. EDI is an essential component in the achievement of a quick-response strategy as it allows the supply chain to respond to real-time data (Barnes et al., 2006). Similarly, radio frequency identification (RFID) uses electronic tags for storing data, attaching a unique serial number to products in order to enable them to be tracked all the way through the supply chain (Stone, 2012). RFID holds much more information than barcodes and the information is read much faster, improving efficiency and accuracy of inventory and stock management (Stone, 2012). Nowadays this is used to understand how people interact with products and what they do with them (Varley, 2019).

Quick-response programmes and supply-chain management

Prior to the computer-aided systems, PDM systems, which appeared during the 1980s, were used to control and manage product information (Ameri & Dutta, 2005). The PDM systems were helpful but also limited in terms of their ease of use as they were very engineering-focused, making them not very user-friendly for users of a non-engineering background. They also failed to engage with areas such as sales, marketing, and supply-chain management as well as customers and suppliers; thus, they did not provide a holistic picture of product development, an aspect that is crucial for fashion. As a result, web applications such as enterprise resource planning, customer relationship management and supply-chain management (SCM) were introduced to support and manage the process more efficiently and support a quick-response (QR) strategy.

QR strategies gained momentum in the late 1990s alongside the advent of fast fashion. These strategies aim to be reactive to sales and produce garments in the quickest possible time in order to meet consumer demand. Stock-management systems can combat lead times between ordering and receiving stock, making it a digital and automated process. Using sales data to support the reordering of key products it intends to reduce any excess stock that is kept for replenishments. Retailers order more frequent, smaller shipments, facilitating a continuous flow of products from suppliers to retailers. This is seen as a co-operative effort between retailer and supplier and requires analysis of sales monitoring and the relaying of this information to the supplier. As a result, the buyer–supplier relationship has changed tremendously and risen in importance. Rather than being adversarial and based on trying to gain the highest profit, QR strategies mean that buyers have to work much more closely with suppliers in order to achieve a common goal. Buyers and suppliers have to trust each other in order to ensure that the right product is delivered to the customer at the right time (Stone, 2012). Yet, strong supplier relationships and technology are not the sole factors that underpin the achievement of QR Additional supply-chain factors can also contribute to a reduction in lead times and forecasting errors, both important elements when striving for QR (Fernie et al., 2010).

SCM has evolved from the QR strategies formed at the turn of the last century. Incorporating all the same benefits of QR, SCM also enables retailers and suppliers to share forecasting information, point-of-sales data, inventory information, and the supply and demand of materials or products (Stone, 2012). Nevertheless, for QR and SCM to work effectively the classification of *Model Stocks* is needed. Model Stocks is the classification of reasonable levels of inventory, or the ideal number of any item in terms of stock levels, enabling a lower level of stock to be available in store or in distribution centres as the stock comes directly from the supply base. The Model Stock amounts need to be maintained and adjusted in line with sales trends and consumer demands, an aspect which is particularly challenging for fashion products as they are unpredictable items that need careful consideration.

Blockchain

Blockchain is a distributed ledger technology that records confirmed and validated transactions in blocks, which are chained together. As each item proceeds through the supply chain each interaction is registered as a 'block' that represents unique information, creating a complete and accurate digital record of the product journey (Lemieux, 2016). Thus, by using blockchain technology, the origin of the garment is clearly traced and can be verified, an aspect that is extremely important in the current climate where transparency of supply chains is being called for. Microchips using blockchain technology can tell a customer with complete certainty whether a piece of clothing is genuine or an imitation, whether it was stolen, and where it was made, and the product's general history. Shoppers could also learn about the composition of a garment, where the fabric was grown, and what chemicals have been used (Chitrakorn, 2019). All this information is accessible via a smartphone, and can help prevent counterfeiting and theft as well as helping retailers to garner greater trust and brand loyalty throughout the product's life cycle, as it can tell consumers not just where an item was made, but also who it was made by, the conditions they worked in, and how much they were paid (Chitrakorn, 2019).

Data-analytics companies

With the development of fast changing products and the increase in consumer demand on the industry, buyers and merchandisers are starting to use data to support them in decision-making. As a result, data analytics is now an industry-standard tool used to get up-to-date pricing and product information. Companies such as Edited and INstock from WGSN are supporting product decision-making with real-time data analytics. The ability to track every commercial trend and product type worldwide live ensures that product decisions are aligned with the market and competitors. Being able to see in real time information regarding competitors' product assortments, pricing strategies, discounts, and sizing availability, as well as making comparisons against their own offerings, is an incredibly powerful tool. As such, buyers and merchandisers need analysis skills more than ever to capitalise on these data-rich platforms in order to make sense of the technology and the information it provides. It is important to be able to absorb great amounts of data and interpret and translate it into useful evidence to support decision-making whilst being both proactive and reactive. On-demand access to data transforms the research capabilities by widening the net of available knowledge, but by itself it could be too big and too daunting to fully assess (Clark, 2015). However, by solely relying on data analytics, there is a risk that the decision-making can become very data-heavy, resulting in a lack of creativity in range planning. In some cases, this can lead to a loss of identity and direction for some retailers as they continue to be reactive and lose the balance of offering what consumers want with their own distinct style. Hence, data analytics provides an excellent direction for what to include in a product range, but it should not replace human decision-making.

Try before you buy

'Try before you buy' or 'buy now, pay later' models were rolled out by many retailers from 2018 onwards and have increased in prominence since. 'Try before you buy' uses payment provider Klarna to enable consumers to order items and then pay for them at a later date. Thus, customers are able to try on clothing or test out consumer goods in the convenience of their own home. Depending on the experience, they can then send back any products they do not want for free or for a small fee. Klarna also offers the option of paying for the item(s) in instalments rather than all in one go. The rise in popularity of services such as this is a result of consumers now wanting more flexible payment and delivery options. Ultimately consumers want choice. 'Try before you buy' offers consumers the convenience of paying when they want to and not having to pay for something that they then decide they do not want and wait for a return.

The upside of this for retailers is that their sales figures are not as inaccurate, as they are not waiting on returns. Furthermore, it can encourage consumers to order multiple sizes and styles without having to worry about the upfront cost, freeing them to try more unusual styles and potentially keeping more items than they originally intended to, thus increasing sales (Brown, 2018a). However, it does mean that money and stock are tied up as retailers have to wait a long time before they receive profits from garments. It also means that garments spend a lot of time out for delivery and back again if a consumer does not want it, meaning it could be then back on the shop floor/website later, after consumer demand has peaked, making it harder to sell.

Artificial intelligence

In fashion, AI has the ability to help brands and retailers with predictive forecasting, capacity planning, and merchandising. Designers, merchandisers, and buyers could all work alongside AI to predict what customers want to wear, before they even know themselves (Abnett, 2016). This means that consumers can enjoy the benefits of better product availability as well as faster, more accurate deliveries. Furthermore, robots are increasingly being used in back-end operations, with many retailers now increasing the number of robots doing their packing operations each year (Brown, 2018b). By automating these processes, retailers will free up employees for more consumer-facing roles, an aspect that is essential as customer service becomes ever more important (Brown, 2018b).

In addition to supply-chain benefits, AI can also help create a smoother browsing experience and improve customer retention through personalisation (Chitrakorn, 2019). For instance, chatbots are now being used in online fashion retailing in order to improve the customer experience (Brown, 2018b). Chatbots, such as the virtual shop assistant Kik on H&M's website, enable consumers to tell the bot what they want and like and it gives them recommendations. Hence, using AI helps retailers to recognise, remember, and recommend certain products to their customers, improving their understanding of them and their needs. However, it is important to note that currently AI is at the beginning of its application and is controversial because of the potential for privacy intrusion and its ability to replace the human workforce (Roncha, 2019).

Innovative technologies influencing the fashion industry

New technologies and applications are being developed continuously, influencing the fashion industry year-on-year. Whilst not all the new technologies will directly impact the role and responsibilities of the buyer and merchandiser on a day-to-day basis, they will address some of the bigger issues within the fashion retail industry and change the consumer shopping experience. Technology, combined with dwindling attention spans (Generation Z has an eight-second attention span compared with Generation X's 12 seconds), means people expect to be delivered relevant content and product faster than ever (Goldfingle, 2019). Below are some of the key technological developments that are changing the fashion industry today and going forward.

Voice-recognition technology

The search for products is evolving and new voice-assisted technologies could change the way that retailers interact with their customers and the way their customers shop. Although the market is still relatively new in the UK, IMRG estimated that by 2020, 20 per cent of all online spend would be driven by voice assistance (Brown, 2018b). Thus, the growth and popularity of devices such as Google Home and Amazon's Alexa have created a new opportunity for retailers by providing them with a virtual shopping assistant in their own home. Customers can tell their voice-assisted technology exactly what they are looking for, perhaps a specific dress, or ask for advice on what to wear, and the virtual shopping assistant can support the customer with all that they need. This prevents consumers from having to scroll through hundreds of items online, making their experience more convenient and personal. The virtual shopping assistants can also offer customers personalised suggestions based on their purchase history and the latest trends (Imms, 2019). In such a saturated market, it is more important than ever to ensure that consumers are able to find the product that they want, and this form of personalisation helps to ensure the right products reach the right customers at the right time.

Visual search

Visual search allows consumers to search for products using photographs or images rather than having to manually type the key word(s) into the search bar. ASOS was one of the first retailers to do this and it works effectively as, in a world where Instagram images are so influential in fashion, consumers can simply insert this image into the search bar and 'buy the look'. Not only does this enable retailers to expand their product reach by recommending a larger selection of products, it also boosts customer engagement (Imms, 2019).

Augmented reality

Augmented reality (AR) is an interactive technology that alters the physical environment with superimposed virtual elements to create an immersive experience (Javornik, 2016). Examples of AR are Magic Mirrors, which overlay a consumer's image with pictures of clothes, as well as filters that can be imposed on a setting or person via a mobile app (Kim et al., 2017; Boardman et al., 2019). Magic Mirrors enable consumers to be able to virtually try on clothing and change the colours and sizes of garments (Hwangbo et al., 2017), potentially improving the customer experience in store as they will not have to wait for fitting rooms. AR could also be used by consumers at home via their smartphone in order to see how garments would look like on them. This will help with consumer decision-making and potentially reduce the rate of returns for retailers. AR will, therefore, broaden the variety of options available for consumers to try on as the experience has no restrictions on the number of items that can be explored. Retailers are also using virtual collections to test consumer reaction prior to any sampling or costing taking place, which will reduce the costly sampling element (Lieber, 2019) and also improve the environmental impact by not having to have as many samples made. By implementing AR technology, buyers can reuse, recycle, and change product templates, thinking more long-term, making range planning much more time- and cost-effective (Lieber, 2019) as well as more sustainable.

Virtual reality

Virtual reality (VR) is a computer-generated 3D immersive illusion which can be interacted with through the use of specialist headsets. Similar to AR, VR is a 'consumer-facing' technology, which means that the consumer can interact with and directly experience it whilst being either in the physical store or at home (Boardman et al., 2019). The American department store Macy's was one of the first stores to create a fully functioning VR retail environment, enabling consumers to virtually walk through the store and purchase items by looking at them from anywhere in the world (Alibaba Group, 2016; Boardman et al., 2019). Furthermore, Coach provided VR headsets in their stores so that their customers could see their latest fashion show (Jian, 2017). This is an area that retailers could capitalise on, as not only would it encourage shoppers to stay in the store longer (Boardman et al., 2019), but it also provides an opportunity to increase consumer demand of certain items and assess consumer sentiment towards a new or upcoming range. Furthermore, VR could be used to highlight the retailer's sustainable or ethical credentials by allowing consumers to see where their items came from by visiting the factory where it was made without leaving a store. In an era where sustainability is now an essential item on the agenda for retailers, VR offers a great opportunity to be more transparent and increase brand's the relationship with customers.

Gamification

Gamification enables consumers to digitally engage with brands through games, competitions, and virtual experiences (Clark, 2019). This is becoming a popular trend in digital marketing. For example, Manchester-based pureplay retailer I Saw It First teamed up with reality TV show *Love Island*, enabling customers to take a 'Which islander are you?' quiz and shop from the clothing that contestants were wearing on the show (Clark, 2019). Thus, gamification adds a fun element to the shopping experience that attracts consumers and can facilitate close relationships between retailers and customers (Pachoulakis & Kapetanakis, 2012). Gamification techniques are also being used within marketing campaigns to personalise product suggestions. Personalisation of the shopping experience is hugely important and can help provide a competitive advantage for retailers due to the enhanced experience that it provides for consumers. Hence, gamification can be used to drive engagement between the brand, consumer, and product.

CHAPTER SUMMARY

This chapter has demonstrated how technological developments have impacted on the fashion industry. Technology has changed the way in which items are produced and marketed as well as the nature of communication both internally and externally for fashion retailers and brands. The entire supply chain is becoming digitised, which can have both benefits and drawbacks, as carefully outlined. For instance, cost analysis can now be done very quickly and efficiently, and digital renderings of products can be produced using CAD, eliminating the need for expensive prototypes (Twigg, 2017). As such, technologies can provide financial benefits for retailers, as they are cutting unnecessary costs, whilst at the same time can be more environmentally friendly with fewer materials being wasted through off-cuts. More recently, technology has been used to gather data on customers, a precious commodity in a world where it is increasingly difficult to stand out and appeal to consumers amongst the crowd. Retailers can now act faster and are more equipped for the ever-changing environment, whilst at the same time offering a more rounded customer experience with chatbots, AI, AR, and VR offering value-added services that can enhance consumer decision-making processes. Going forward, technology will continue to have an impact on the fashion industry, with production becoming increasingly automated. Retailers are now using technology to provide more exciting and compelling experiences to increase customers back into stores (Boardman et al., 2019).

References

Abnett, K. (2016). 'VisionQuest: 3 technologies shaping the future of fashion', 22 February, Business of Fashion, available at: www. businessoffashion.com/articles/fashion-tech/digital-fashion-tech-in-2016-messaging-virtual-reality-3d-printing.

Alibaba Group. (2016). 'Buy+ The first complete VR shopping experience', YouTube, available at: www.youtube.com/watch?v=-HcKRBKlilg.

Ameri, F., & Dutta, D. (2005). 'Product lifecycle management: Closing the knowledge loops', *Computer-Aided Design and Applications*, 2(5): 577–590.

aRks. (2016). 'Multidisciplinary creative duo Samuele and Rosanna of aRks Studio present "Coral" – their first 3D printed bikini collection', n.d., available at: www.arks3d.com/en/press.html.

Ashdown, S.P., Loker, S., Schoenfelder, K., & Lyman Clarke, L. (2004). 'Using 3D scans for fit analysis', *Journal of Textile and Apparel, Technology and Management*, 4(1): 12.

Bak, D. (2003). 'Rapid prototyping or rapid production? 3D printing processes move industry towards the latter', *Assembly Automation*, 23(4): 340–345.

Bambauer-Sachse, S., & Mangold, S. (2011). 'Brand equity dilution through negative online word-of-mouth communication', *Journal of Retailing and Consumer Services*, 18(1): 38–45.

Barnes, L., Gaynor Lea-Greenwood, M., Hayes, S., & Jones, N. (2006). 'Fast fashion: A financial snapshot', *Journal of Fashion Marketing and Management*, 10(3): 282–300.

Blazquez, M., Zhang, T., Boardman, R., & Henninger, C.E. (2019). 'Exploring The Effects of Social Commerce on Consumers' Browsing Motivations and Purchase Intentions in the UK Fashion Industry', in Boardman, R., Blazquez, M., Henninger, C.E., & Ryding, D. (eds), *Social Commerce: Consumer Behaviour in Online Environments*. London: Palgrave Macmillan, pp. 99–116.

Boardman, R., Henninger, C.E., & Zhu, A. (2019). 'Augmented Reality and Virtual Reality – New Drivers for Fashion Retail?', in Vignali, G., Reid, L., Ryding, D., & Henninger, C.E. (eds), *Technology-Drive Sustainability: Innovation in the Fashion Supply Chain*. London: Palgrave Macmillan, pp. 155–172.

Brown, H. (2018a). 'Hit or miss: Testing retail's technology developments', 5 December, Drapers 2018, available at: www.drapersonline.com/business-operations/hit-or-miss-testing-retails-technology-developments/7033169.article.

Brown, H. (2018b). 'Five ways the online world will change in 2018', 1 February, Drapers, available at: www.drapersonline.com/retail/ecommerce/five-ways-the-online-world-will-change-in-2018/7028746.article.

Brownbridge, K., Sanderson, R., & Gill, S. (2016). 'Aspirational bodies: Fashioning new beauty ideals', *Interdisciplinary.net,* pp. 1–12.

Bye, E., & LaBat, K. (2005). 'An analysis of apparel industry fit sessions', *Journal of Textile and Apparel, Technology and Management,* 4(3): 1–5.

Chaffey, D. (2019). 'Global social media research summary 2019', 12 February, Smart Insights, available at: www.smartinsights.com/social-media-marketing/social-media-strategy/new-global-social-media-research/.

Chitrakorn, K. (2019). '5 technologies transforming retail in 2018', 19 January, Business of Fashion, available at: www.businessoffashion.com/articles/fashion-tech/5-technologies-transforming-retail.

Christodoulides, G., Michaelidou, N., & Siamagka, N. (2013). 'A typology of internet users based on comparative affective states: Evidence from eight countries', *European Journal of Marketing,* 47(1/2): 153–173.

Clark, J. (2015). *Fashion Merchandising; Principles and Practices.* Basingstoke: Palgrave.

Clark, T. (2019). 'Fashion retail gets its game on', 17 July, Drapers, available at: www.drapersonline.com/news/fashion-retail-gets-its-game-on/7036733.article.

D'Avolio, E., Bandinelli, R., & Rinaldi, R. (2015). 'Improving new product development in the fashion industry through product lifecycle management: A descriptive analysis', *International Journal of Fashion Design, Technology and Education,* 8: 108–121.

Drapers. (2019). 'Report: Mapping the multichannel customer journey: Connected consumer 2019, Rebecca Thompson', 25 September, available at: www.drapersonline.com/business-operations/special-reports/mapping-the-multichannel-customer-journey-connected-consumer-2019/7037722.article.

Fenton, A., Timperley, N., & Boardman, R. (2019). 'Visible Change and Inspiring Others: Making Events that Challenge Innovation', in Fenton, A., Fletcher, G., & Griffiths, M. (eds),

Strategic Digital Transformation: A Results-Driven Approach. Abingdon: Routledge, pp. 149–156.

Fernie, J., Fernie, J., Sparks, L., & McKinnon, A. (2010). 'Retail logistics in the UK: Past, present and future', *International Journal of Retail & Distribution Management,* 38(11/12): 894–914.

Gill, S. (2015). 'A review of research and innovation in garment sizing, prototyping and fitting', *Textile Progress,* 47(1): 1–85.

Goldfingle, G. (2019). 'Keeping up to speed with the customer', 15 May, Drapers, available at: www.drapersonline.com/news/keeping-up-to-speed-with-the-customer/7035810.article.

Guerrero, J. (2009). *New Fashion and Design Technologies.* London: A&C Black.

Heater, B. (2018). 'Adidas joins Carbon's board as its 3D printed shoes finally drop', 18 January, Techcrunch, available at: https://techcrunch.com/2018/01/18/adidas-joins-carbons-board-as-its-3d-printed-shoes-finally-drop/.

Huang, Y., Leu, M.C., Mazumder, J., & Donmez, A. (2015). 'Additive manufacturing: Current state, future potential, gaps and needs, and recommendations', *Journal of Manufacturing Science and Engineering,* 137(1): 1–10.

Hwangbo, H., Kim, S.Y., & Cha, K.J. (2017). 'Use of the smart store for persuasive marketing and immersive customer experiences: A case study of Korean apparel enterprise', *Mobile Information Systems,* 2017: 1–17.

Imms, K. (2019). 'Four tech innovations pushing retail boundaries', 3 October, Drapers, available at: www.drapersonline.com/news/latest-news/four-tech-innovations-pushing-retail-boundaries/7037763.article.

Javornik, A. (2016). 'Augmented reality: Research agenda for studying the impact of its media characteristics on consumer behaviour', *Journal of Retailing and Consumer Services,* 30: 252–261.

Jian, E. (2017). 'Virtual reality: Growth engine for fashion?', 28 February, Business of Fashion, available at: www.businessoffashion.com/articles/fashion-tech/virtual-reality-growthengine-for-fashion.

Kim, H.-Y., Lee, J.Y., Mun, J.M., & Johnson, K.K.P. (2017). 'Consumer adoption of smart in-store technology: Assessing the predictive value of attitude versus beliefs in the technology acceptance model', *International Journal of Fashion Design, Technology and Education*, 10(2): 26–36.

Kozinets, R.V., De Valck, K., Wojnicki, A.C., & Wilner, S.J. (2010). 'Networked narratives: Understanding word-of-mouth marketing in online communities', *Journal of Marketing*, 74(2): 71–89.

Lemieux, V.L. (2016). 'Trusting records: Is blockchain technology the answer?', *Records Management Journal*, 26(2): 110–139.

Lieber, C. (2019). 'Would you buy a virtual pair of Nikes?', 8 July, Business of Fashion, available at: www.businessoffashion.com/articles/fashion-tech/virtual-fashion-digital-products.

Mangold, W.G.W., & Faulds, D.D.J. (2009). 'Social media: The new hybrid element of the promotion mix', *Business Horizons*, 52(4): 357–365.

McCormick, H., Zhang, R., Boardman, R., Jones, C., & Henninger, C.E. (2019). '3D Printing in the Fashion Industry: A Fad or the Future?', in Vignali, G., Reid, L., Ryding, D., & Henninger, C.E. (eds), *Technology-Drive Sustainability: Innovation in the Fashion Supply Chain*. London: Palgrave Macmillan, pp. 137–154.

Mountney, H., & Murphy, D. (2017). 'See now buy now how ready are you?', n.d., Kurt Salmon, available at: www.accenture.com/t20170531T020308Z__w__/us-en/_acnmedia/PDF-53/Accenture-Strategy-DD-See-Now-Buy-Now.pdf.

Pachoulakis, I., & Kapetanakis, K. (2012). 'Augmented reality platforms for virtual fitting rooms', *International Journal of Multimedia & Its Applications*, 4(4): 35.

PLM. (n.d.). 'Product Lifecycle Management (PLM)', n.d., available at: www.product-lifecycle-management.com.

Roncha, A. (2019). 'Fashion Brand Management', in Varley, R., Roncha, A., Radclyffe-Thomas, N., & Gee, L. (eds), *Fashion Management: A Strategic Approach*. New York, NY: Red Globe Press, pp. 105–129.

Segonds, F., Mantelet, F., Maranzana, N., & Gaillard, S. (2014). 'Early stages of apparel design: How to define collaborative needs for PLM and fashion?', *International Journal of Fashion Design, Technology and Education*, 7(2): 105–114.

Shapeways. (2018). 'About us', n.d., Shapeways, available at: www.shapeways.com/about.

Shaw, M.J. (2017). *e-business Management*. Chams: Springer.

Sivadas, E., & Jindal, R. (2017). 'Alternative measures of satisfaction and word of mouth', *Journal of Services Marketing*, 31(2): 119–130.

Stone, E. (2012). *In Fashion*. 2nd ed. New York, NY: Fairchild.

Twigg, M. (2017). 'Is the old sourcing model dead?', 14 September, Business of Fashion, available at: www.businessoffashion.com/articles/global-currents/is-the-old-sourcing-model-dead.

Vanderploeg, A., Lee, S., & Mamp, M. (2017). 'The application of 3D printing technology in the fashion industry', *International Journal of Fashion Design, Technology and Education*, 10(2): 170–171.

Varley, R. (2019). 'Fashion Marketing', in Varley, R., Roncha, A., Radclyffe-Thomas, N., & Gee, L. (eds), *Fashion Management: A Strategic Approach*. New York, NY: Red Globe Press, pp. 43–57.

Yap, Y.L., & Yeong, W.Y. (2014). 'Additive manufacture of fashion and jewellery products: A mini review', *Virtual and Physical Prototyping*, 9(3): 195–201.

CHAPTER 4

The buying cycle and critical path

Introduction

This chapter outlines the entire buying cycle that fashion buyers and merchandisers will follow in order to conduct their role and responsibilities. The chapter discusses the purpose and importance of the buying cycle and provides a holistic overview of what occurs in each of the stages. The chapter also describes the nature of the critical path and analyses how essential it is as a tool used by buyers and merchandisers.

Learning outcomes

By the end of this chapter you will be able to:

* Outline the key stages of the buying cycle;
* Describe the critical path and how it is used by buyers and merchandisers;
* Discuss the importance of the critical path in buying and merchandising.

The buying cycle

The fashion buying cycle refers to all the processes involved in the creation of a product range. The buying cycle includes everything from the design of a product to the production, shipping, allocation, delivery to store, and, finally, sale to the customer. Buyers and merchandisers are involved in all of the different stages of the buying cycle. The cycle will vary depending on the company, the market, and the product retailed. Most own-label fashion retailers will follow all the stages of the buying cycle (but the order in which they do so may vary slightly), and even the smaller, independent retailers will adhere to the majority of the stages. Different retailers will also use different terminology for the different stages within the buying cycle.

The traditional buying cycle took 12 months from concept to customer, which meant that orders were placed for bulk manufacturing six months before the range was launched into stores (Goworek, 2007). Although this is still true for some fashion retailers, such as luxury retailers, those selling classic items, or slow-fashion retailers, most fast-fashion retailers' buying cycles are now much quicker, and start much closer to the launch date. Figure 4.1 depicts a contemporary fashion buying cycle.

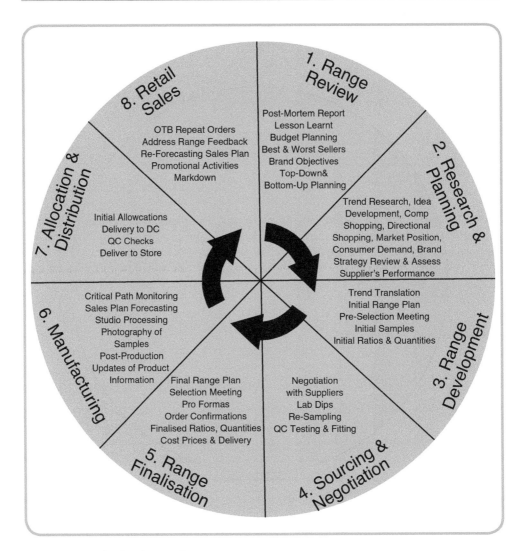

Figure 4.1   **The buying cycle**

The buying cycle involves the research and design of a product, the creation of samples and fabric testing, manufacturing the product and getting it delivered to the UK distribution centre, allocating it to most appropriate stores, and selling it to the customers, then monitoring and reacting to the sales figures. The buying cycle is a fluid concept but is generally followed in some form by the majority of own-label fashion retailers, with some implementing it faster than others. Nevertheless, for all fashion retailers, buyers and merchandisers are involved throughout the whole buying-cycle process, with buyers taking the lead at some stages and merchandisers taking the lead at others.

Stages of the buying cycle

As Figure 4.1 outlines, the fashion buying cycle consists of eight stages. The buying cycle is generally followed in the order that the stages are depicted in Figure 4.1 as, in some cases, activities need to be completed in order to progress to the next stage. Therefore, overall the buying cycle is a linear and sequential model, although in some instances, when products have issues, or ideas and plans change, products can move backwards if necessary. Each of the stages is summarised briefly below, whereby the various activities that occur during them and the responsibilities of buyers and merchandisers during those stages is outlined. These stages will be discussed at greater length and in much more detail throughout the following chapters of this book.

1. *Range review* – the range-review stage requires the buying and merchandising teams to address the product performance and financial outcomes of the previous season. Buyers and merchandisers will do this with the aid of a post-mortem report, a document containing all the sales data from the previous season, outlining the key best and worst sellers. The purpose of the range-review stage is to inform financial planning and the upcoming product range plan. The range-review stage enables buyers and merchandisers to develop ideas of what the ranges, assortments, and products could be for the upcoming season, particularly in terms of the budget available, expected margins, and financial expectations for departments, categories, and product areas. The planning and range review are done from a top-down (trend-forecasting-driven) and bottom-up (consumer-driven) approach to ensure that all areas of the business are considered and a well-executed and researched plan is developed. Department and category budget plans as well as a skeletal range plan with initial quantities will be developed to support the next stage: research and planning.
2. *Research and planning* – once the skeletal plan of ranges and budgets are compiled the research and planning can begin. This stage is conducted in order to aid and support the development of the planned ranges, assortments, and specific products, specifically considering the brand or retailer's signature style, corporate strategy, and target consumer's expectations. Product, trend, market, consumer, and supplier research is conducted at this point and shared collectively with the various teams within the departments so that there is a shared vision of identity and also no overlap of ideas or duplication of efforts. In particular, trend concept boards, consumer boards, competitor shops, directional shops, and supplier appraisals/reviews will be created and shared.
3. *Range development* – once all the research and planning has been collated and shared within the teams, the range plan can now be developed into a more formalised assortment. Trends and ideas are translated into the initial range plans with breakdowns of colours, prints, fabrics, and quantities. Initial samples and product costings are requested from suppliers. Pre-selection meetings take place during this stage, whereby buyers and merchandisers present the initial range plan to the whole buying and merchandising teams, including senior management. Aspects that are presented and discussed at the pre-selection meeting include the computer-aided-designed

range plan, initial samples, colourways, sizes, and quantities, as well as financial information. Decisions about each product in the range plan is made within these pre-selection meetings, considering which samples will be taken forward for finalisation and whether these will have any alterations or amendments.

4. *Sourcing and negotiation* – once the products and samples from the pre-selection meeting have been finalised and the alterations and amendments made clear, this information is forwarded to the appropriate supplier, where an accurate sample is produced in the correct colour, fit size, and acceptable fabric-quality level. Accurate cost prices, quantity, the recommended retail price, a breakdown of size ratios, and required delivery time are also generated at this stage. Once these aspects have been decided the product is ready to be finalised.

5. *Range finalisation* – this stage involves the finalisation of all completed and accurate products. Products are finalised by the approval and sign-off of the sealed sample along with the pricing and manufacturing information. This information feeds into the pro formas for confirmed orders to suppliers. Until this point changes can still be made to products as new information and decision-making can change the assortment plan, but once it is finalised it cannot be altered as it is approved for bulk manufacture.

6. *Manufacturing* – this stage of the buying cycle is where the products are produced by suppliers (manufacturers). Although, in the majority of cases, this process is conducted externally to the buying and merchandising team, it is a stage that must be carefully monitored. The critical path is an essential tool that can be used here by buyers and merchandisers to check the progress of an item and its expected shipping and delivery times. Communication throughout the supply chain is crucial to ensure that there are no issues with production or any delays with transportation, so that the items will arrive at the retail warehouses as expected.

7. *Allocation and distribution* – deliveries from the various suppliers need to be processed within the warehouse to make sure that the product ranges are ready to be sent to stores or sold online. The boxed or hung garments need to be checked and categorised for easy distribution to the many different-sized stores in various geographical locations. Different levels of stock will be allocated to different stores based on their size and location and the type of consumers there. As not all stores will receive the same number of products, personalised store deliveries are processed and dispatched at this point to ensure that the required delivery time to the store is met and that products are available to buy online on time.

8. *Retail sales* – the final stage in the buying cycle is the trading period itself. This is where products are available for sale to be bought by customers. Sale figures are monitored carefully by merchandisers to gauge the performance of the product range. The sales information is used to inform rebuys, promotional activities, planning for the next season, and even products that are still in the development stages.

The schedule is usually planned out by buyers and merchandisers in reverse order, starting with the launch date of the range. This is because buyers and merchandisers plan when the optimum time will be to launch a specific product range that will suit their target customer and the conditions in the marketplace in order to maximise sales. The stages of the buying cycle primarily involve buyers and merchandisers but some stages also involve other departments, such as the designer in the design stage, the garment technologist in the sampling stages, and marketing at various points so that they know how to promote the range when it launches into stores (where visual merchandisers and store managers will also take a lead role). The relationship between buyers and merchandisers with other departments (discussed in detail in Chapter 2) during different stages of the buying cycle is highlighted below.

The buyer and merchandiser roles within the buying cycle

Managing the buying cycle requires excellent teamwork and communication skills between the buyer and the merchandiser. Buyers and merchandisers each have different roles within the buying cycle. Some of the stages involve both the buyer and merchandiser's input, whereas in other stages the buyer takes the lead or the merchandiser takes the lead. Figure 4.2 illustrates the different relationships with other departments within the buying cycle.

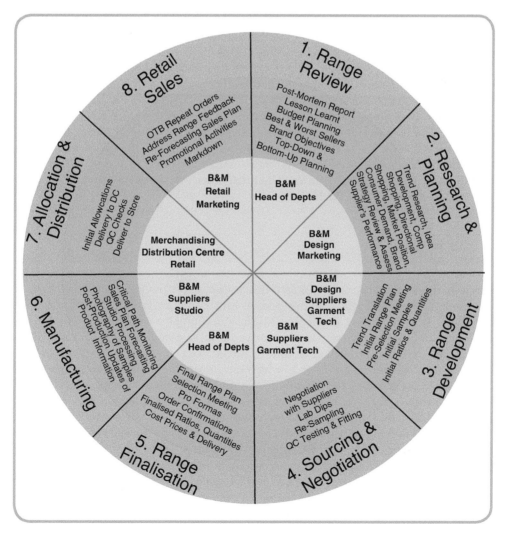

Figure 4.2   Relationships with other departments within the buying cycle

The changing nature of the buying cycle

Different types of retailers have different buying cycles with varying speeds to market. Nowadays fast-fashion retailers produce smaller ranges that are delivered much more frequently in order to create a sense of 'newness' in stores, refreshing their product offering regularly for the contemporary consumer. Although the stages of the buying cycle are generally the same for most retailers, it is not uncommon for additional stages to be added or for some stages to be skipped. The buying cycle needs to be a flexible and agile model that allows for change dependent on the retailer and the ever-changing, volatile market. The unpredictable nature of the market and the need for fast-fashion retailers to be reactive to consumer demand questions whether every product needs to go through the full buying cycle in contemporary fashion retailing. For instance, it could be argued that some of the early stages within the buying cycle that are associated with product development may not all be needed in order to create a commercially viable product, especially for short-term fads or on-trend hero pieces where speed-to-market is of the essence and these pieces are not designed to carry over for multiple seasons. With the increase of demand-driven forecasting, in-season buying, and short lead times, if the stages or activities are not entirely necessary then products should be able to move speedily through them or even skip them entirely. A positive of this, alongside it being quicker to market and ensuring that it is available for sale during the peak demand, is that it would be a more sustainable production method as there will be less sampling and fewer airmiles travelled by the product from supplier to retailer. However, the downside to this is that the less fabric testing and sampling conducted, the riskier it is in terms of the quality level of the garment as errors or inaccuracies may be missed, which could lead to an increase in product returns (potentially then eventually ending up in landfill, which is obviously less sustainable).

The buying cycle for fast-fashion retailers

Fast-fashion retailers have revolutionised the concept of the buying cycle. Their business model has seen a huge increase in the speed at which products moved through the cycle. Rather than the traditional 12 months, fast-fashion pureplay retailers can have buying cycles of just 12 weeks, or even as short as two to three weeks if sourced from the UK, from design to online. Product development is conducted at an enhanced level of speed for these types of retailers and brands, which can impact the holistic process and create differences in the activities and tasks that are normally seen in the buying cycle. In some instances, products may not pass through all of the stages if they are not required to, or, more commonly, there are stages and tasks happening in tandem in order to accelerate the speed. If the buying cycle is started too far in advance of the product launch date, the forecasting of trends and customer demand may be inaccurate and the range not very popular or successful in terms of sales. However, implementing it too close to the season can result in higher manufacturing costs as the supplier has to be close to the domestic market or operating in the domestic market (a near-shoring or re-shoring sourcing strategy is implemented), or even poorer quality of garments due to rushing and missing out particular stages, such as all of the sampling stages. Nevertheless, the balance of being the first to market with a key product is the key objective for these businesses. Hence, over the last decade buying cycles have become much faster and are now more flexible and agile as they have to be very reactive to demand. As a result, fashion product development for online fast-fashion retailers is not precisely sequential as it is in the traditional buying cycle, but is a series of linked activities that overlap, requiring concise planning for time, resources, and people in order to address the implications of rapidly changing consumer demand and speed of delivery to the market (Parker-Strak et al., 2020).

A critique of the buying cycle

The buying cycle helps to provide an element of structure to the role of the buyer. It illustrates the sequential nature of the role and the variety of activities that occur within each stage. These activities and tasks will vary in time and effort for each product in the range. This is due to the challenging nature of product development and the relationships with external suppliers, as some products will move swiftly through the cycle whilst others may be slower or stall in certain sections due to unforeseen circumstances. The challenging demand-driven retail environment that exists also impacts how buyers and merchandisers are managing the roles and the responsibilities that they have.

As a result, buyers are increasing the amount of in-season buying that they do (using their open-to-buy budget) in order to ensure that they stock all of the current trends that will appeal to their target market. Therefore, nowadays fast-fashion buyers order smaller quantities of items either just before or actually during the trading season to 'top up' their ranges with on-trend items that are less risky as consumer demand is more predictable when much closer to or actually in the season. A more frequent buying strategy may result in higher overall costs, but it could still be more profitable for the company as a whole as markdowns and leftover stock will be reduced because the buyer has a more accurate idea about consumer demand (Bruce & Daly, 2006). This shows that range planning is just as much demand-driven as it is forecast-driven, a shift that has occurred over the last few years, emphasising the importance of bottom-up factors such as social media influencers in dictating what people want to wear. Furthermore, it is now questionable whether the traditional buying cycle of one year exists at all for fashion brands, or whether it is only luxury brands/show-fashion retailers that can afford to have such an extended amount of time. Either way, the relationship between buyers and suppliers is more important than ever (an aspect that will be discussed further in Chapter 8).

The critical path

A critical path (Figure 4.3) is a schedule of key dates for product development and manufacturing. It is known in industry as a critical path because it is critical that these dates are met if the product ranges are to be launched for sale at the intended time (Goworek, 2007). Thus, the critical path is a tool that is used by buyers, merchandisers, and suppliers to map out the key stages of development, production, and delivery of a product from the product-development stages to when it is launched onto the shop floor. It essentially

Department	Womenswear
Product style number	DR34560
Product description	Gio Maxi Dress
Supplier	GMA Textiles
COO	Turkey
Quantity	350
Product development approved	28/03/2020
Sample approval	14/04/2020
Pre-selection meeting	21/04/2020
Garment fitting approval	28/04/2020
Selection meeting	11/05/2020
Order confirmation date	25/05/2020
Fabric order confirmation	27/05/2020
Bulk production start date	09/06/2020
Shipping start date	25/06/2020
DC arrival date	04/07/2020
Product launch date	14/07/2020

Figure 4.3   **Example of a basic critical path document**

puts the dates and deadlines on each of the key stages of the buying cycle in order to ensure that the product is on time and will not be late for the date that it is due to be launched into stores. This ensures that buyers and merchandisers know exactly what stage of the buying cycle each product is up to and can monitor its progress and ensure that it is running on time.

As with the buying cycle, the critical path is planned in reverse order, starting with the launch date then working backwards to ensure that each stage will be completed on time and to see when each stage needs to begin in order to achieve this. This document, therefore, essentially deals with the lead times of each of the stages when producing a product. A product's lead time is the amount of time taken for the planning, purchasing, and production steps to be implemented before the item is available to be sold to customers (Granger, 2015).

Each item in the product range will have its own critical path with its own key set of dates, as not all items in the same range are necessarily being manufactured by the same supplier and some items take longer to plan and create than others, such as fashion, sequined, and embroidered items, vs basic T-shirts and leggings. Thus, the lead times of products will vary depending on their classification and the factory's size and location and how busy it is, as well as whether it does any outsourcing. This highlights the complex nature of the buying and merchandising teams' roles of monitoring the many critical paths of product ranges and the much more complicated nature of the fashion industry compared to all other industries!

Creating a critical path

In order to create a critical path, different companies use different computer software (similar to Excel). The critical path document is available to be accessed and updated by all members of the buying and merchandising teams for transparency in order to ensure that all members are up to date with the progress of all items.

The key dates and deadlines are generally set by senior managers, such as buying directors, and then communicated to the rest of the buying and merchandising teams. Once the buying and merchandising teams know the key dates they can start planning product ranges and the key sign-off meetings (pre-selection meeting and final selection meeting), as well as booking meetings with different departments, such as design and marketing, and trips to suppliers, at key times. The staff that work on specific stages of the critical path, such as the buyer, merchandiser, the designer, and quality assurance (QA), will have weekly meetings to keep abreast of the situation regarding different products. Some key dates are fixed and cannot be moved, such as the launch date, but others, such as the sampling stages, are slightly more flexible, with extra time factored in to account for any issues that may occur. Furthermore, some stages are very structured and take very specific amounts of time that cannot be speeded up, such as the shipping of garments, but there are other areas that buyers for fast-fashion retailers may choose to speed up, or cut out altogether, such as sampling, fabric testing, visiting trade shows, and negotiating face-to-face, for the necessity of fast lead times.

The buyer needs to be familiar with the quality standards and lead times of the supplier in order to accurately project how long it will take to complete all of the relevant approvals, and build in time for the possibility of samples being rejected and having to be resubmitted. This is not easy as no garment range is ever the same, but estimations can be made based on historical data, such as how long it took suppliers to make similar garments for previous seasons' ranges. Extra time is usually factored into the critical path in order to allow for rejections, remakes, and general delays in order to ensure that the product will definitely be ready in time for the launch date. Consistent lateness on the part of the buyer, designer, or supplier in developing and approving various aspects of each of the garments by critical dates would result in garments not being available to the consumers at the required time (Goworek, 2007). Hence, if the product does not meet the critical path deadlines then this could result in a loss of sales and profits for the retailer. Furthermore, cultural and religious holidays need to be accounted for, especially in a global sourcing world, in order to allow for factory shutdowns and delays in delivery. For example, factories in China will stop working over Chinese New Year, and Muslim countries will have reduced working hours during Ramadan and Eid. However, if buyers factor in too much extra time then the product will be designed and manufactured too far away from the launch date, running the risk of it being inaccurate in terms of the forecasted consumer demand. Monitoring the critical path of a garment range is one of the major responsibilities of the buyer and also forms a large part of an assistant buyer's role. Most buyers are responsible for hundreds of garments within a range for more than one season at a time; thus, the critical path is crucial to helping them monitor the many processes involved (Goworek, 2007).

The importance of the critical path

The critical path is so-named due to it being absolutely 'critical' in the management of the delivery of a product range from the design stage to the shop floor on time. It is essential that products are not late for their store launch date, as this date is carefully calculated to be the optimum time to capitalise on consumer demand. As such, monitoring the critical path is an important responsibility of the buying and merchandising teams and will form a key part of the job descriptions of admin assistants/assistant buyers/ merchandisers as well as allocation analysts.

As previously mentioned, the launch of each product range is carefully timed to meet the target customers' needs at the exact moment that it is predicted that they will want the item. As such, if the product is late then the key window of opportunity for maximising sales and profits will be lost. Therefore, without the careful monitoring of the timings of each product using the critical path, the retailer/brand could miss the peak level of demand. Moreover, if some of the items are late this will result in incomplete ranges in stores/online. This will diminish the overall effectiveness of the range as it is designed to be presented as a whole, and missing garments could mean the overall look is compromised as it will appear unbalanced, such as having a disproportionate number of tops compared to bottoms, or a lack of dresses. Furthermore, when the late product finally arrives then a lot of the range may have already sold out, and thus the product may look almost random in the store/on the website and not go with other items around it, again compromising the overall image of the brand/product mix. This will also cause there to be gaps in the physical store that were meant to be filled, resulting in the store looking empty and unfinished, which is not an attractive proposition for customers. This also raises the issue of space and the lack of capacity for products in physical stores when the item does finally arrive, as new ranges that are on time for their launch date will be prioritised and the late item will go straight into sale, therefore, again, hitting profit margins. Hence, the critical path is an extremely important tool for buyers and merchandisers as it enables them to plan out each of the stages, including any additional time needed to allow for any hold-ups or issues, and keep each product in the range on time to be ready for the launch date. This is 'critical' as launching a product range on time is key for maximising profits (Cremer & Willes, 1998).

CHAPTER SUMMARY

The buying cycle involves eight general stages followed by buyers and merchandisers in order to design and produce a product range. The stages have been briefly summarised in this chapter, yet are further explored in the following chapters of this book. The buying cycle is usually sequential in nature but it has now evolved to be more flexible and agile than ever in order to suit the contemporary fashion retail market. The cycle itself will vary between each brand/retailer depending on the nature of that business (i.e. what market it is competing in, such as fast fashion vs slow fashion) and the type of product being produced (e.g. basics vs fashion items, dresses vs T-shirts). There are risks in implementing the buying cycle either too far in advance of the product launch date, such as inaccurate forecasting of trends and customer demand, as well as in implementing it too close to the season, such as higher manufacturing costs or poorer quality of garments due to rushing and missing out particular stages, such as all of the sampling stages. The critical path is therefore an essential tool used by buyers and merchandisers to monitor each garment as it is produced, manufactured, and shipped, then allocated and distributed to the store to be sold to the customer on time. Late deliveries of products to stores can cause a number of different problems, as discussed in this chapter, all of which ultimately can lead to a loss of sales and profits for the retailer.

References

Bruce, M., & Daly, L. (2006). 'Buyer behavior for fast fashion', *Journal of Fashion Marketing & Management*, 10(3): 329–344.

Cremer, R., & Willes, M. (1998). *The Tongue of the Tiger: Overcoming Language Barriers in International Trade*. River Edge, NJ: World Scientific.

Goworek, H. (2007). *Fashion Buying*. 2nd ed. Hoboken, NJ: Blackwell.

Granger, M.M. (2015). *The Fashion Industry and its Careers*. 3rd ed. New York, NY: Bloomsbury.

Parker-Strak, R., Barnes, L., Studd, R., & Doyle, S. (2020). 'Disruptive product development for online fast fashion retailers', *Journal of Fashion Marketing and Management*, accepted for publication.

Range review

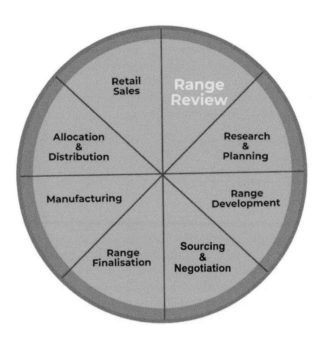

Introduction

Central to the product development process for all buying and merchandising teams is a review of the previous season's range and product performance. This valuable information informs the initial plans and ideas for the future season's ranges and products. The purpose of the review is to inform the planning process – a time-consuming element, but the efforts and time spent doing this at the beginning of the range plan rather than towards the end result in better-organised operations that can focus on driving sales online and in store (Koumbis, 2014). This chapter will outline the range-review process through a detailed look at the 'post-mortem' report and how it shapes the planning of future ranges. Aspects such as the analysis of historical sales figures, like-for-like sales, and sales forecasting will be discussed, showing how all this information feeds in to the merchandise plan.

Learning outcomes

By the end of this chapter you will be able to:

- Discuss the importance of reviewing past seasons' product ranges in the planning of future ranges;
- Describe the process of reviewing a past season's product range;
- Define the post-mortem report;
- Identify what aspects make items bestsellers or worst sellers;
- Describe the process of analysing like-for-like sales and its importance in range planning;
- Define sales forecasting and describe the process of conducting it;
- Describe the merchandise plan and how it is used by buyers and merchandisers in range planning.

Macro-environment review

The buyer needs to consider many different elements that may have impacted on the previous trading season for the retailer. A large majority of these aspects will form the post-mortem report, which will be discussed later in this chapter. As well as the internal aspects focused on products, it is also important to also consider some of the external (macro) aspects that influenced trading in general as well as specific markets and consumers (micro). The macro environmental analysis can be conducted focusing on PEST (political, economic, sociocultural and technological) factors.

- Political – the political climate can have a huge effect on consumer sentiment. For instance, if there is uncertainty over a general election, or the recent upheaval caused by the Brexit referendum, people may not be focused on shopping as they may be worried about their living situation.
- Economic climate – if the current economic climate is positive and flourishing then it will reflect positively upon consumers. On the other hand, talk of recessions, rising unemployment, the falling pound, and general financial uncertainty makes consumers consider spending less on items such as clothes and become much more cautious in terms of their shopping habits. However, this can vary depending upon the target customers of a brand and what their priorities are.
- Sociocultural trends – changing attitudes and bigger society trends can also impact purchase decision-making for consumers. For example, consumers' increased awareness of and rising interest in sustainability has changed how they are shopping. This could impact on the retailer's market share, and buyers may need to consider including more sustainable lines or more sustainable methods of product development as a result.
- Technological changes – technology is constantly evolving and new developments can have a huge impact on the fashion industry. Examples of this have been the rise in people shopping through their smartphone (meaning that retailers must ensure that their mobile apps/mobile sites are optimised) and the number of social media influencers that have such a power and sway over what people buy now.

Micro-environment review

The micro-environment review involves an analysis of the changes in the retailer's direct market and in the behaviours of its target consumers. The buyer will analyse the market as a whole, looking at their direct competitors and their performance as well as consumer attitudes. This is important, as increased competition in the market and changing customers' opinions on brand identity can increase and decrease sales opportunities.

The sharing and discussion of the information gathered from the macro and micro market analyses will generally happen in form of a meeting that will allow the teams from the different categories within the department to share their good practice, concerns, and ideas for the future season and range plan. Working collaboratively across the different categories allows a more collective approach to the start of the season and range plan. Sharing the main strategic goals for the brand as well as key suppliers and product ideas will result in a more cohesive product mix and clear brand identity.

The importance of conducting a range review

Buyers and merchandisers constantly review product progress throughout the development and trading parts of the buying cycle as it helps to ensure that the products will be on time for their set launch date and that they achieve the intended financial margins required. However, it is also vital that a review is done at the end of the season to analyse what sold well, how could it have sold better, what did not sell at all, and what can be taken forward into the next season. This can be in terms of products, colours, styles, and fabrics, as well as suppliers, categories, and departments overall. Critically analysing the product range after the trading season enables buyers and merchandisers to reflect upon the work that they have done, what actions should have occurred to support a more successful selling period, and how this can be used to inform future plans and development.

The range review often takes place in the form of a presentation to the buying and merchandising teams, and, in some cases, the designers and garment technologists too, although this may depend on the brand's structure and size. The post-mortem report, samples, sales figures, and sell-through and return rates will support the discussion of the previous season's product ranges. A full breakdown of the previous season is conducted with the intention of uncovering what is relevant and important for the upcoming season. The ability to learn about what worked well from other buyers and merchandisers is valuable and can highlight common issues and best practice in order to help and support each other. The buying of fashion products is an incredibly complex and unpredictable experience; thus, sharing best practice and developing a supportive environment facilitates a better working environment.

The post-mortem report

At the end of each season buyers and merchandisers will undertake a post-mortem report, analysing the performance of each product, range, and category, as well as the factors that had both a positive and negative impact on this. The purpose of the report is to understand the lessons learned from the previous season and use this knowledge for the next season to inform the product range and future plans. Post-mortem reports will vary from retailer to retailer and, as such, include the key information and discussion points that are specific to their business goals and objectives. However, the main purpose they serve is to inform and aid the development of the next season's range plan, product assortments, and the key pieces to include, as well as budget plans.

Aspects included in a post-mortem report

- Best and poor sellers;
- Lessons learned;
- Markdowns;
- Margins;
- Sell-through rates;
- Number of product returns;
- Net sales – sales achieved after the customer returns and deductions are adjusted;
- Gross sales – the total sales before the customer returns and deductions are accounted for;
- TY – this year's trading figures;
- LY – last year's trading figures;
- YTD – the year to date.

What makes a best/worst seller?

The terms 'bestseller' and 'worst seller' are often heard in retail to describe a product's performance in relation to its intended sales target. A product can be considered a bestseller if it sells faster than expected at full price, thereby achieving its full intended profit margin. A product is considered a worst seller if it does not sell in the expected time frame and requires discounting to achieve any rate of sale. The following aspects could be considered when analysing the performance of an item and what made it a best or worst seller:

- Style;
- Price;
- Fabric;
- Trend;
- Sizing/fit;
- Print/pattern;
- Colour.

For example, take the following dress (Figure 5.1), an item that was a bestseller at the time.

Product	Bestseller analysis
	The price (RRP) – making this dress very affordable and excellent value in comparison to competitor product. It also fits in with the customers' expectations and other product price points
	The trend – the trend translation has been effective and suitable for the type of customer, brand style, and launch time within the season
	The fabric – a good-quality lightweight polyester that was suitably cost-effective, did not crease, and was therefore suitable for the holiday season that the product was promoted for
	The style – suitable flattering cut that suited most body shapes and sizes, and applicable for full size breakdown
	The colour and print – on-trend colour and print that has been matched and reflected well from trend translation. Not too risky for most consumers and flattering on most complexions

Figure 5.1 Analysis of a bestseller dress

This dress was a bestseller for a number of different reasons. For instance, the floaty style is very flattering on any body shape and so the dress had universal appeal due to the loose, forgiving fit. It skims over the stomach, does not cling to the thighs and covers the arms – three of the areas that women are most self-conscious about. This made it quite a safe buy for consumers, and the oversized style meant that the fit would not need to be perfect, which would minimise the likelihood of returns. The loose material also makes it cool for hot summer days but it can easily be worn with a jacket and boots to make it a bit warmer, so it is quite a versatile piece. Similarly, it can be dressed up with heels for a night out, with smart shoes and a smart jacket for the office, or with sandals for a casual look. The print itself is very on-trend for the season, as animal print had a huge revival that year. Moreover, although it is clearly identifiable as the animal-print trend with the Dalmatian spots, it is not too 'out-there' in terms of the colour scheme (white and black is very safe), making it acceptable to many consumers, not just the more daring fashion-forward ones. Finally, the price point was £39.99, making it reasonably affordable.

Analysis informs range planning

Once buyers and merchandisers have analysed which styles were best and worst sellers, they will use this data to inform their future ranges. Some items will be carried forward, some will be dropped, and some will be reworked. In order to maximise profits, bestsellers can be regarded as proven 'winners' that have been tried and tested in the market and will likely to be carried forward to future seasons with minor amendments. Similarly, poor sellers will likely be discontinued and the mistakes that were made learned from. Although this may be a true reflection for some items, in reality the process is not that simple. It is much more complex than that: bestsellers will get carried forward, and worst sellers will be dropped. The aspects that contributed to making it a best/worst seller need to be analysed in-depth and taken into account when making any decisions, as highlighted in Figure 5.2.

As Figure 5.2 shows, the analysis of best and worst sellers is multifaceted, and, therefore, each garment must be considered individually. For instance, if a style has sold well, or out-performed expectations (such as the grey coat in Figure 5.2), then the buyer may decide to carry it forward for another season, making minor amendments to refresh it and keep it current. However, as with the dress in the above example, some styles may have sold well due to the market conditions and particular fashion trend at the time, and therefore would not be expected to sell as well in future seasons, so will not be carried forward. Hence, some bestsellers are very specific to that season and their success will not be repeated if tried again.

On the other hand, a product may be a worst seller because the timing was wrong; people may not have been ready for that particular trend at that time as it was introduced too early, or the weather was unseasonably warm or cold for that time of year. In this instance, the garment may be given another chance and carried over for when consumers are more accepting of the trend or the weather is more in line with expectations. Infor-mation can be gathered from websites such as WGSN, Drapers and Edited on predicted trends and sales patterns in order to see whether another period in time would be better to launch this product.

Nevertheless, if a product sold poorly due to its style, then this suggests that the buyer has not correctly gauged what the target market wanted, so the product will be discon-tinued and further analysis and research into their target consumer's preferences will be conducted. This highlights the importance of conducting in-depth consumer research and understanding the needs and wants of the target market.

Finally, if the poor sales performance is due to fit issues (something which is becom-ing an increasingly serious issue, reducing retailers' profits due to the high number of returns) then analysis of the fit will be conducted. As a result, further sampling and testing stages may be factored in for future garments, and a supplier appraisal may be warranted, after which the garment may or may not be improved and carried forward.

After the review meeting and thorough analysis of the post-mortem report, buyers and merchandisers will have a framework of successes and key ideas on which they can build for the upcoming season. They will combine this key information with their research (dis-cussed at length in Chapter 6) in order to ensure that their decision-making for the new range is effective. Some of the information that will be combined with the post-mortem report to plan out the new range will be very generic, such as the buying strategy that the brand intends to achieve long-term, whereas some of the information will be very specific and open to interpretation dependent on the category or department each of the buyers and merchandisers is focusing on. At this stage, buyers generally concern themselves with product, styles, ranges, and assortments, whereas merchandisers focus on the budgets and breakdown of product quantities and ratios across a category. Before design concepts have been developed it is possible to estimate the total value of the range by defining the num-ber of styles with provisional quantities (Goworek, 2007). Merchandisers have a good idea from the previous sales figures, the initial quantity ordered, and the previous overall budget spent of how they can allocate the budgets for the upcoming season. This emphasises the importance of the range-review process and the value of the post-mortem report from both a product aesthetics and style perspective, but also for the financial and category and assort-ment breakdown. This information will all feed into the creation of the *merchandise plan*.

Product	Product description and classification	Bestseller or worst seller?	Carrying forward for next year?
	Dress	Bestseller	No – this item was very much a product of its time. It encapsulated the current trend, which was the main reason for its popularity, but this trend is not set to continue for next year and so is not likely to be as popular. Therefore, the product was a short-term fad and will be discontinued.
	Jeans	Bestseller	Yes – this item is set to continue to be popular next year and can transcend seasons. It will be continued as it is selling well, and more colourways may be added to capitalise on this.
	Grey coat	Bestseller	Yes, with alterations – This is a classic item that will sell well next year as it is not based on any trend. The product will be altered slightly; e.g. change from buttons to a zip and include beige fabric under the collar/lapels to keep it fresh.
	Red jumper	Worst seller	Yes, with alterations – although this was a poor seller, analysis shows that the timing was not right. The weather was uncharacteristically warm in autumn and so sales of jumpers are down overall. The item will be carried over as it may increase in popularity if the weather is colder.
	Dress	Worst seller	Analysis shows that this dress sold well originally but there were a high number of returns due to fit issues. This indicates that the style of dress is popular, but the sizing and style/fit/shape of the garment needs to be readdressed. Work will be done with the supplier to improve this, or a new supplier will be sought to recreate this style of dress with a better fit for next year.
	Dress	Worst seller	No – poor sales figures due to unpopular style. Item will not be carried forward as it is not popular with the target market.

Figure 5.2   **Range analysis for future planning**

The merchandise plan (also known as a buying and merchandise plan)

In every business it is important to measure performance against a pre-determined criterion, and fashion is no exception (Jackson & Shaw, 2001). At the beginning of every buying season, forecasts are made, which predict the sales for specific products, product categories, and departments overall. Sales forecasts are based upon previous sales histories and performances, as well as predictions of future market demand. Retailers must cover all of their costs and ensure that a sufficient income surplus is achieved in order to be considered profitable. In order to implement this, heads of merchandising will establish the buying budget for the whole buying team, which is then split across each of the main buying areas. It is the merchandiser's responsibility to advise and cooperate with the buyer on how the budget should be allocated, and to make clear the margin that must be achieved for each product and each product category. They will also allocate the amount of stock that is required in order to meet customer demand and secure sufficient levels of profitability. Hence, it is the buyer who principally decides what is bought and included in a product range; however, it is the merchandiser who decides how much of a product is actually bought and the number of sizes and different colourways. Thus, the merchandiser plays a key role, working alongside the buyer to achieve the right balance of products within a range through the consideration of previous sales history combined with forward sales and trend prediction (Jackson & Shaw, 2001). As such, the financial management of buying is typically the responsibility of the merchandiser, and this is based upon the merchandise plan.

The merchandise plan is the intended stock and sales amount planned for a season. The plan is initiated approximately six to 12 months ahead of the trading period. However, a more trend-led or fast-fashion retailer will work much closer to the season. Starting the planning process too far in advance can be dangerous as it can fail to pick up more recently emerging style trends (Jackson & Shaw, 2001). The unpredictable nature of the fashion industry, coupled with consumer demand and a lack of brand loyalty, makes working as close to the season as possible the preferred option when focusing on product specifics; however, it is still very important that the initial plan is finalised in advance. First, a sales plan is developed whereby the buying and merchandising team will try and fix some key sales ratios upon which the future planning process will be based (Jackson & Shaw, 2001). This could be a percentage or numerical increase. Once this figure is approved, a stock plan is created, meaning that the overall new sales plan is then split across the different categories, which then feeds into the intended forecast sales plan. In general, last year's trading performance forms the basis against which a merchandise plan is created (Shaw & Koumbis, 2014). Figure 5.3 illustrates a previous year's sales and the intended growth for the category, and how this is split across the different styles.

It is really important that there is a merchandise plan in place as fashion products have extremely varied and changeable sales patterns, making them very unpredictable. The sales of fashion items can be affected by many different factors, such as fashion fads, weather conditions, seasonality, and special occasions. The ultimate goal for a merchandiser is to achieve the planned level of buying profit and margin intended.

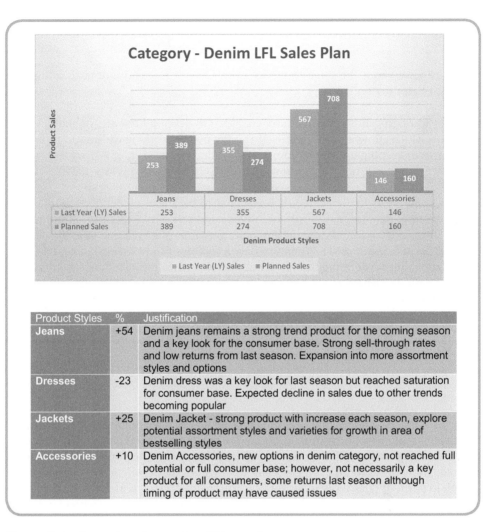

Figure 5.3   **Examples of growth within a category**

The aim is to sell as much stock at full price as possible in order to increase the level of profit made, as selling at a reduced markdown price will have a negative impact on the profit margin.

Merchandisers will allocate some specific sales ratios based on the post-mortem report, starting with overall financial sales that need to be achieved. Once a financial amount has been decided it is then necessary to divide it across the months and specific seasons or occasions to break down exactly how much each period is intended to achieve. This will vary depending on the customers and the brand, and it will also change each year. Merchandise planning is a demanding task, requiring logic and intuition to ensure that the business carries the right product range at any point in time. The best merchandisers have analytical, estimating, and forecasting skills, which enable them to see both macro and micro trends as they occur throughout trading (Jackson & Shaw, 2001).

Like-for-like and growth

Most businesses want the same thing: to grow. Growth is so important to a business because it helps to develop:

- The brand's exposure, which, in turn, enables it to develop itself and its staff;
- Profits, which allow it to support itself and the people working within it;
- In terms of keeping up with its competitors within the market;
- Further opportunities for expansion when a gap in the market is ascertained.

Whatever strategy is implemented, it is essential to be ahead of the market and to be proactive rather than reactive. Businesses never stand still; they either move forward and grow or they slide backwards and decline. Sales growth is often referred to as like-for-like (LFL) (Jackson & Shaw, 2001). When you have a complex product to sell, such as fashion items that are prone to unpredictable demand-driven consumers and market influences, it can sometimes be hard to see how well you are actually doing. As trends emerge from season to season, using LFL enables buyers and merchandisers to see exactly where growth has occurred. LFL measures true sales turnover growth as opposed to total growth and is regarded as a better index to use in order to assess business performance (Clark, 2015).

Understanding demand and sales forecasting

Once the financial amount that needs to be achieved has been planned, it then needs to be converted into how much stock is required to meet that target. The merchandiser consults the range plan in order to make recommendations on the quantities that need to be sourced. There needs to be a sufficient amount of stock to meet demand and encourage growth in terms of sales, a key indicator of success for the business and a target that tends to increase each year. A strong growth in sales the previous year can be a good indicator for growth for the following year, although an element of fashion knowledge, experience, and 'intuition' must pay a part.

Nevertheless, forecasting sales on the sole basis of historical sales figures is not sufficient enough to anticipate future performance. There needs to be a consideration of external factors and how they are likely to have an impact on product performance, as well as what the target customer's needs may be. It is key that the forecast sales plan responds to specific retail events during the year and product ranges correspond to consumer demand during these events. Consumers purchase products for specific reasons, occasions or activities, or sometimes develop a need for a product because of attitudes and lifestyle activities at specific times of the year. Understanding when these occasions, events, or situations will be enables buyers and merchandisers to react and drive sales to specific products, an aspect that is anticipated and reflected in the sales forecast plan. Figure 5.4 illustrates a retail calendar with a variety of different consumer occasions and events that can impact on budget and range planning.

As retailers now operate internationally, understanding each of the individual target consumer profiles is more important than ever when forecasting sales. There are different cultural holidays that need to be considered, such as Valentine's Day in the UK vs Singles' Day in China, and Independence Day in America or Bastille Day in France. Sometimes

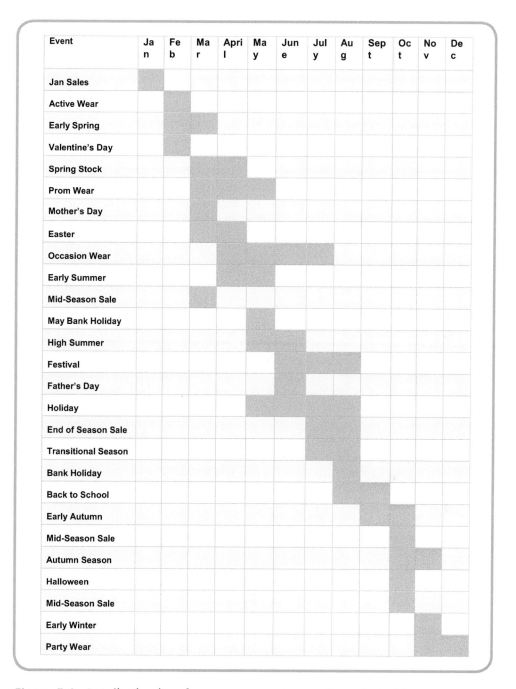

Figure 5.4   Retail calendar of consumer occasions and events that impact range planning

different cultural influences can spread, such as the participation of many UK retailers in Black Friday, an event centred around Thanksgiving in the US, and, more recently, a celebration of Singles' Day by UK retailers. This means that certain promotions and sales patterns need to be carefully planned by fashion brands.

Taking advantage and promoting products with specific occasions and events in mind is used in all forms of retail, not just in fashion. However, with the rise of social media, the interactions between the brand and the consumer are now closer and more frequent than ever before, providing more opportunities to drive sales. Brands can offer discount promotions or alert their customers to new stock deliveries as well as items that are specific to retail calendar events. Gaining an advantage in an extremely fierce competitive market is vital and needs to be considered when forecasting sales.

Retailers need to ensure that they have a sufficient amount of stock available for a period of time before their customers are able or want to buy it. When forecasting sales, consideration to the wardrobe planning stage is important as consumers purchase products prior to the planned wearing time. These times need to be carefully considered, particularly with much shorter selling seasons and unpredictable product life cycles. Thus, a comprehensive understanding of the customer and their demands is vital to the success of forecasting sales.

Flexible planning

Good merchandise management should always be able to cope with the obvious peaks and troughs of trade (Jackson & Shaw, 2001). Having a flexible attitude to planning also helps the process. As discussed previously, there are many occasions and events that can impact trading. However, it is important to note that both planned and unplanned factors can influence sales and these can sometimes be out of the control of the buying and merchandising team (Jackson & Shaw, 2001). A *planned* circumstance is something that they buyer and merchandiser knows will happen. This planned situation generally occurs every season, or every year, and is usually expected. For example, buyers and merchandisers know that there will be colder weather during the winter months and warmer weather during the summer in the UK The weather can be one of the most significant factors that impacts on product sales, affecting not only the products consumers decide to purchase but also influencing whether or not they are inclined to go shopping (Goworek & McGoldrick, 2015). Planned events also include sales periods, such as mid-season sales, that will impact on the consumer's attention. Understanding the types of products that are linked to the different occasions, planned events, and the time of the year at which they occur makes for better planning.

An *unplanned* circumstance, on the other hand, is the situation or event that buyers and merchandisers are not expecting. This could include unseasonable weather that retailers are not necessarily prepared for, political or terrorist activities, or episodes that distract national attention. In some cases, an unplanned factor can have a positive impact, such as celebrities or influencers gaining media attention wearing a particular product. Although this situation is generally planned as part of promotional campaigns, it can sometimes occur accidentally and create a positive impact around the product in question. However, it is important to remember that if consumers are focusing their attention on particular products at certain times, there will always be products that they are not looking at or purchasing as a result. Thus, good merchandisers require quick thinking and reaction times as well as experience in order to cope with all the sudden unplanned factors that tend to occur when they are least expecting them (Jackson & Shaw, 2001).

The sales forecast plan

Once the initial budget plans and growth strategies have been identified for the different categories across a department and the retail calendar of planned events has been factored in, the sales plan is then broken down over the season's trading period in order to create a *sales forecast plan*. A sales forecast plan is created to enable the merchandiser to forecast exactly how many sales need to be made per month and per week. Jackson and Shaw (2001) identify the three key facts and ratios that emerge from sales forecast plans:

1. *Seasonal sales variation* – autumn/winter products traditionally command higher sales figures due to more higher-priced garments and holiday seasonal products;
2. *Seasonal sales peaks* – some categories will have more concentrated sales peaks than others; for example, swimwear sees high sales but during a very narrow time period in preparation for people's summer holidays;
3. *Sales ratios* – sales ratios are usually 2:1 in terms of tops vs bottoms, as consumers will buy a higher proportion of tops over a season than they will bottoms.

It is important to remember that whilst the information on retail planned occasions is available and these key general rules give buying and merchandising teams some ground rules for forecasting, the sales forecast plan needs to contain an element of flexibility. A truly flexible plan is always reflective of the customer in terms of their purchase behaviour and their expectations. Acknowledging where the target customers' focus will be in regard to products and purchasing items for their wardrobes and lives will aid in developing an understanding of where the sales peaks and troughs are when forecasting. An effective sales forecast plan will take advantage of the opportunities where possible and provide a full breakdown of a numerical amount of products required to sell each month and then each week. This can then be used to support product development and range planning. However, it is impossible to set a plan that will never need changing; thus, the variable and changing sales pattern of fashion products makes it essential that re-forecasting occurs once products are actually trading. Therefore, the merchandiser analyses the sales forecast plan to create daily, weekly, monthly, and seasonal sales plans in order to monitor sales and performance, and to compare against actual sales once trading begins.

Buyer and merchandiser instinct

As demonstrated throughout this chapter, a large proportion of the planning and decision-making for future ranges relies upon data and historical seasons' sales patterns. However, there is also an element of instinct that is required by the buyer and merchandiser. Buyers and merchandisers need to understand the brand that they are working for and their overall strategy and objectives in order to react instinctively and keep in line with this when making decisions. Each company will have its own objectives that will influence the financial and product decision-making on a daily or seasonal basis. For instance, some brands aim to push boundaries in terms of fashionability, and this will be reflected in the product assortments and styles that they develop. Other brands will focus on commercialising trends into products for mass appeal on the high street, whereas others are very focused on their margins, and thus like to 'sell it cheap and sell it fast'. As such, each brand/retailer requires a different approach to buying and merchandising, and it is essential that this is understood when going to work for that company.

There is information available to support and guide the decision-making process from a variety of internal and external sources. This is all very useful but buyers and merchandisers need to avoid getting information-overload and ensure that they remember to follow their instincts. Thus, there needs to be a strong balance between the factual information and buyer/merchandiser instincts and experience when planning a product range. It is the elements of insight, experience, instinct, and risk management that are harder aspects to measure, but all form part of the decision-making that occurs within fashion buying and merchandising, from the early stages of budget and range planning right down to specific product discussions that take place throughout the buying cycle. There are times when data, research, and knowledge need to be questioned. A buyer or merchandiser will organically develop their intrinsic bank of information and experience that they will need to rely on, suddenly at times, in order to react to consumer demand. Hence, no spreadsheet or digital device is a replacement for the human brain which pulls on experience, information, and instinct to help balance decision-making and risk management.

CHAPTER SUMMARY

This chapter has provided a comprehensive overview of the range-review stage, detailing how previous sales performance and current growth (LFL sales) are analysed. The previous best and worst sellers' information is fed into the creation of the merchandise plan, which is used as a basis for range planning. Once this has been established, thorough market, trend, and consumer research is conducted in order to determine which styles will make up the product range, as discussed in Chapter 6. Key here is also the fact that the experience and instinct of buyers and merchandisers is essential in order to make a smooth transition.

References

Clark, J. (2015). *Fashion Merchandising; Principles and Practices*. Basingstoke: Palgrave.

Goworek, H. (2007). *Fashion Buying*. 2nd ed. Hoboken, NJ: Blackwell.

Goworek, H., & McGoldrick, P. (2015). *Retail Marketing and Management: Principles and Practice*. Harlow: Pearson.

Jackson, T., & Shaw, D. (2001). *Mastering Fashion Buying and Merchandising Management*. London: Palgrave.

Koumbis, D. (2014). *Fashion Retailing: From Managing to Merchandising*. New York, NY: Bloomsbury.

Shaw, D., & Koumbis, D. (2014). *Fashion Buying*. New York, NY: Fairchild Books.

6 Research and planning

Introduction

A significant amount of consumer, market, and trend research is conducted by buyers and merchandisers when planning a new product range. The fashion industry and its consumers are notoriously hard to predict due to fashion's fast-paced nature, an aspect that has become even more apparent since the development of the internet and social media. Yet, there are still ways of being able to forecast the direction of change and what consumers may want at certain times of the year, and buyers must do this whilst also ensuring that their brand's overall mission and corporate strategy are adhered to. The buyer will conduct the market, consumer, and trend research which will then inform the merchandise plan, a tool used by the merchandiser to forecast sales for the upcoming range. This chapter explores the different types of research conducted by buyers and merchandisers before they plan out their new product range, all of which will inform the merchandise plan.

By the end of this chapter you will be able to:

- Identify all the different types of research and planning that goes into a product range;
- Discuss the importance of aligning a new product range with the brand's overall strategy and identity;
- Discuss the importance of undertaking extensive consumer and market research in order to understand the brand's target consumer and their behaviour/preferences;
- Identify the different trend-forecasting tools and methods used by buyers, and discuss their relative merits;
- Critically discuss how trend forecasting has changed in the last decade and the transition from solely top-down to the rising importance of bottom-up information;
- Explain the significance of the merchandise plan and outline how it can be used by merchandisers when planning a product range.

Brand strategy

When creating a new product range, buyers and merchandisers need to ensure that it is aligned with the overall brand strategy and brand values. The brand's *mission statement* and *corporate objectives* must be consulted and the new range consistent with the overall direction and identity that the company wishes to portray.

Mission statement

A company's mission outlines why it exists in the first place. A mission statement distinguishes the company from its competitors and declares the purpose of its existence (Campbell & Yeung, 1991). It describes what the company is and what its values are. A mission statement helps a brand to present itself favourably to the public, as well as identifying and responding to various stakeholders (Rajasekar, 2013). Mission statements should be informative, inspiring, enduring, concise, clear, and conducive to both employees and customers, encouraging them to form an emotional bond with the brand (David et al., 2014).

Corporate strategy

A *corporate strategy* refers to the overall plan for a company (Porter, 1987). Put simply, it is how the company will achieve its mission. It produces the principal policies and plans for achieving goals, and defines the strategy that the company is to pursue, the kind of organisation it is or intends to be, and the nature of the economic and non-economic contribution it intends to make to its shareholders, employees, customers, and communities (Andrews, 1997). Corporate (or business) objectives are set at the high level and are quite distinct from any more detailed functional objectives set for the functional areas of a business, such as the buying strategy. Decisions based on the corporate strategy will define the central image of the company and the position it will occupy in the market. Corporate strategy is focused on aspects such as growth, internationalisation, consolidation, market positioning, and competitive advantage (Varley & Clark, 2019). It generally considers the next one to five years, outlining the overall targets for the business, namely making a profit as well as aspirational or corporate social responsibility (CSR) targets.

Examples of corporate objectives would include targets for:

- Sales revenue – a traditional measure of the size and strength of a business (if revenue is growing then the business is growing);
- Profit;
- Return-on-investment;
- Growth – sales volume and profit;
- Market share;
- Shareholder value – particularly important for publicly-quoted businesses where senior management are tasked with growing the value of the business;
- Corporate image and reputation – an aspect which is becoming increasingly important and links closely with CSR, product and customer service quality, and business ethics.

Once the corporate strategy has been consulted, buyers can devise the *buying strategy*. The buying strategy implements the ethos of the corporate strategy through the selection of products or brands that are purchased and through the product differentiation and development strategies (Varley & Clark, 2019). An example of how the buying strategy is aligned with the corporate strategy could be as follows:

Corporate objective for a multi-brand fashion retailer

Grow and strengthen own-brand offering in order to achieve a higher gross margin and improve the brand recognition.

Buying strategy: ensure that 60 per cent of products in range are own-brand.

Corporate objective for an own-label fashion retailer

Increase the quality of products and the positioning of the brand in terms of product quality in the marketplace to reduce the rate of returns.

Buying strategy: ensure that 90 per cent of products bought have a quality rating (AQL) of 5.

This will then be broken down further when considering range planning, the product mix, and pricing architecture, and reviewing suppliers.

Example	Buying Strategy	Advantage
A retailer is placing all its efforts on marketing its own branded good as an area of growth	The buying strategy may be to ensure 65 per cent of all purchased products are own-brand	Higher gross margin achieved on all branded goods Increased brand recognition
A retailer is placing a lot of emphasis on increasing quality	The buying strategy may be to ensure 90 per cent of all products received have a five-star quality rating when inspected	Tighter control of quality leads to customers' repeat business Fewer returns Higher profits achieved Measurable targets received
The number of suppliers is too large and unmanageable making buying less efficient	The buying strategy may be to reduce the supplier base by 20 per cent over a three-year period	Costs of communication and administration can be reduced Concentrated business with a smaller network of supplier can give higher negotiating power, although it can lead to over-reliance on specific suppliers and a threat to efficiency
A retailer is placing efforts in developing a new product line that targets a new market	The buying strategy may be to ensure 30 per cent of the overall product assortment is suitable for the new target market	Increased market share and brand recognition

Figure 6.1   **Examples of buying strategies**

Figure 6.1 outlines a variety of corporate objectives and the buying strategies that would be employed in order to support the development and achievement of that objective. The buying strategy is used to underpin all decision-making in terms of product development, range planning, and sourcing in order to fulfil the corporate objective.

Brand positioning

Brand positioning determines where the brand sits in relation to its competitors in the minds of consumers. Thus, a brand's positioning relates to its competitors in the market and how it is viewed by the public, an aspect that can change over time due to changing consumer needs, expectations, and perceptions (Roncha, 2019). Determining a brand's positioning in the marketplace is important as it enables brands to measure themselves against their direct competitors and assess which areas they may need to improve on. Perceptual maps can be created in order to demonstrate how the brand is perceived by their customers in relation to their competitors in the market. The axis could be whatever the brand is using to measure itself against its competitors; for example, price, fashionability, quality, or sustainability.

Market research

As well as considering the brand's heritage, personality, and values, extensive research needs to be conducted on the market that it is competing in when creating a new product range. With such a fast-paced market characterised by fierce competition on a global scale, effective and thorough market research is essential to the success of a range.

Comparative (comp) shops

Comparative shops (or 'comp shops' as they are commonly known in the industry) consist of a buyer visiting competitors' stores either on the high street or online in order to assess their product offering. The competitor's whole product range will be analysed, in terms of the price architecture, quality of materials, colourways, and style/fashionability, as well as any promotional activity. Buyers purchase items from competitors during these trips and dissect them when they get back to head office.

Comp shops are useful for a number of reasons. Firstly, they allow buyers to see if there are any gaps in their own product range. For example, if a buyer identifies that competitors are all stocking a particular type of scarf, such as silk scarves, and they do not sell silk scarves, the buyer may realise that they have missed a rising trend of consumer interest in silk scarves, and so use their open-to-buy budget to buy a range of silk scarves in order to maximise profitability and not lose sales to their competitors. Product pricing is also reviewed during comp shops. Buyers need to make sure that their product offering is competitively priced against other retailers and brands selling similar or the same products. In a fierce selling environment where consumers are less brand loyal than ever, a small difference in price can make all the difference when trying to win sales. Competitors' promotional activity is also important to monitor as it can be matched in order to not lose sales. Promotional activity on certain items or ranges are also a potential indicator of items that are not selling as well as they were predicted to. Hence, buyers can adjust their own strategies accordingly.

Retail data analytics

The development of technology and the availability of online information has driven a surge in capabilities in terms of product analysis. In particular, brands' and retailers' expansions into multi- and omnichannel retailing has widened the available measures with which the merchandiser can analyse their business. As a result, there has been an increase in data analytics companies that can support retailers with active and customised competitor monitoring in real time. This enables merchandisers to have the ability to drill down into the data to support product development with competitor benchmarking. One of the hardest things in fashion product development is understanding how a new product will perform without a real sense of how it will sit in the wider market. Retail data analytics is a supportive tool to aid product decisions using real-time data by helping detect trends, discover new brands, and spot gaps in a retailer's own assortment and its competitors'. Data analytics are incredibly useful when used in the early range-planning and research stages of the buying cycle as well as during the trading stage. Easy access to information can support a reactive and proactive response to new trends and market gaps, and identify any missed opportunities. Consequently, buyers and merchandisers are now required to have further analysis skills in order to be able to interpret all the data that they are presented with.

Thus, the development of fast-paced trends, complex product development, and heightened consumer demand has forced the industry to utilise metrics and rely much more on data. However, in some cases this has started to stifle creativity in range planning. As a result, brands are in danger of losing their distinct identity and direction. Being constantly reactive can impact negatively on range assortment and volume of product styles as the brand is not producing anything that is distinctly unique. Therefore, it is important to have a balance of reactive and original products, offering what the consumer wants and what is competitive, but also keeping it aligned with the overall corporate strategy and mission statement. Furthermore, despite the benefits of possessing huge amounts of data for helping with range planning, data cannot replace human decision-making, so must not solely be relied upon.

Consumer research

It is essential that buyers gain an in-depth understanding of their consumers in order to ensure that their offering appeals to their target market. A brand or retailer's target market can be defined as the customer whose wants and needs should be met by the company's products (Varley, 2019). Thus, target markets are specific groups of customers that the retailer intends to make regular customers (Stone, 2012). By researching their specific target market, the buyer can ensure that their product range will be accurately aligned to the consumers' tastes, styles, and preferences.

In order to identify the wants and needs of their target market, the retailer/brand must first identify their target market, a process which is achieved through the segmentation of the market. *Market segmentation* refers to 'the separation of the total consumer market into smaller groups' (Stone, 2012, p. 31). Markets are segmented in four major ways: geographics (focusing on where people live), demographics (age, gender, etc.), psychographics (more in-depth studies focusing on customers' personalities and lifestyles), and behaviour (based on consumers' opinions of products and services) (Stone, 2012).

Consumer demographics can be used to detect consumer niches in order to determine the purchase intentions for specific product offerings (Kwon et al., 2007). This will help retailers satisfy and retain their target consumers (Dholakia & Uusitalo, 2002) as well as helping retailers improve their communication with their customers (Parment, 2013). Buyers need to analyse their customers' lifestyles and outlooks in order to determine how they buy and what they buy, to maximise the saleability of the product range. If the buyer and merchandiser can understand their customer's needs, they can develop products that provide superior value for them; then price and distribute them effectively, resulting in high sales (Stone, 2012).

There are several ways in which consumers can be analysed by their demographic information for market-research purposes, such as:

- Age and generational cohort;
- Gender;
- Typology (fashion leaders vs fashion followers);
- Culture;

- Income;
- Geography;
- Employment/occupation;
- Religion;
- Ethnicity, race, or nationality;
- Education;
- Family situation

Some of these will now be discussed.

Age and generational cohorts

Consumers can be classified as part of a generational cohort based on the year that they were born. Generational cohorts give researchers a tool to analyse changes in views over time, providing a way to understand how different experiences (such as world events and technological, economic, and social shifts) interact with the life cycle and ageing process to shape people's views of the world (Dimock, 2019). Whilst younger and older adults may differ in their views in general, generational cohorts allow researchers to examine how today's older adults felt about a given issue when they themselves were young, as well as analysing how the trajectory of views might differ across generations (Dimock, 2019).

Each generation experiences a unique occurrence of events that defines its outlook on life (Tapscott, 2008). Generations are inherently diverse and complex groups, not simple caricatures (Dimock, 2019). Each generation shares a unique set of values and attitudes that sets it apart from other generations (Parry & Urwin, 2011). People can be roughly divided into the following generational cohorts (generational cut-off points can vary between sources but most agree that these dates are approximately representative):

Baby boomers (born in approximately 1946–1964)

The key event which formed the marker for this generation in Western society was the end of World War II (McCrindle, 2006), as there was a huge baby boom when the men came home from war (Tapscott, 2008). The Depression and war years were replaced by economic growth and full-time employment (McCrindle, 2006). Austerity was replaced by technological advancement and more freedom, as well as an increase in immigration (McCrindle, 2006). The large number of baby boomers means that they have had a big impact on societies.

Baby boomers are generally very idealist and driven, hard-working, and believe that personal sacrifices must be made in order to achieve financial success (Glass, 2007). They grew up as television developed and media became more accessible, changing their lifestyles and connection to the world in a fundamental way (Dimock, 2019). Baby boomers have lived through immense changes and adapted to them, and so they are a flexible generation that embraces things such as technology (McCrindle, 2006). They have a revolutionary outlook and events such as the US moon landings inspired them into thinking that they could do anything (Parment, 2013). As the baby boomers age, they continue to be big spenders and will have a significant impact on the retail market (Clodfelter, 2012). As one of the largest and wealthiest generations, baby boomers cannot afford to be ignored by fashion brands or retailers.

Generation X (born approx. 1965–1979)

Generation X grew up during the advent of computers, an aspect that shaped their lifestyle and ways of working, making them more digitally savvy than baby boomers (Mintel, 2019a). Although social media tends to be thought of as a marketing tool to target millennials and Generation Z, Generation Xers are also prolific users of social media, particularly Facebook (Mintel, 2018a). They are a very hard-working generation, characterised by their experiences of their parents being made redundant in the 1980s recessions (McCrindle, 2006; Parry & Urwin, 2011). This also led them to see jobs as more temporary than the previous generation (Filipczak, 1994). Generation X are generally more sceptical and not as loyal as the generations before them, as well as very independent (Glass, 2007). They place a lot of emphasis on their work/life balance and stress its importance, believing this is something that baby boomers did not do (Glass, 2007). Furthermore, they are more open about personal issues than baby boomers are, such as approaching the menopause, and they seek information and advice from their peers both on and offline (Mintel, 2019a). Generation X are also less concerned about their appearance than other generations (Mintel, 2019a), meaning that fashion retailers need to think carefully how to target them.

Generation X are under pressure to care for and support not only their children, but also their ageing parents, whilst still working either full- or part-time, meaning that they have a lack of free time (Mintel, 2019a). This implies that convenience is valued very highly by this generation (Mintel, 2019a). However, this seems to have bred a 'live in the moment' spending style amongst this generation, who spend more on hobbies and meals out than they do on fashion due to the idea that they should enjoy the little disposable income they have (Mintel, 2019a).

Generation Y/millennials (born approx. 1980–1995)

Millennials are the most wanted generation as birth control and abortions were widespread when they were born; thus, their parents chose to have them (Glass, 2007). Furthermore, as families had fewer children and were financially more secure, parents of this generation were more dedicated in raising them (Glass, 2007). Generation Y are more ethnically diverse and better educated than previous generations (Howe & Strauss, 2000). Having grown up being aware of the 9/11 terror attack and the wars in Afghanistan and Iraq, millennials are also very politically active (Dimock, 2019). They are digital natives, having grown up with the advent of the internet as well as a vast amount of technology and new advances being developed regularly (Glass, 2007). This makes them unafraid of new technology, unlike the previous generations (Glass, 2007), and this digital knowledge sets them apart from their parents (Tapscott, 2008). They use technology to integrate their work life with their home and social life and seek the freedom to change jobs when they wish (Tapscott, 2008).

Millennials entered the workforce amidst an economic recession, causing many to experience a 'slow start' on their career path, a factor which has shaped many of their life choices and outlook (Dimock, 2019). Millennials are the first generation since the nineteenth century to be worse off than their parents (Lavelle, 2019). They want freedom of choice and freedom of expression and, thus, they expect to have a wide variety of sales channels, product types, and brands available to them (Tapscott, 2008). Academic research has found that millennials have a higher purchase frequency and make more impulse purchases compared with other cohorts (Pentecost & Andrews, 2010). Millennials are generally very confident people with high levels of self-esteem, as well as optimists and team players, and are accepting of authority, following the rules (Howe & Strauss, 2000; Glass, 2007; Bolton et al., 2013). Yet, they are also materialistic (Bolton et al., 2013). Despite older generations being the most optimistic about their financial situation in the years ahead, this is not translating into a greater willingness to spend, and it is millennials that are driving current and future retail sales (Mintel, 2018b), highlighting their particular importance to fashion brands.

Generation Z (born approx. 1996–2010)

Generation Z are even more ethnically diverse than the previous generation. They have been brought up surrounded by technology from the very beginning of their lives. The iPhone launched in 2007, when the oldest Generation Zs were approaching 10, and by the time they became teenagers the primary means of communication was via mobile phone (Dimock, 2019). Smartphones are the decisive difference between this generation and the one before it, and this device has opened up new ways for children to engage with each other socially (Mintel, 2018c). The nature of being 'always connected' through social media and on-demand entertainment are assumed as a way of life, as opposed to previous generations who have had to adapt to them (Dimock, 2019). Gen Z expects various new devices and technology to be widely available in order to provide them with autonomy and faster transactions as well as more informed shopping decisions (Priporas et al., 2017).

Generation Z want to travel and have exciting new experiences (Mintel, 2018c). Although research has found no significant differences between Generation Z and Generation Y in terms of their decision-making styles, Generation Z are more sensitive to price yet more overwhelmed with the multitude of information than consumers from Generation Y (Smalej, 2017). They are very fashion conscious due to the influence of social media, and update their wardrobes very frequently as they are accustomed to fast fashion. Indeed, this generation are huge consumers of influencer content, meaning that brands have had to adapt their strategies to incorporate influencer marketing in order to target this generation effectively (Mintel, 2018c). Yet at the same time, Generation Z are much more aware of and concerned about the environmental impacts of fashion.

Generation Alpha (born approx. 2011–2025)

Generation Alpha are the children of millennials. They have grown up with all of the technology of the previous generations, and, for a lot of them, their whole lives have been documented on social media, from their ultrasounds being uploaded to Facebook to their baby pictures littering their parents' Instagram. It is too early to tell right now, but it will be interesting to see how this generation are shaped by their experiences growing up and how it will affect their shopping habits.

The ageing population and what it means for buyers and merchandisers

The world's life expectancy is slowly increasing, mainly as a result of improved diets and healthcare advances. The age of retirement in the UK has also increased, which has had an impact on the past traditional stereotypes of age, as 40 years ago the age of 60 may have seemed elderly whereas today that person is much more active and often still working. Today's older people are healthier, better educated, and more active than previous generations, and will live much longer (Stone, 2012). This has had a significant impact on the fashion retail market.

The ageing population in the UK has provided fashion retailers with an opportunity to create collections suited to an older target market. However, the change in age dynamics may create a test for the women's fashion market, because an interest in clothes shopping decreases dramatically amongst older generations (Mintel, 2012). Their interests and purchases vary dramatically from younger consumers, providing a challenge for retailers to meet the demands of the 'new old' (Stone, 2012). Furthermore, female consumers over 55 years old are almost twice as likely to shop at retailers that have a wide size range than younger consumers, as over-55-year-olds are more likely to be overweight or obese (Mintel, 2014b). Therefore, the ageing population means that fashion retailers should design clothes that fit larger body shapes and have a wider range of sizes available in their stores (Mintel, 2014a). The rise in 'plus size' or 'curve' lines that multiple fashion retailers have introduced in the last few years shows that they are already capitalising on this. Fashion retailers are also becoming increasingly interested in the older market as the youth market has become so saturated. As a result, they are exploring ways in which fashion trends can be extended to suit the tastes of older consumers (Twigg, 2012). Older women have more disposable income to spend than younger women, and are now spending more on clothes and shoes for themselves than they have done in the past (Mintel, 2014c). Furthermore, women in the over-55s age group view quality as one of the most important aspects when buying clothes, much more so than younger women do, and they also want value for money (Mintel, 2014b).

There has also been an increase of blurred target age ranges in terms of the garments produced by fashion brands. Whilst some fashion brands/retailers still have very specific target markets, such as high-street fast-fashion retailers who often target 16- to 24-year-olds, others are much broader in their definitions of their target market, such as department stores who are often targeting anyone aged 25-plus. In recent years, the boundaries of targeting a specific target age range are blurring amongst retailers, as 25- to 34-year-olds are shopping more in 16- to 24-year-old-targeted retailers. This, coupled with the ageing population, has resulted in many brands emphasising that their clothes can appeal to all ages, thus creating an unprecedented challenge for fashion buyers and merchandisers when range planning.

Gender

Fashion brands and retailers should also consider the gender that they are targeting and their characteristics, as well as what those consumers look for in a product and how they shop, when planning a product range. Fashion consumption has traditionally been associated with women. However, men are now taking a greater interest in fashion than ever before, creating more opportunities for fashion brands/retailers to target them. Research has shown that gender has a significant impact on a person's weekly and yearly expenditure on fashion items (Pentecost & Andrews, 2010) so it is important to be aware of this when planning to launch new collections. For instance, women purchase clothes more often and are more likely to buy items on impulse than men (Pentecost & Andrews, 2010). This suggests that ranges that are smaller but released more frequently may be more appealing to women. Furthermore, Mintel (2019b) found that men tend to buy clothes less often than women do, but when they do go shopping they tend to buy in bulk. Research also shows that men tend to show a greater affinity to branded clothing than women (Mintel, 2019b), which is important to note for branded buyers. Finally, and very important to note going forward, women show a higher level of sustainable consumption behaviour both in overall behaviour and tendency to reuse products (Bulut et al., 2017). This implies that sustainability needs to be at the core of the brand's values and buying strategy in the future.

However, gender differences in terms of clothes shopping may minimise in the future. Current research suggests that men's shopping behaviour may be changing to incorporate more traits that have previously been linked with female shopping behaviour (Shepherd et al., 2016). As gender fluidity has become more accepted and is on the rise, retailers and brands are responding to this. For example, in 2018, ASOS launched a 'Collusion' line, consisting of products that were gender-neutral and could be worn by both men and women. This indicates that gender fluidity is now an important concept to consider for buyers and merchandisers.

Consumer typologies: fashion followers vs fashion leaders

Consumers can also be classified in terms of the time it takes them to adopt the latest fashion trend. Buyers and merchandisers can use this information to ascertain how the trend should be translated to their product, when they should introduce a trend to their consumers, when the peak sales period will be, and when they should start discounting the item. This can be achieved by applying the Diffusion of Innovation model (Rogers, 1983). The Diffusion of Innovation shows the amount of time it takes for the innovation to be filtered through the population of consumers, thus measuring the product's life cycle. Using the Diffusion of Innovation, fashion consumers can be classified according to their behaviour of acceptance of a specific style over a period of time. There are five categories of fashion adopters:

1. Innovators (the first 2.5 per cent of the population to adopt the product/trend);
2. Early adopters (the following 13.5 per cent to adopt it);
3. Early majority (the following 34 per cent to adopt it);
4. Late majority (the following 34 per cent to adopt it);
5. Laggards (the last 16 per cent to adopt it).

In general, fashion diffuses from fashion innovators and opinion leaders to early fashion adopters. The diffusion then moves on to the peak stage where a large number of consumers begin to adopt fashion. The adopters at this stage can be called fashion followers and consist of the early majority and late majority of shoppers. Eventually the number of fashion adopters starts to fall down when the trend is already established; thus, the diffusion process moves to the decline stage, where the late adopters, known as laggards, adopt the fashion The model, therefore, acknowledges that fashion consumers adopt new trends and will buy new products at different times. Buyers need to ensure that their products are the appropriate level of fashionability for their target customers in order to not alienate them by being either too fashion-forward or too outdated (Jackson & Shaw, 2001).

The Diffusion of Innovation is, therefore, a useful tool for buyers and merchandisers to use when range planning. However, the model is not without its faults. It is retrospective, so there is no way of knowing how accurate it will be for new products going forward; it can only ever be an estimation of the pattern of demand for a product. It is diagrammatic and does not tell us why a product was accepted or not, why this was a pattern of demand, why the rates of acceptance were so high, and why it is a success. As each product is different (an aspect that makes the fashion industry particularly challenging for buyers and merchandisers!), the likelihood of it following the diffusion curve so neatly is not very realistic, especially with such a fast-paced and unpredictable market. There are lots of external factors that could have an impact on the diffusion of a product that the model does not consider, such as celebrities/influencers, trends, or events. Furthermore, it is important to note that the rate, extent, and timescale of demand for fashion products vary enormously; for example, classic garments technically never really go out of fashion so do not enter the decline phase, nor do they have a 'peak' like fashion garments. Thus, buyers need to bear in mind that not just one fashion trend emerges at a time; each trend may have different levels, rates, and lengths of acceptance. Nevertheless, what has happened in the past is a useful indicator of what *might* happen in the future, so the model is still a useful tool.

Fashion leaders (innovators and early adopters)

Fashion innovators and early adopters comprise 2.5 per cent and 13.5 per cent of the population respectively and can therefore be classified as fashion leaders. Fashion leaders are generally risk takers, have higher education and income levels than the average population, and are very socially active (Varley, 2019). They are opinion leaders, usually highly active on social media and very influential in terms of their style. In comparison to fashion followers, fashion leaders are more conscious of their clothing style and appearance and are more likely to consider fashion as a means of symbolising their social status, prestige, and success (Park et al., 1999; Beaudoin et al., 2000). A true fashion leader is always seeking uniqueness (Stone, 2012). People look up to fashion leaders for style advice and fashion inspiration and so they are very influential in terms of product sales. In the contemporary fashion industry, buyers for super-fast-fashion companies often work directly with fashion leaders to create their 'own range' for the brand, a process called 'brand collaboration', such as Dani Dyer for In the Style and Rhianna for River Island. This adds a level of prestige to the product range and creates added interest through the media buzz surrounding it.

Fashion followers (early majority, late majority, and laggards)

Fashion followers represent the majority of high-street fashion consumers. Without followers the fashion industry would collapse, because they are the consumers of mass-produced fashion (Stone, 2012). There are various reasons why people become fashion followers, from a feeling of insecurity to the admiration of others, or even a lack of interest in the new (Stone, 2012). Fashion followers are fashion brands' key consumers, and so buyers must tailor the majority of their range to meet their needs and wants.

Cultural differences

Fashion brands often operate internationally, selling products to many different countries and cultures. Culture can be defined as 'the values, beliefs, norms, and behavioural patterns of a national group' (Leung et al., 2005, p. 357) or as the collective programming of the mind which distinguishes the members of one group or category of people from another (Hofstede, 1980). Culture is a multi-faceted construct but fundamentally it means the way, and why, we do things, as well as how we develop as a consumer (Roncha & Gee, 2019). Culture includes everything a person has learned about social norms, values, customs, traditions, religions, and beliefs (Roncha & Gee, 2019).

Hofstede (1980) conducted a detailed study in order to understand cultural differences for strategy development from 1967–1973. The study garnered 116,000 respondents throughout 72 countries in 20 different languages. One of the key dimensions in Hofstede's framework was the difference between *individualist* and *collectivist* cultures. Individualism/collectivism represents the extent to which members of a society are concerned with their personal interests and the welfare of their families (Hofstede, 1980). Low scores on the individualism scale indicate that members of a society view themselves as part of a larger group. Countries such as Korea, China, Japan, Brazil, Chile, and Columbia scored very low on the individualism scale, indicating that they are collectivist cultures. In a collectivist culture, people are likely to be concerned with their role as members of a group, meaning that group norms are particularly relevant. A sense of 'group protection' is fostered where people feel part of a community and develop strong relationships with other people in that community, seeking group harmony. On the other hand, in an individualist culture such as the US, Canada, the UK, and Australia, people are likely to be concerned with their own self-interests and have a much lower dependency on others. Concepts such as independence and 'me against the world' are prominent in individualist cultures.

Culture is central to how individuals engage with the world around them. The way people dress is a material aspect of culture that has importance economically as well as socially (Workman & Lee, 2011). It is important for buyers to be aware of cultural differences as not all garment ranges will appeal to particular cultures, and some products may need to be adapted in order to make them more culturally appropriate. For instance, certain cultures advocate more modesty when dressing than others, and so sleeves, as well as hemlines on dresses and skirts, will need to be adapted to be longer, and necklines brought up higher. The symbolisation of colour is also important for buyers to be aware of when designing product ranges for different cultures. For example, black is the traditional colour of mourning in the UK and US, whereas in Japan and the Far East it is white (Roncha & Gee, 2019). Furthermore, the colour red symbolises good luck and prosperity in China and is often worn throughout the year by people when their birth year matches the current Chinese zodiac animal.

Idea generation: directional shops

Directional shops are undertaken by buyers to gain inspiration for their upcoming product ranges. Buyers may travel abroad to get an authentic look at cultures, streets, markets, and artwork. Buyers will bring back samples and objects that have inspired them on their trip in order to act as a starting point for a new range. Photographs are taken and notes and sketches will be made for information and ideas. For instance, if a Moroccan theme is forecast to be on-trend the following year, buyers may visit Morocco and walk around the local markets and speak to the people, gaining ideas on prints, colours, and fabric that may help them stand out from their competitors and offer something unique that will appeal to consumers. Research can come from different levels of the market, from street wear, vintage garments, and social media, as well as looking at the brands and retailers that the target market would aspire to buy from. What is important here is how buyers interpret the inspiration and information that they gather. They must use their knowledge of their customer, the market, and their past sales figures in order to inform how to apply it to their upcoming product range.

Inspirational and directional research is a key part of product development and enhances how a final product can look and feel. All products need a point of difference in order to differentiate them from competitors' product assortments. Ideas on fastenings, style details, colour combinations, finishing touches, and even linings are considered to provide this point of difference. It is these points of difference that can sometimes be the key influencing factor when consumers are comparing products from retailer to retailer.

However, it is worth noting that these trips can be expensive and time-consuming, and so some retailers have stopped buyers doing them in order to save costs and maximise the time spent on developing the range and getting it on the shop floor as quickly as possible to maximise profits. This is particularly the case for fast-fashion retailers and smaller retailers. With the vast amount of information and images available on the internet, such trips are less important than they used to be.

Trend forecasting

A fashion trend is the direction in which a fashion is moving. Brands need to ascertain whether it is moving towards or away from maximum consumer acceptance (Stone, 2012). They can do this using trend forecasting. Trend forecasters use their knowledge of fashion design, marketing, current affairs, trends, and history combined with consumer and business information in order to predict the future fashion trends (Granger, 2015). Trends need to be forecast well in advance so that buyers will understand what will appeal to consumers in order to develop garments to meet those demands and ensure that they are available to be sold at the right time. Forecasting companies provide information on future trends relating to colour, fabric, silhouettes, design themes, patterns, prints, and styling details up to 18–24 months ahead of the season (Granger, 2015). Buyers need to be selective in the trends that they choose to adopt as they must suit their company ethos and target customer. If buyers get this wrong then the product range will not sell and items will have to go into markdown, thus diminishing profits.

Buyers are not responsible for generating trend-forecasting information, but for observing and analysing the data created by trend-forecasting companies and other sources in order to inform the design of their product range. It is good practice for buyers and merchandisers to have a strong awareness of the current season's trends; however, it is the design team who will develop and plan for the key trends that are specific to the retailers' target consumer. They will translate the key looks that the buying team need to buy into for the season. The buying team will then use the trend information developed from design to influence their product assortments as well as their own trend research and knowledge to influence any in-season buying and product development.

Trend-forecasting tools

Fashion trend prediction is used by fashion professionals including buyers and designers to help them produce and buy what is predicted to be popular in a forthcoming season (Dillon, 2012). The following section outlines some of the key sources of trend-forecasting information consulted by buyers when planning a new product range.

Trend-forecasting packages

Trend-forecasting packages are a traditional way for fashion companies to gather future trend information. The packages consist of trend boards and sketches detailing the trends up to 18 months in advance of the current trading season. The packages are produced and sent to fashion brands/retailers every six months and are expensive to subscribe to. This means that for smaller independent fashion retailers they can be too costly. Yet, the depth of information included in these forecasting packages is seen to be worth the investment for many companies.

Trend-forecasting magazines

Trend-forecasting magazines are another long-standing traditional way for fashion businesses to get fashion trend information. The magazines are a more accessible way of gathering trend-forecasting information in terms of price and they are also produced more frequently than trend-forecasting packages, usually every month. However, the magazines are not as detailed as the packages and mainly focus on the colours and fabrics that will be on-trend.

Trend-forecasting websites

The first trend forecasting websites were founded in the late 1990s to early 2000s, revolutionising the trend-forecasting industry. The advent of these internet-based trend-forecasting companies meant that buyers could access trend-forecasting information on a daily basis, an aspect that is essential in such a fast-paced industry that is so prone to change. As well as details on key colours and prints for the upcoming seasons, trend-forecasting websites often provide detailed reports and commentaries on the trends. Unlike traditional trend-forecasting companies, trend-forecasting websites also consider trends that are generated from the 'bottom up' as opposed to just the 'top down', with researchers scanning social media sites such as Instagram and Pinterest, as well as 'street style' snaps, in order to discover any movements from fashion leaders. The internet enables trend forecasters to constantly post updates, adding any surprises that may have been missed previously or as a result of unexpected events or occurrences.

Fashion weeks

There are four main fashion weeks that occur over a four-week period twice a year (February and September) every year: New York, London, Milan, and Paris. The fashion weeks show designers' collections for the following season (e.g. in February the designers show the product ranges for the following September or autumn/winter). The fashion weeks are very prestigious events that buyers from all across the fashion industry visit in order to get inspiration for their own brands. In recent years, more 'fashion weeks' have sprung up in other cities around the world, making them more accessible. For instance, there are now fashion weeks in Denmark, Australia, Brazil, Canada, New Zealand, India, Japan, China, and Hong Kong. This creates further opportunities for inspiration for both fashion buyers and consumers alike. However, it is the traditional four fashion weeks that are still the biggest and most prestigious, attracting the top luxury brands and acting as a showcase of their latest designs on a global stage.

On the other hand, fashion weeks have changed in recent years. Gone are the days where they were invitation-only to buyers, and very closed events. Now they generate a lot of publicity, and invitations are extended to influencers and PR companies in order to promote the events and the brands and collections showcasing at them. Furthermore, brands often stream the catwalk show on their websites and their social media platforms, enabling their consumers to see them. As a result, it can be argued that this increased access to trend and product information has shortened consumers' attention span when it comes to fashion, making their appetite for rapid change more prevalent than ever (Stone, 2012). Retailers now weigh the costs of sending buyers to attend the fashion weeks, as well as global trade shows, as opposed to just staying in the office and gathering information on each of them through internet sources, as both are expensive ways of conducting research, making them inaccessible to smaller brands.

Trade shows

Trade shows consist of huge exhibitions whereby suppliers from all over the world display either their garments or fabric (depending on what type of trade show it is) to visiting buyers. They usually take place twice a year, around February and September to correspond with the traditional seasons, enabling buyers to place order with suppliers up to six months in advance. Trade shows are important for buyers to attend as, even if they are not planning on purchasing fabrics/garments, they provide inspiration for colour palettes, prints, and fabrics, so can inform buyers' ranges overall. There are two main types of trade shows: fabric trade shows and garment trade shows. Each trade show covers a specialist area (e.g. yarn), and the buyer visits those which are the most relevant to their retailer/department.

Fabric trade shows

Examples of fabric trade shows are detailed in Figure 6.2.

Fabric trade show	Location	Time of year	Details
Pitti Imagine Filatti	Florence, Italy	January and July	International event that presents yarn and knitting. The visitors include international buyers and designers looking for inspiration from the unique yarns and knitting designs
Premiere Vision	Paris, Moscow, New York, Sao Paulo, Shanghai	February and September	One of the biggest trade shows. Brings together the best in manufacturing, fabrics, and specialists from sportswear to denim
Tex World	Paris, Moscow, New York, Sao Paulo, Shanghai	February and September	Texworld offers buyers variety of products from basics to creative high-end fabrics. Specializes in cotton, denim, drapery and tailoring, embroidery and lace, jacquard, knitted fabrics, linen and hemp, prints, shirting, silk, silky aspects, sportswear and functional fabrics, trims and accessories, wool and woollen materials
Tissu Premier	Lille, France	February and September	Tissu Premier is a fast-response show for fashion brands and volume retailers. Presents the work of approximately 60 textile producers that specialize in supplying volume retail chains.
Munich Fabric Start	Munich, Germany	February and September	Fabrics, trims and accessories, innovation, sourcing, and fashion prints and patterns from more than 1,000 suppliers

Figure 6.2   **Examples of fabric trade shows**

Garment trade shows

Examples of garment trade shows are detailed in Figure 6.3.

Garment trade show	Location	Time of year	Details
Pure	London	February and August	Womenswear brands, with selections from emerging designers to established ready-to-wear designers
Jacket Required	London	February and September	Premium clothing trade show for forward-thinking style. Showcases a curated collection of contemporary menswear, womenswear, and selected accessories
Moda	Birmingham	February and August	Menswear, women's apparel, and accessories brands from various levels of the market
Fashion SVP	London	January and August	Sourcing show presenting over 100 leading global apparel producers

Figure 6.3   **Examples of garment trade shows within the UK**

For buyers, there are several advantages of going to trade shows. First, they are great sources of inspiration for upcoming seasons. Buyers are able to see a wide range of colours, fabrics, and garments in person which will help them to make better-informed decisions. Second, trade shows also enable buyers to meet potential suppliers. Meeting in person is a much more effective way to build up the buyer–supplier relationship and put the buyer in a much better position for the negotiation.

However, there are also disadvantages of going to trade shows. They are time-consuming and involve a lot of travelling, thus preventing the buyer from carrying out the rest of their duties. This is particularly relevant in the contemporary fashion industry where lead times are pushed to be as short as possible and buyers are having to be very reactive to consumer demand. This reason alone means that the majority of the super-fast-fashion brands will not attend them. Furthermore, it is expensive for the buyer to travel to them, eating into the companies' profits. Yet, for buyers who cannot attend many (or any!) trade shows, trade sources such as Drapers and WGSN have full details of all the shows and exhibitors on their websites, keeping them informed, and so this mitigates some of the risks of not attending them in person.

From top-down to bottom-up

Trend forecasting has traditionally been conducted using the previously discussed resources, facilitating a top-down approach; i.e. brands told consumers what was on-trend that season. With the advent of the internet and Web 2.0 platforms such as Instagram,

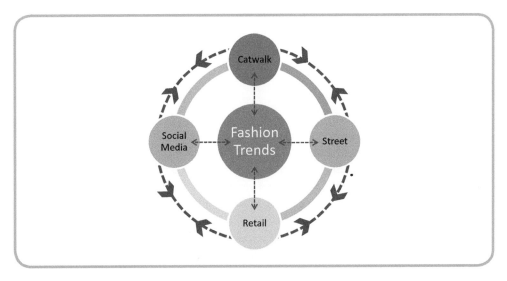

Figure 6.4   Circular example of how trends and social media influence range planning

blogs, and YouTube, this has changed. The last decade has seen the power shift more towards consumers, with 'street style' becoming just as important as the traditional fashion weeks in determining trends, and consumers following fashion leaders on Instagram for fashion inspiration, rather than traditional media such as magazines. Thus, the rise of celebrity and influencer culture has resulted in less certainty for buyers when trend forecasting, as it is much more difficult to predict what consumers want. Trends can spring up very quickly on social media, leaving the buyer scrambling to keep up and ensure that they sell items that meet consumers' needs. Political and social events are also starting to impact trends, and these are being reflected on the catwalks as well as on the high street and social media Nowadays most brands need to consider a combination of 'street style' from influencers and social media with their traditional trend-forecasting tools, conducting a circular top-down and bottom-up approach (Figure 6.4).

The future of trend forecasting

Christopher et al. (2004) believe that the fashion products can no longer be forecast at all. Although this is an extreme view, it is becoming increasingly difficult to forecast fashion trends based on the greater influence of bottom-up factors such as influencers and social media, as discussed above. The live-streaming of the fashion week shows mean that the designer's garments and ideas are on display instantly, creating instant desire for consumers (a concept which has come to fruition with the see-now-buy-now model adopted by Burberry in 2016). Yet, whilst on-demand manufacturing is certainly rising in importance and can be used to generate a competitive advantage for retailers, the abolition of trend forecasting altogether is unlikely. The extensive research that is conducted by trend-forecasting companies and the cyclical nature of fashion trends means that their predictions are generally fairly accurate, and it is only a few unexpected influences each season that disrupt this. Buyers and merchandisers can, therefore, plan the majority of their range confidently using trend-forecasting research, and set aside a portion of their budget (the open-to-buy budget) for in-season buying in order to react to unforeseen trends.

CHAPTER SUMMARY

This chapter highlights the extensive research and planning that buyers and merchandisers do whilst developing a product range, from market research, past sales analysis, consumer research, and trend forecasting, all the while ensuring that it is aligning with the brand's mission and values. Fashion retailers now have more opportunities in terms of market segmentation, in that they can look at inter-generational needs and wants, make clear splits between different generations, and/or follow different characteristics, such as whether or not someone adopts trends early or late. Consumers, particularly fashion leaders, are now more influential than ever before in dictating fashion trends, as the move from top-down to bottom-up surges on through the further developments of technology and social media. Consumers are now in charge of what is being sold, through their adoption, acceptance, and rejection of the styles that are offered (Stone, 2012).

References

Andrews, K.R. (1997). 'The Concept of Corporate Strategy', in Foss, N.J. (ed.), *Resources, Firms, and Strategies: A Reader in the Resource-based Perspective*. Oxford: Oxford University Press, pp. 52–59.

Beaudoin, P., Moore, M.A., & Goldsmith, R. (2000). 'Fashion leaders' and followers' attitudes toward buying domestic and imported apparel', *Clothing and Textiles Research Journal*, 18: 56–64.

Bolton, R.N., Parasuraman, R., Hoefnagels, A., Migchels, N., Kabadayi, S., Gruber, T., Komarova Loureiro, Y., & Solnet, D. (2013). 'Understanding Generation Y and their use of social media: A review and research agenda', *Journal of Service Management*, 24(3): 245–267.

Bulut, Z.A., Cimrin, F.K., & Dogan, O. (2017). 'Gender, generation and sustainable consumption: Exploring the behaviour of consumer from Izmir, Turkey', *International of Consumer Studies*, 41: 597–604.

Campbell, A., & Yeung, S. (1991). 'Creating a sense of mission', *Long Range Planning*, 24(4): 10–20.

Christopher, M., Lowson, R., & Peck, H. (2004). 'Creating agile supply chains in the fashion industry', *International Journal of Retail & Distribution Management*, 32(8): 367–376.

Clodfelter, R. (2012). *Retail Buying: From Basics to Fashion*. 4th ed. New York, NY: Fairchild Books.

David, M.E., David, F.R., & David, F.R. (2014). 'Mission statement theory and practice: A content analysis and new direction', *International Journal of Business, Marketing, and Decision Sciences*, 7(1): 95–110.

Dholakia, R.R., & Uusitalo, O. (2002). 'Switching to electronic stores: Consumer characteristics and the perception of shopping benefits', *International Journal of Retail & Distribution Management*, 30(10): 459–469.

Dillon, S. (2012). *Fundamentals of Fashion Management*. New York, NY: Bloomsbury.

Dimock, M. (2019). 'Defining generations: Where millennials end and Generation Z begins', 17 January, Pew Research Centre, available at: www.pewresearch.org/fact-tank/

2019/01/17/where-millennials-end-and-generation-z-begins/.

Filipczak, B. (1994). 'It's just a job: Generation X at work', *Training*, 31(4): 2127.

Glass, A. (2007). 'Understanding generational differences for competitive success', *Industrial and Commercial Training*, 39(2): 98–103.

Granger, M.M. (2015). *The Fashion Industry and its Careers*. 3rd ed. New York, NY: Bloomsbury.

Hofstede, G. (1980). *Culture's Consequences: International Differences in Work-Related Values*. Beverly Hills, CA: Sage.

Howe, N., & Strauss, W. (2000). *Millennials Rising: The Next Great Generation*. New York, NY: Random House.

Jackson, T., & Shaw, D. (2001). *Mastering Fashion Buying and Merchandising Management*. London: Palgrave.

Kwon, H.H., Trail, G., & James, J.D. (2007). 'The mediating role of perceived value: Team identification and purchase intention of team-licensed apparel', *Journal of Sport Management*, 21: 540–554.

Lavelle, D. (2019). 'Move over, millennials and Gen Z, here comes Generation Alpha', 4 January, *The Guardian*, available at: www.theguardian.com/society/shortcuts/2019/jan/04/move-over-millennials-and-gen-z-here-comes-generation-alpha.

Leung, K., Bhagat, R.S., Buchan, N.R., Erez, M., & Gibson, C.B. (2005). 'Culture and international business. Recent advances and their implications for future research', *Journal of International Business Studies*, 36(4): 357–378.

McCrindle. (2006). *New Generations at Work: Attracting, Recruiting, Retaining & Training Generation Y*. Norwest Business Park: McCrindle Research.

Mintel. (2012). *Women's Fashion Lifestyles – UK*, May. London: Author.

Mintel. (2014a). *Clothing Retailing – UK*, October. London: Author.

Mintel. (2014b). *Fashion for All Ages – UK*, November. London: Author.

Mintel. (2014c). *Womenswear – UK*, May. London: Author.

Mintel. (2018a). *Reports – Social and Media Networks – UK*, May. London: Author.

Mintel. (2018b). *Reports – Consumers and the Economic Outlook – Quarterly Update – UK*, March. London: Author.

Mintel. (2018c). *Reports – Technology Habits of Generation Z – UK*, September. London: Author.

Mintel. (2019a). *The Generation X BPC Consumer – UK*, February. London: Author.

Mintel. (2019b). *Reports – Menswear – UK*, March. London: Author.

Park, J.H., Cho, E.H., & Rudd, N.A. (1999). 'Fashion Opinion Leadership and Appearance Management Behavior', in Owens, N.J. (ed.), *Proceedings International Textile and Apparel Association*. Monument, CO: ITAA, p. 85.

Parment, A. (2013). 'Generation Y vs. Baby boomers: Shopping behavior, buyer involvement and implications for retailing', *Journal of Retailing and Consumer Services*, 20(2): 189–199.

Parry, E., & Urwin, P. (2011). 'Generational differences in work values: A review of theory and evidence', *International Journal of Management Reviews*, 13(1): 79–96.

Pentecost, R., & Andrews, L. (2010). 'Fashion retailing and the bottom line: The effects of generational cohorts, gender, fashion fanship, attitudes and impulse buying on fashion expenditure', *Journal of Retailing and Consumer Services*, 17(1): 43–52.

Porter, M.E. (1987). 'From competitive advantage to corporate strategy', *Harvard Business Review*, 65: 43–59.

Priporas, C.V., Stylos, N., & Fotiadis, A. (2017). 'Generation Z consumers' expectations of interaction in smart retailing: A future agenda', *Computer in Human Behaviour*, 77: 374–381.

Rajasekar, J. (2013). 'A comparative analysis of mission statement content and readability', *Journal of Management Policy and Practice*, 14(6): 131–147.

Rogers, E.M. (1983). *Diffusion of Innovations*. New York, NY: Free Press.

Roncha, A. (2019). 'Fashion Brand Management', in Varley, R., Roncha, A., Radclyffe-Thomas, N., & Gee, L. (eds), *Fashion Management: A Strategic Approach*. New York, NY: Red Globe Press, pp. 105–129.

Roncha, A., & Gee, L. (2019). 'International Growth Strategy in Fashion Markets', in Varley, R.,

Roncha, A., Radclyffe-Thomas, N., & Gee, L. (eds), *Fashion Management: A Strategic Approach*. New York, NY: Red Globe Press, pp. 59–78.

Shepherd, A., Pookulangara, S., Kinley, T.R., & Josiam, B.M. (2016). 'Media influence, fashion, and shopping: A gender perspective', *Journal of Fashion Marketing and Management*, 20(1): 4–18.

Smalej, O. (2017). 'Styles of making purchasing decisions by consumers from Z generation and Y generation', *International Journal of Retail & Distribution Management*, 31(2): 95–106.

Stone, E. (2012). *In Fashion*. 2nd ed. New York, NY: Fairchild Books.

Tapscott, D. (2008). *Grown up Digital: How the Net Generation Is Changing Your World*. New York, NY: McGraw-Hill.

Twigg, J. (2012). 'Adjusting the cut: Fashion, the body and aging on the UK high street', *Aging & Society*, 32: 1030–1154.

Varley, R. (2019). 'Fashion Marketing', in Varley, R., Roncha, A., Radclyffe-Thomas, N., & Gee, L. (eds), *Fashion Management: A Strategic Approach*. New York, NY: Red Globe Press, pp. 43–57.

Varley, R., & Clark, J. (2019). 'Fashion Merchandise Management', in Varley, R., Roncha, A., Radclyffe-Thomas, N., & Gee, L. (eds), *Fashion Management: A Strategic Approach*. New York, NY: Red Globe Press, pp. 155–173.

Workman, J.E., & Lee, S. (2011). 'Materialism, fashion, consumers and gender: A cross-cultural study', *International Journal of Consumer Studies*, 5(1): 50–57.

Range development

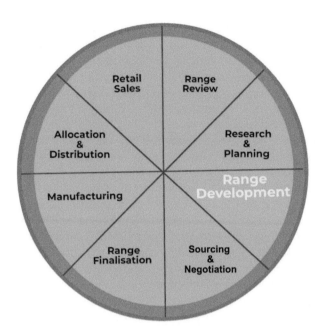

Once all the research and planning has been conducted, buyers and merchandisers can move onto the range-development stage. This involves the amalgamation of the trend-forecasting research and consumer/market research to translate it into a product that reflects the brand identity and will meet consumer demand. This chapter will outline the key stages of range development and the responsibilities of buyers and merchandisers throughout this stage.

By the end of this chapter you will be able to:

• Describe the trend-translation process and its importance in range development;
• Identify key product characteristics and classifications;
• Outline the key elements that need to be considered when developing a product range;

- Discuss the width and depth of a product range and how different fashion retailers use this strategically;
- Analyse how to reduce risk in range planning.

Trend translation

The development of new products is key to a business's success and the continuation of customer loyalty. Thus, increasing the frequency and 'newness' of fashion collections has become crucial to the survival of many fashion companies (Tran et al., 2011). As trends are determined and showcased incessantly throughout the seasons, consumers expect to see these trends reflected in the products sold on the high street and online. Therefore, buyers must ensure that they sell the key trends throughout the season in the form of products that their customers want to wear. This involves the process of *trend translation*.

Trend translation is the process whereby the original trend ideas are developed into product variations that reflect the brand's identity and signature direction as well as the tastes of their target market. Once trend-forecasting research has been conducted, a clear vision is presented of the key looks, colours, styles, details, and fabrics that are important for the season. Consideration of how to apply those trends, concepts, and ideas to the product ranges and assortments is the next step in product development. Hence, trend translation involves the analysis of the tone of the trends predicted and applying it to designs or products that fit the brand and its consumers (Dillon, 2012).

It is the translation of these trends, concepts, and ideas into commercial products that drives fashion product development. Informative and conflicting information needs to be assessed to help determine the final outcome to ensure that the product is translated as appropriately as possible. A common question arises here: why translate the trend, and not just copy it? Trend translation gives the products that a brand sells a point of difference. It enables the brand to stand out from its competitors and grow its market share. Moreover, it is expected from its customers and so the brand must live up to these expectations.

The key factors that impact trend translation, including both internal and external factors, are listed below:

- *Fashion information* – trend information provided by forecasting agencies, catwalk influences, celebrities, press and social media;
- *Supply chain* – how a product will be manufactured and where it will be manufactured. Two key areas are the lead time taken and product costs, both of which can heavily influence how a product looks, fits and feels;
- *Competitive information* – understanding what a brand's competitors are doing is vital and will inform many subtle decisions made regarding a product. The priority is to make sure that the products being developed have a point of difference in the market, providing the target customer a reason to purchase them over a competitor's offer;
- *Brand identity and market positioning* – the brand identity and corporate strategy is essential to keep in mind during product development, and extremely influential during trend translation. Brands have a distinct market position and it is important to maintain it. When developing products, it is key to make sure that they incorporate the right level of fashionability in order to uphold the market position;

- *Consumer information* – what the customer expects to buy is a good starting point for a range. Therefore, it is crucial to understand the type of customer, their specific needs, and how external factors influence them when developing the range. Selling a product at the correct time for the customer is crucial, so buyers and merchandisers must know when their customers will be ready to purchase a new product or trend. This is dependent on the trend and product style, but also on different types of customers and their stance in relation to the diffusion of innovation (see Chapter 6 for further information). Making sure that the right product gets to the right customer at the right time is vital; trying to sell a product too late or too early can be an expensive mistake for a brand/retailer;
- *Historical sales* – information from previous sales patterns and customer purchase history can be very beneficial to trend translation. Not only can historical sales inform retailers of the best and worst sellers, but also the pricing structures and profit margins that need to be considered when developing a range of products. Key data on customer preferences in terms of colours and sizes is extremely useful when planning and developing products. This information acts like a skeletal plan for future ranges.

These factors (Figure 7.1) all impact and influence the ideas for a product. It is a combination of this information mixed with the buyer's experience, expertise, and instinct that collectively aid product development. Truly understanding a brand's signature style and consumers' expectations are key to the most successful trend translations. Understanding what elements need to be diluted or reflected within the financial restraints of a product is really important. Good buyers understand this process and execute it with careful consideration. The methods of trend translation will vary and can really depend on the type of product that is being considered. However, there are two key ideas that can help the translation of trends and concepts to create a commercially viable product: *diluted/ direct reflection* and *timing*.

Dilution or direct reflection

In many cases the trend that is illustrated on the catwalk and by trend forecasters needs to be diluted in order for it to be appropriate and suitable for the target consumer for

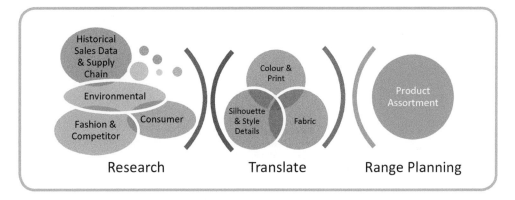

Figure 7.1   Factors that influence trend translation and range planning

high-street retailers. Although the garments, ideas, and trends look incredibly inspiring, they may not be practical for everyday life. Also, in some cases, the target consumer may not be confident enough nor want to wear a product that is extremely directional or 'on trend', preferring a gentler nod to the trend with a garment that is appropriate and fits in with the rest of their wardrobe. Thus, fashion retailers need to reflect the appropriate level of fashionability in their products, or risk alienating customers through being either too forward or too old-fashioned in the designs they offer (Jackson & Shaw, 2001).

Mixing key colours with more subtler shades, or only using them on trims and smaller aspects of a product is a form of dilution. Simplifying on-trend styles and details to a more appropriate level helps to develop a more commercial product for retail. Indeed, the elements of the trend that are discarded are just as important, if not more important than what is included. Hence, an understanding of what to leave out is just as relevant as understanding what to keep for the buyer. How a brand translates a trend will differ across the market; every brand will have a complex set of requirements that are important to its target customers and how they will receive a trend.

Figure 7.2 illustrates a simplified version of trend translation, taking a trend idea and diluting it in several forms to make a more commercially viable product for the brand and consumer.

Timing

Selling a product at the correct time for the target customer is also crucial. A key priority for buyers and merchandisers is ensuring that the product launch is neither too early nor too late to meet their customers' needs. Hence, knowing when the target customers will be ready to purchase a new product or trend is essential in range planning and trend translation.

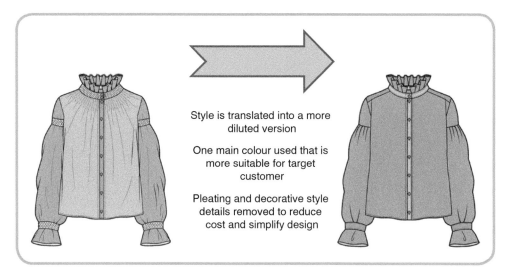

Style is translated into a more diluted version

One main colour used that is more suitable for target customer

Pleating and decorative style details removed to reduce cost and simplify design

Figure 7.2 **Trend translation example**

Each product follows the *Product Life Cycle,* a theory that advocates that all products have a defined life cycle, and, thus, that no product can go on selling forever (Jackson & Shaw, 2001). Understanding where the product is in its life cycle will help with product development and the translation of trends. Buyers and merchandisers can use the product's life cycle to ensure that they launch the product at the correct time to meet consumer demand and monitor its progress throughout it in order to know when to promote it and/or put it into markdown.

Product Life Cycle

Once a product has been developed and released to the market it will go through the sequential stages of:

- *Introduction* – where the product is launched in manageable or small volumes in order to monitor performance and acceptance by the more fashion-forward consumers;
- *Growth* – where the product's sales start to grow and it becomes accepted by mass consumers. The product is now widely available and purchased by consumers on a large scale – it is at this stage where large profits can be made in fashion (Jackson & Shaw, 2001);
- *Maturity* – sometimes referred to as *saturation.* This is where the product is widely worn by many customers and practically all types of fashion retailers across the market are selling this product type. Price promotions and discounts start to appear as the more fashion-forward customers start to reject the style due to its vast popularity and wide availability;
- *Decline* – the product style starts to decrease in sales at this stage. Heavy discounts are now in place in order to attempt to clear the stock, and the style will not be considered for inclusion in the upcoming ranges.

Product styles and trends will move through these stages at a variety of different paces and in some cases even they may even pause. Buyers and merchandisers need to ensure that they have an understanding of where styles and trends are within their life cycle in relation to their target market. This knowledge supports not only the development of a product style but also how many of the styles will be bought and if any promotional activities are needed.

Range planning

Once the buyer has conducted thorough market research, consumer analysis, and trend forecasting, as well as an analysis of the post-mortem report (discussed in Chapter 5) and liaison with the merchandising team, they are now ready to start planning the product range. A product range can be defined as a cohesive collection of garments and/or accessories and shoes that follow a particular trend or colour palette. There is no set number of items that make up a product range – it can vary from range to range, from retailer to retailer, and from brand to brand; however, around ten to 20 items is the norm. The full range will not be stocked in every store (mainly due to space constraints), so particular products from it will be selected based on the type of store and the type of consumers that shop in that store (this is discussed in more detail in Chapter 11). On the other hand, flagship stores and online stores will provide the full range to consumers. A product range must contain a variation of different styles, colourways (usually one or two dominant colours that are trend-driven/specific to the season, as well as several neutrals), and sizes that will appeal to that brand's target market. The product range must remain true to the brand's identity and maintain expectations in terms of quality, fit, and price (Grose, 2012). It needs to provide a balanced assortment of product classifications, primarily being made up of classic/basic items and fashion items, depending on the retailer.

PRODUCT RANGE

A product range is a coordinated set of items that are sold by a brand or a retailer. There is no fixed number that defines a garment range, although typically ranges will be made up of between ten and 20 items.

The range should comprise of a balance of different products based on their classifications, type (e.g. tops vs bottoms ratio), and price architecture. The type of brand or retailer and its strategic direction also impacts on the approach, product assortments, and even types of products that are suitable to include in the range. There are four key aspects that need to be considered at every product decision made:

- *Market positioning* – is the product suitable in terms of its fashionability and quality at the level of the market that the brand trades at? If not, it may be unlikely to sell. Brands must ensure that they are competitive in the market in terms of their product offering, and that they maintain their perceived market position each season.
- *Target customer* – truly understanding the identity of the target customer is vital to product development. Different types of customers expect various different types of products at very different times, and understanding who the customer is and when they are ready to purchase certain trends or products helps make sure that the correct products are developed at the right time.
- *Customer expectations* – to be successful, retailers must bring new products to the market which can completely satisfy customers' expectations, as well as the business desire to increase profitability (Levtushenko & Hodge, 2012). Understanding customer expectations is key to product development. Ideals on price and quality can influence customer decision-making, so it is important to consider all of their expectations, good and bad, and that they are addressed when range planning.
- *Retail calendar* – there are various events and activities throughout the year that are specific to certain types of customers. There are some very generic themes – such as party season during December and holiday season during June and July. However, there are also very specific occasions, such as festival season, that are focused on a certain customer type.

Product classifications

A product range needs to have a good mix of product types, from fashion items to basic and classic items. Classifying products into certain types helps to support with volumes and quantities of the product needed. This is extremely helpful when range planning and can help determine the risk factor a product may potentially have, in order to allow strategies to be put in place to combat this. Figure 7.3 illustrates the product-classification categories and also shows the risk and demand expectations of each category.

Products can enter at any part of the pyramid and can move down the categories from season to season, depending on the trend adoption from the consumer, new trends available, and product popularity. The price points, colourways, and fabrics will also determine classification. For example, the same product in two different variations can be two different product classifications (e.g. plain black vs bright pattern).

When range planning, the buyer needs to consider how the range will look collectively, and make considerations for how the products will be visually merchandised together either in-store or online. Considerations regarding visual merchandising support the selling of products, whether they are singular or part of a look, and further the buyer's understanding of how products will sit within the whole range. Most products will always sell as separates, but it is important that they coordinate with each other within the range and that they complement each other too.

Product classification will determine the volumes ordered by the merchandising team. For example, buyers and merchandisers do not expect to sell as many hero items as basic items, as basic items have universal appeal, whereas hero items will only appeal to a particular segment of consumers. Thus, using the product-classification method when range planning allows the buying and merchandising teams to control any risks that there may be with products. It also allows ranges to have a balance of different product types, reflecting the different types of customers that they cater for.

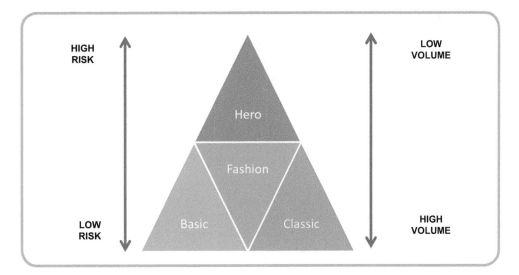

Figure 7.3   **Product classifications**

Customer interpretation is key to product classification, as understanding how the consumer will receive the product within a range is vital. Timing and competitor products as well as aspirational influences will impact how a consumer perceives a product and influence if they are ready to buy the product or not, which can determine and influence its product classification. Therefore, product classifications can differ from brand to brand depending on their market positioning and target consumer; a fashion item for one retailer may be a basic product for another.

Basics

Basic items are products that are seen as a staple in the wardrobe. They are the products that we all expect to own and purchase on a replacement basis. Basic items are, therefore, functional items that rarely change and are considered a necessity. Basics are easier to forecast, as consumer demand for these items is steady and constant all year round. This means that the supply chain is relatively stable and consistent year-on-year, requiring very little change. The lead times can be long, and the cost to produce these items is low. The volumes are high as the demand is considered high. As such, they are usually the first items to be included in the range due to their defined sales history. Examples of basic items include black/white T-shirts, grey vest tops, and black leggings.

Classics

A classic is a style that satisfies a basic need and remains in fashion acceptance for an extended period of time (Stone, 2012). Like basics, classics also encompass items that are 'staples' in people's wardrobes. Classic items are acceptable during any time and in any place. The design of the items is simple, which keep them from becoming dated (Stone, 2012). They are usually comfortable and aesthetically appealing, including items such as black blazers, jeans, white shirts or blouses, black trousers, and a little black dress. Like basics, classic items are much easier to forecast, and lead times are long. Items that have originally been fashion and sold can become a classic item, and in some cases these products will be bestsellers. They are retained for more than one season in the same form or are slightly amended to update the fabric or colour.

Fashion

Fashion items are products that are widely accepted by most of the target customers. These products are available in a variety of colourways and fabrics, making them appealing to different consumers. They are trend-driven products but are acceptable to all customers. Fashion items are not usually stocked for more than one season, but some bestsellers may carry over to the next.

Hero

Hero products are trend-driven products that encompass the key looks for the season and are seen as being the 'must haves' in order to translate a trend. They are, therefore, high-risk products as they are completely new to the market in terms of trend translation. As a result, retailers may stock them in low volumes as they are a much harder product to sell. Although they may be the key look for the season for some of the target market, they may not appeal to all consumers. Hero products may need more time and visibility on the high street before all consumers will purchase them. An understanding of the brand's customer and how they may react to hero products helps buyers to determine their presence in range planning. However, hero products also serve a purpose in capturing the attention of consumers and are used to drive attention to product ranges either online or in-store. It is for this reason that brands often include hero products in their promotional and marketing campaigns, as well as store window displays and key visual merchandising areas online and in-store.

Fad

A fad is an item that suddenly sweeps into popularity, affects a limited section of the population, and then quickly disappears again (Stone, 2012). Fads are influenced by the mood and certain trends at the time, encompassing a stand-out feature or exaggerated detail that appeals to the consumer. Fads are linked to many things, such as a particular behaviour, a fashion trend, music, dance moves, and even food. Fad products' availability can be so rapid that in some cases it is not possible to be included within range planning. Social media has facilitated celebrity product exposure, an aspect that can heavily influence fads and fashion products. Fads usually arise and are driven by a desire to be a part of a group and are usually adopted by younger consumers. Fads are usually easily imitable and so tend to saturate the marketplace in a short space of time, resulting in consumers tiring of them quickly. Fads are bought in low volumes as they are the riskiest kind of products to sell and will only appeal to a small number of consumers. Nevertheless, they need to be included in the range so that the brands are seen to be 'current'. Hence, these types of products are generally seen in fast-fashion retailers whose business objectives are to create and sell the latest look or product and be the first to market to sell it.

Key elements that need to be considered in the range plan

There are some vital elements that are required for each range plan, aspects that are specific to each brand. Below is a list of some of the general aspects that are considered when developing a range plan, compiled from Grose (2012) and Goworek (2007):

- *Number of garments to be included in the range (product mix)* – there needs to be a sufficient choice of garments within the range to satisfy the consumer and provide enough variety. However, there should not be too much choice as that can add confusion in the overall look and identity of the range, as well as being costly and wasteful to produce.
- *Proportion of different types of garments included* – there needs to be a variety and a clear plan of how many tops vs bottoms. Historical sales will aid this decision and the merchandiser will give a clear breakdown of ratios for each type of style required.
- *Ratio of product classifications* – the range needs to be clearly balanced in terms of how many classics/basics vs fashion products there are, as well as which product(s) will be the hero product, with enough open-to-buy budget left for any potential fads.
- *Colourways or prints available in each style* – each of the styles in the range will be available in various colourways or prints. These are specific to the trend, style, and consumer expectations. For example, many products, regardless of whether they are a basic or a fashion product, tend to be offered in the colourway black too due to its universal appeal. The range plan shows the variety of colour options per style available.
- *Fabric composition of each style* – information on the fabric composition of each of the styles must be gathered. The composition of fabric is illustrated in percentages; for example, *80% polyester and 20% polyimide*.
- *Cost price (CP) of each style* – the cost price needs to be affordable and enable the retailer to generate a profit once the selling price is determined. This information shows, at a glance, what the retailer is paying the supplier for each of the styles.
- *Selling price (RRP) of each style* – the selling price needs to be realistic in terms of the target market's expectations and in keeping with the brand's position in the market.
- *Sizes to be offered* – the full size range needs to be determined, along with whether the item will also be included in different fits, such as petite, tall, plus size/curve, and/or maternity.
- *Which supplier to use for each style* – this information provides a greater understanding of the supplier portfolio and a breakdown of styles that they are responsible for.
- *Order quantities* – the amount of products per colourway or print of each of the styles that is being ordered must be decided.

KEY TERMS

CP = cost price
RRP = recommended retail price
COO = country of origin

Figure 7.4 illustrates a typical range plan. As demonstrated, a range plan comprises of a creative visualisation of the product range. The creation of a product range appears to be very focused on the creative element initially, but the numerical and financial information is just as important. Ultimately, the sole purpose of the product range is to make money for the retailer, so the financial information needs to be portrayed and communicated across the buying and merchandising teams.

Figure 7.4 Visual CAD illustrated range plan

Range-planning approaches

There are two main range-planning approaches in the fashion industry: (1) predominantly classics/basics, and (2) fashion-focused.

1. *Predominantly classics and basics* – some brands rely on simple styling (often focusing more on quality than fashion) and therefore include predominantly classic and basic items in their ranges. This range-planning approach relies heavily on past sales data. The products included in the range are much-lower-risk than fashion products and can often transcend seasons, having longer product life cycles. As a result, speed-to-market and lead times are not as important and there is less pressure on buyers to be fast and responsive comparatively to fast fashion. They are also not as driven by the latest key silhouettes unless they really fit the brand identity. The fashion element of their range will come from key colours/fabrics and specific styles rather than trends.

2. *Fashion-focused* – brands that aim to offer their consumers the latest trends rely much more on fashion or hero items in their ranges. Trend forecasting is much more important in informing these ranges. Short lead times will minimise the risks of these items as the closer to the season they are produced, the more accurate the trend forecasting and prediction of consumer demand is. Brands who are known for being more fashion-forward require a more collaborative approach between merchandisers, designers, and buyers. They participate in the whole process from sales analysis, design, and product development to production in order to minimise the risks. The quicker a fashion product can go from design to retail, the more chance there is to gain maximum sales; therefore, fast lead times also help to reduce risk.

There are three main methods of producing the silhouettes for a range, each of which can be used in combination as well as individually: (1) original and new design, (2) modification of an existing style, and (3) catwalk copies.

1. *Original and new design* – this involves the creation of styles entirely from an initial idea. This type of product development will begin with the design team and will go through a lengthy product-development process. This form of product development tends to be seen in higher-priced products, so is generally not seen in high-street fashion but more in luxury fashion brands. It can be very expensive in terms of both time and money as there is no historical data which it can be based on. This form of product development originates from a designer's influence rather than the buying team, and thus has a much more creative and design-focused aspect to its product development. Design identity is heavily incorporated into these products to give them a point of difference from each other and the brand's competitors.

2. *Modification of existing style* – this method is most commonly seen in high-street fashion product development where most products are connected to a style from a previous season. Historical sales analysis is drawn upon to aid the sampling, making it a much more cost-effective method as the patterns and the technical specs have already been developed. This also helps to minimise risk as there is some certainty of sales due to bestsellers from previous seasons being carried forward with minor modifications made to details, colours, fabrics, etc. This is sometimes the most

preferred form of product development as there is less risk involved, because much of the technical pack, quality-checking and fit testing has been done, thereby cutting down a lot of the time-consuming sampling and fitting processes. This method is also a much more sustainable option of product development as there is less waste and sampling required.

3. *Catwalk copies* – this method involves garments being adapted or modified from products designed by other brands. This is done through the use of photographs or actual garments. During the biannual fashion weeks, designer labels, couture housesm and ready-to-wear brands showcase their ranges a season ahead (i.e. the ranges shown in September will not be available for sale until February/March), thus enabling high-street retailers to 'copy' sections. High-street brands do this to enable mass-market consumers to find cheaper, replica versions of designer items.

How do mass-market brands get away with 'copying' styles?

Many mass-market brands owe part of their success to the creation of items that are clearly 'inspired' by more premium or luxury brands, or even other mass-market brands. Copying can land a buyer in tremendous legal difficulties, especially if they get involved with large global companies who are prepared to go to international law courts to protect their garment design (Jackson & Shaw, 2001). Buyers need to not only take responsibility for the products they are purchasing, but also make sure they conduct their product development in an honourable and ethical manner; however, it is impossible for every garment to be completely new and unique (Jackson & Shaw, 2001). In a world where there are new products available almost on a daily basis, it seems that all products are influenced and inspired by another. Thus, with fierce competition and new and up-and-coming brands fighting for market share, there is a very limited number of genuinely original garments on the high street.

Copyright laws

Brands that imitate designers must be careful as there are various copyright laws that they need to abide by. Copyrighting and patenting are legal ways of registering a design or an idea or invention (Jackson & Shaw, 2001). The Design Registration Scheme is a way to officially protect specific designs. In a climate where originality feels like an unknown element, and exposure to images and products is higher than ever, brands and designers sometimes take legal action to ensure that their designs are not able to be imitated by copycats, in order to remain unique and the only one in the market. For instance, Christian Louboutin, the luxury shoes and accessories brand, has been embroiled in a number of lawsuits across the world regarding its trademark red soles. Furthermore, in 2019 Kim Kardashian West filed a $10m (£7m) lawsuit against online fast-fashion retailer Missguided, accusing the brand of profiting by replicating an outfit she posted on Instagram designed by Kanye West. Missguided had posted a dress similar to one worn by Kim Kardashian West with the caption: 'The devil works hard but Missguided works harder' – pointing to a pre-order page for the style. Missguided responded to the complaint with a statement: 'Missguided shoppers know the score. We're about the look, without the celeb bucks. For the record, as much as we love her style, we're not working with Kim on anything' (Brown, 2019). Kim Kardashian West won the lawsuit filed in California against Missguided USA and was awarded $2.7m (Whelan, 2019).

Hence, fast-fashion retailers need to tread carefully in this area. Although their business model is often focused on celebrity-inspired looks at an affordable price, there is a fine line between 'inspiration' and 'copying' at the expense of the designer (Brown, 2019). Designers spend a lot of time, money, and effort perfecting certain items and so it is unfair to see a copycat item produced and made widely available at a fraction of the price, which is why they often take legal action to protect themselves. Thus, fast-fashion retailers must engage in the trend-translation process properly and create an item that fits their brand and target consumer, inspired by the original design but not a copy of it, in order to operate in an ethical manner.

Range-plan product assortment

Product assortment refers to the different types of products within a range. The product assortment is very important as it is the crux of how a brand can differentiate itself from its competitors. Detailed planning of the product range needs to be conducted in order to ensure that the product assortment is balanced and attractive to the consumer, as well as being aligned with the core values of the brand. Retailers must adjust the variety and depth of their assortments to changing consumer tastes and profiles (Mantrala et al., 2009). This can be achieved through the balance of the width and depth of a range.

Scope of a range: width vs depth

When developing a product range, buyers and merchandisers must also consider the width and depth of their assortment. The *width* of a product range refers to the different styles and shapes that are offered; how wide the choice is for consumers. Thus, the wider the choice (or greater the width), the more styles that are on offer for customers. The range *depth*, on the other hand, refers to the number of colours, prints, sizes, and price points available in each of the styles. Customers expect products to come in a variety of colours and sizes; however, too much variation in fabric and colour can also make your range look inconsistent and confusing. Hence, when developing a range, balance is needed. Achieving the right balance between the width and depth of a product range is based on the target customer's expectations.

Historical sales in terms of the best and worst sellers from previous seasons will influence the width and depth of future ranges. Buyers and merchandisers will monitor competitors' variations of styles and options available, and are always considering how to expand gain more market share and therefore more product sales. The brand strategy can impact on the width or depth of a range as the direction that the brand is intending to move forward with may influence product variations. It is important that the brand strategy is considered and that the buying strategy for the range supports this direction.

For example, if the direction for the brand is to reduce the amount of styles available, but offer more variations of colour and prints in key styles, this will reduce the width and increase the depth of a range.

Generally, trend-driven fashion brands have a wide product assortment in order to provide a comprehensive offer for their consumers with plenty of choice of styles. This is known as a *broad and shallow strategy*. A broad and shallow range assortment consists of a wide selection of garment styles but with a limited number of quantities of them made. This requires a much more extensive form of product development, as more time is spent in the initial creative aspects of the product-development process ensuring that all the key silhouette options are considered and represented. As a result, this has a much higher cost, as time and effort need to be spent in the sampling options and getting the product perfect for manufacturing. This is then reflected in higher price points for customers, but as the products tend to be more trend-driven, retailers are able to charge a little more for them as customers accept paying more for them. These ranges need to be constantly updated in response to changing trends and development of consumer demand, and a flexible approach to the width and depth needs to be considered because of this.

Other, more classic brands offer a narrower product range with much less variety of styles, but they have a deep selection in terms of colourways and sizes within those styles. This is known as a *deep and narrow strategy*. This method of range development minimises the amount of product-development activities as there is little time spent on creative development. These ranges can, therefore, be much more efficient to manufacture and much more cost-effective. This means higher profits for the retailer as it is able to forward-order this type of product, and as a consequence, has lower prices for the customer. However, as a result there is a lack of exclusivity and variety in the products in the range. These brands may choose to be 'category specialists' and focus on one particular type of product offer in order to be the market leader in that category, such as Levi's for jeans. Variety can be achieved through the number of different styles (within that category; e.g. for Levi's high-waisted jeans vs low-rise jeans, bootleg cut vs skinny jeans), sizes, fits, prices, and quality levels, as well as brands if it is a multi-brand retailer.

The correct range-development approach is vital to the success of the range but also for cohesion within the retail environment. Offering too many products can cause confusion and potentially lose customers. Therefore, in order for the range to be clear and understandable to the customer, it is vital to get the correct range width and depth for the target market level.

Size availability

Consumers want a full range of sizes available for every product; as broad as possible in order to suit the whole market (e.g. size 4–34). However, this is not profitable for a retailer to offer, as many of the smallest sizes and the largest sizes will be left over at the end of the season and could end up making a loss. Furthermore, the sizes in the middle may sell out very quickly and leave an uneven size selection available. As a result, buyers must ensure that they offer a wide enough range of sizes to keep the customer happy, but narrow enough so that it is still profitable, minimising the amount of stock left over. Research into the target customer is essential here, especially as size often increases with age, so retailers targeting an older age group should buy more larger sizes. In general, buyers should buy less of the smallest and largest sizes (such as sizes 6 and 8; 18 and 20) and stock more of those in the middle (size 10–16). This is particularly important for more trend-led pieces, such as hero and fad products, as their lifespan is not very long, meaning that the retailer only has a very limited selling period in which to sell out of them.

Price architecture

Price architecture is important to get right as this is a factor used in consumer perceptions of brand positioning (Varley & Clark, 2019). Brands often have different levels of price architecture for different types of products and product ranges. For instance, basics will be at the bottom level of the price architecture, with a classic pair of jeans in the middle band, and a highly embellished hero piece in the top band with the highest price point. Having a variety of different price points helps to make brands more accessible to consumers. All retailers have some form of logical price policy. Consumers have an expectation of what they will pay for a product from a retailer. Price points need to be understandable and logically stepped, with each level perceived to be good value for money. The differences in fabric quality, design, and style will all impact on price points. Product prices will also help to determine the volumes that are planned by the merchandisers. In some cases, the highest-priced products will have lowest volume but higher margins, whereas the lowest-priced products will be high volume but low margin as they tend to sell more in bulk.

Reducing the risk in range planning

There are a number of ways that buyers and merchandisers can minimise the risk in range planning, such as:

1. *Reduce the levels of riskier merchandise* – most fashion consumers err on the cautious side when purchasing, so buyers must ensure that their range includes fashion elements, but should underbuy the extremes of fashion. Nevertheless, buyers should still ensure that there are enough risky items so that the range looks fashionable to consumers. As such, buyers employ a strategy of 'selling short' of riskier merchandise, deliberately running out before the end of the season.
2. *Tailor it to meet your target consumers* – when consumers believe that real thought has gone into the range that they are offered, and that it is tailored towards their specific needs and preferences, they will be more receptive to it. However, if consumers have too much of a selection to choose from, they will become frustrated. Therefore, buyers must produce a range that speaks to consumers on a personal level but with a limited selection.
3. *Getting the size balance right* – customers want their size to be available and for the garment to fit well. Good buyers spend time ensuring that the fit of the garment is right. Good merchandisers spend time ensuring that there is an appropriate size range available.

Where to begin?

In the initial stages of product development, it is good practice to begin with a larger number of products for the range than is needed. That way, buyers can see what is really necessary and what are the best items to include. Near-completed ranges are presented at the pre-selection meeting. At this point styles can be withdrawn from a range for many reasons, such as:

- Issues with quality or fit;
- Lead times are too long;
- It is too expensive/not meeting a profit margin;
- It is too similar to an existing style;
- It has not got a strong enough presence within the range;
- It does coordinate well with the rest the range.

Creating a successful range

Maintaining the correct balance between the width and the depth of a range depends on the target market. Buyers and merchandisers will start with the sales history and the previous season's best and worst sellers in order to identify what customers expect to buy from the retailer. Consumers do have an expectation each season to see a certain variety of products and a mix of new ones, so buyers and merchandisers need to find a balance between retaining bestsellers to maximise sales and developing new trend-led products that customers want to see in order to stay fashionable. Next, buyers need to ensure that the distribution between different product classifications is appropriate, balancing the number of classic, basic, fashion, hero, or fad items in the range. It is also very important to consider the season that the range is selling in as there are some aspects that change from season to season due to specific events and the weather. For example, for womens-wear brands in the UK, traditionally the autumn/winter season sells more coordinates due to the nature of the weather and how consumers like to dress, and the spring/summer season sells more dresses. Thus, the weather, consumers' shopping habits, and the retail calendar will all impact upon the range's width and depth, as well as the trends forecasted to be popular that season. Furthermore, the delivery of the product must be considered when thinking about the products within a range as it is important to ensure that there is maximum selling time before the next ranges are delivered. In trend-driven high-street fashion retailers there is approximately eight weeks' selling time available before consumers expect to see the next available ranges. For example, a Christmas range must be in-store and ready to sell by the end of October and sold out by the end of December.

Range coordination

Successful product ranges consist of garments that can all be worn together, in order to increase sales. Ranges traditionally contain more tops than bottoms to help this process. Therefore, fabrics and colours need to be carefully considered so that they can be mixed together. The concept of coordinates provides consumers with confidence that their look is pulled together and fashionable, while giving them the option of selecting among garments that meet their personal needs (Keiser & Garner, 2013). The balance of how this is done will depend on the specific customer and the brand. Maximising the full potential of a range is crucial to its success. Having a combination of basic, fashion, and hero products also aids coordination of the different variations of outfits that a range can offer. In some cases, using a specific fabric, such as a print or texture, throughout the range will clearly demonstrate how the items are coordinated, and is an effective means of fabric usage and more cost-effective too. If a customer hopes to purchase clothing but cannot find all the product categories necessary to put together an outfit (variety), his or her preferred style in the category (depth), or the proper size, then the retailer has failed and may not be able to induce the customer to return (Mantrala et al., 2009). Hence, if the retailer fails to provide the expected assortment, customers will defect and buy from their competitors, causing losses in both current and future sales.

Product assortments for pureplay retailers and long-tailing

Product development, management, and ordering has traditionally been limited by store size, the environment, and promotional availability. There is a predetermined number of products that can be displayed at any one time. For instance, product ranges for stores have to consider hanger appeal and work collectively to show clear coordination. This provides a much more effective approach to visual merchandising within the store and helps the saleability of a collection.

This is different for online retailers, who do not have a shop floor to consider. Unsurprisingly, having an endless amount of space available to stock as many products as possible has an impact on product assortments and portfolios for online retailers. Thus, operating online allows the buying and merchandising teams to grow or reduce categories if necessary without having to consider restrictions of space. This also means that buyers can add individual products that are reactive to trends or customer demands on an ad hoc basis. This flexible range-planning approach is one of the distinct advantages of product development in pureplay companies. However, there still needs to be available space in the warehouse to stock the items. Furthermore, there still needs to be a balance in and consideration of the overall product offering for the consumer to make sure there is not a saturation of products, or even products that are too similar to each other.

Increased market segmentation and niche lifestyle consumers have given way to the approach called 'long-tailing' (Anderson, 2006). The long-tail effect and the opportunity to offer a much wider product range sourced from a wider supplier base means that a greater number of options can be offered for sale (Anderson, 2006). The long-tail effect recognises the falling costs of production and the opportunity to develop wider individualistic product assortments (Clark, 2015). Therefore, it allows for a much broader and shallow range assortment. For a merchandiser this potentially endless range-planning process can change the characteristics of a completed range plan (Clark, 2015). Keeping volumes small but increasing product styles allows a retailer to target more consumers by offering a huge variety of styles. This is particularly suitable for retailers that target global customers who require a vast variety of products, as the environments and cultural and logistical elements are completely different.

CHAPTER SUMMARY

This chapter has outlined the many different aspects and considerations required when developing a product range. Trend-forecasting information is translated into a tangible product representing the brand identity and one that will appeal to the customer base. Trend forecasting can vary depending on the retailer and is further influenced by, for example, the weather, celebrity endorsement, special events, and social media influencers. The width and depth of a range, including a balance of different product classifications, must be determined in line with the target market, market environment, and seasonality. Buyers will largely modify existing styles based on historical data on past bestsellers for upcoming ranges to minimise the cost and time of the product-development process. A good size range and mix of exciting trend-led products with more classic items will help to contribute to the success of a range.

References

Anderson, C. (2006). *The Long Tail: How Endless Choice Is Creating Unlimited Demand*. London: Random House.

Brown, H. (2019). 'Super-fast fashion: From screen to store in seven days', 28 March, Drapers, available at: www.drapersonline.com/7034964.article.

Clark, J. (2015). *Fashion Merchandising; Principles and Practices*. Basingstoke: Palgrave.

Dillon, S. (2012). *The Fundamentals of Fashion Management*. Worthing: AVA.

Goworek, H. (2007). *Fashion Buying*. 2nd ed. Hoboken, NJ: Blackwell.

Grose, V. (2012). *Fashion Merchandising*. New York, NY: Bloomsbury.

Jackson, T., & Shaw, D. (2001). *Mastering Fashion Buying and Merchandising Management*. London: Palgrave.

Keiser, S., & Garner, M.B. (2013). *Beyond Design – The Synergy of Apparel Product Development*. New York, NY: Fairchild/Bloomsbury.

Levtushenko, O., & Hodge, G. (2012). 'Review of cost estimation techniques and their strategic importance in the new product development process of textile products', *Research Journal of Textile & Apparel*, 16(1): 103–124.

Mantrala, M.K., Levy, M., Kahn, B.E., Fox, E.J., Gaidarev, P., Dankworth, B., & Shah, D. (2009). 'Why is assortment planning so difficult for retailers? A framework and research agenda', *Journal of Retailing*, 85: 71–83.

Stone, E. (2012). *In Fashion*. 2nd ed. New York, NY: Fairchild.

Tran, Y., Hsuan, J., & Mahnke, V. (2011). 'How do innovation intermediaries add value? Insight from new product development in fashion markets', *R and D Management*, 41: 80–91.

Varley, R., & Clark, J. (2019). 'Fashion Merchandise Management', in Varley, R., Roncha, A., Radclyffe-Thomas, N., & Gee, L. (eds), *Fashion Management: A Strategic Approach*. New York, NY: Red Globe Press, pp. 155–173.

Whelan, G. (2019). 'Kim Kardashian West win Missguided lawsuit', 4 July, Drapers, available at: www.drapersonline.com/news/latest-news/kim-kardashian-west-wins-missguided-lawsuit/7036582.article.

8 Sourcing and negotiation

Introduction

Once the product range has been finalised it needs to be produced into a tangible set of garments that can be retailed to the customer. The majority of retail organisations outsource their production to factories all around the world, with some notable exceptions, such as Zara, which has a vertically integrated supply chain, producing and manufacturing all items in-house. Outsourcing enables companies to access external organisations in order to make use of skills that are either unavailable or too expensive internally (Varley & Pickard, 2019). By paying manufacturers to produce their products, retailers do not have to invest in and maintain expensive equipment and machinery, so it is often a more cost-effective way to run their business.

Buyers need to decide where to get their products manufactured, how they should be transported to their UK distribution centre, and which factory offers the best value in terms of skills, lead time, and cost. Due to the number of suppliers available, sourcing fashion garments is now more complicated than ever before, with products from the same range being made in several different countries at the same time, all of which need to be delivered to the distribution centre and then put on the shop floor and/or online to be sold to the customer. Buyers need to balance getting the best products (in terms of quality and style) for the best price, with an acceptable order quantity with the supplier that can be manufactured and delivered within the strict time constraints.

Learning outcomes

By the end of this chapter you will be able to:

- Describe the different types of sourcing and the shift from local to global sourcing in the last few decades;
- Discuss the advantages and disadvantages of global sourcing for UK fashion retailers;
- Explain and discuss the role of the fashion buyer in sourcing fashion products;
- Identify the main garment-producing regions around the world;
- Identify how buyers select and appraise suppliers;
- Recognise the importance of the buyer–supplier relationship for long-term success and profitability for retailers;
- Discuss the negotiation process between buyers and suppliers, and identify successful negotiation tactics.

What needs to be sourced?

There are various aspects that are commonly outsourced by fashion retailers. The most common examples are as follows:

- Fabric – this makes up the outer and inner garment, such as linings;
- Trims – decorative trims such as piping, sequins and beads, and embellishments;
- Interfacing – to stiffen collars and cuffs;
- Fastenings – zips, buttons, drawstrings, poppers, and hooks and eyes;
- Labels – brand label, fabric content and country-of-origin label, and care labels;
- Packaging – swing tickets, hangers, and garment-protection sleeves.

Strategic sourcing vs single sourcing

Single sourcing is where the retailer uses one supplier to manufacture its products. This simplifies the process and can create a good working relationship between the buyer and supplier based on loyalty and a long-term commitment to working together. This also means that the retailer will be a priority for the supplier as they will want to maintain its business, and so the delivery dates for samples and bulk orders are more likely to be kept to time. However, this is also a risky strategy as if something unfortunate happens to the supplier, such as their machinery breaking or it is discovered that they have been operating unethically, the retailer has a high dependency on them and, thus, a lack of alternatives to turn to. This may result in, at worst, a failure to deliver the product range to the shop floor, and, at best, the products going straight to markdown and significantly diminishing the profit margin. As a result, many retailers employ a *strategic sourcing* strategy, whereby they select a number of different suppliers to manufacture their products based on the best value for money in terms of cost, quality, and lead time. This minimises the risks in the sourcing strategy, as if there are issues with one supplier then there are others that can be depended upon. Having a strategic sourcing strategy also enables the buyers to select the suppliers on merit and work with those that are innovating, potentially achieving a competitive advantage as a result. Yet, having too many suppliers can make the process very complicated for buyers to manage, not only in terms of their own time, but also in attempting to coordinate a product range and getting each product to the distribution centre on time. Buyers will have to monitor many different critical paths and ensure that they are all keeping to time in order to try and stay on top of it. Furthermore, the supplier is less likely to prioritise the buyer's order if they are working with several different retailers as their loyalties may lie elsewhere with retailers that have placed a larger more profitable order. As such, buyers are now under pressure to reduce their supplier base in order to streamline the process and minimise the risks involved in strategic sourcing (Shaw & Koumbis, 2014).

From local to global sourcing

Global sourcing refers to an arrangement between a retailer and a supplier that is outside of the market where the final product is sold to its end customer (Holweg et al., 2011). The sourcing of products from UK retailers began to decline significantly from the 1980s onwards, with the term 'off-shoring' (sourcing products from international emerging markets) becoming the 'thing to do' by retailers in order to cut costs and increase profit margins (Bearne, 2018). UK manufacturers were also often limited in how many items they could produce at one time; by sourcing internationally, retailers were able to order larger volumes for much lower prices. The Multi-Fibre Agreement (MFA) (1974) required retailers in 'developed' economies to abide by laws dictating specific quotas for each type of product, limiting the amount of exports that the company could purchase from 'developing' countries. This system was abolished in 2005, whereby restrictions on imports of clothing and textiles were completely phased out, enabling increased penetration of cheaper garments. After the abolition of quotas due to the MFA, in January 2005 there was a huge increase in Chinese exports to the UK (Goworek, 2007). Hence, by the early 2000s the opening up of international borders and the abolition of import quotas from China meant that the UK clothing and textiles sector reached its lowest number of employees, totalling only about 90,000 workers (Bearne, 2018).

Global sourcing often aims to procure the delivery of a product or service from low-wage economies in order to gain access to low-cost skilled labour, low-cost raw materials, and other economic factors like tax breaks and low trade tariffs.

As consumers now expect low prices for fashion garments, there has been an increasing pressure on buyers to find cheaper manufacturing costs in order to keep prices low but maximise profits. Clothes are unique in this capacity as the cost of virtually everything else has increased (e.g., food, fuel, houses). This is linked to the rising cost of labour in the UK due to the introduction of the minimum living wage, coupled with the fact that many techniques involved in garment manufacturing are done by hand and are irreplaceable by machine. As a result, in order to keep the cost of clothing down, retailers can no longer afford to source their manufacturing and production of garments in the UK, and clothing manufacturing has inevitably shifted towards the cheapest producing nations. By sourcing items globally, retailers can remain competitive with low-cost items inherent in fast fashion.

Global sourcing has changed the nature of the industry in terms of the production and manufacturing times, going from the short lead times delivered through domestic sourcing to long lead times. When the UK manufactured most of its own fashion requirements, foreign travel and international communications were limited, but the average buyer is now expected to spend long periods of the year working abroad with their manufacturing base, developing new ranges and continually looking for new product opportunities. Thus, cheaper products from the Far East, Middle East, Eastern Europe, Pacific Rim, China, Bangladesh, and India have fundamentally changed the way in which UK buyers work.

Advantages of global sourcing

- *Cheaper manufacturing costs* – the primary reason that retailers choose to source their products from abroad is because it is more cost-effective than getting them manufactured domestically. Thus, global sourcing is an attractive option for fashion retailers as it enables them to purchase large order quantities for low prices and gain a competitive advantage in the market.
- *Specific skills in certain countries that are unavailable elsewhere* – retailers will source certain types of products, materials, or prints internationally due to their lack of availability at home. For example, retailers wanting to incorporate a unique batik print may turn to Indonesia, as the country specialises in this technique. Sourcing original designs and prints from countries that specialise in them is beneficial for retailers as customers are always striving for uniqueness; thus, retailers will be able to gain a competitive advantage through the innovation and design of their prints and fabric.
- *Better-quality material* – some material can only be found, or may be of better quality, in certain places in the world. For example, silks from China and Japan are renowned for being the best quality, as the silkworms are fed mulberry leaves, whilst Belgium and Ireland are famous for linen, Italy for its leather production, and India for cotton.

Disadvantages of global sourcing

- *Long lead times* – as the items are being manufactured outside of the domestic market, the time taken to get the items delivered to the distribution centre is considerably longer. Major production of garments can take eight to ten weeks (Carr & Hopkins Newell, 2014) and when shipping is added to that (approximately six weeks from China and the Far East), this results in a considerable amount of time.

Thus, the orders need to be placed earlier and further away from the season to enable there to be enough time to have the garments ready for the ideal selling period. The earlier the product range is finalised and ordered with the manufacturer, the less accurate it is likely to be in terms of predicting and anticipating consumer demand, as well as 'in trend' and colour forecasting, thus making sale forecasts more difficult. Whilst visiting suppliers in domestic markets will take the buyer a day or two, visiting suppliers on the other side of the world can take up to a week, or even two weeks if buyers visit multiple suppliers in the same region. Spending so much time away from the office visiting suppliers means that buyers will have less time to perform their other responsibilities. Long lead times are also problematic if the item is a bestseller and the buyer wants to reorder it in order to capitalise on sales. The time taken for it to be manufactured and shipped is often too long and the opportunity to capitalise on that short sales window, before the product matures, is lost. Therefore, speed-to-market is now a priority for fast-fashion retailers and so having a shorter lead time may now outweigh the cost advantage of sourcing from further afield when deciding which factory to use. A 2019 report by McKinsey & Co found that top-performing 20 per cent of fashion retailers prioritised speed-to-market in their sourcing strategy (Brown, 2019).

- *Delivery issues through risk of natural disasters or volatile political situations* – long times spent in transit are also risky, because buyers have a lack of control over the merchandise and with long distances to travel items could get lost or damaged easily. Unforeseen wars or political conflicts within or around the country of manufacture could disrupt the supply chain dramatically and the merchandise may not make it to the UK as a result. Incidents of political unrest can occur at any moment across the world, and these could be in countries where the garments are being manufactured as well as ones on the delivery route. For example, in 2016 the so-called Islamic State issued a direct threat against fashion buyers visiting Bangladesh, causing many retailers to reassess their sourcing strategies (Geoghagan, 2017). Therefore, buyers must be cautious when selecting which countries to get their garments manufactured in, and devise a contingency plan in case anything goes wrong. There may also be unforeseen strikes at the factory or at the ports, holding up the merchandise and delaying the delivery. As a result, absolute delivery dates can never be guaranteed, and late arrivals can have a serious negative impact on profits. With timing being so important, buyers and merchandisers calculate the exact time that the product range needs to hit the shop floor/website in order to optimise consumer demand and maximise profits, and thus the unpredictability of delivery issues makes this very stressful and difficult to manage. Not only would the merchandise not be made available when planned (the peak selling period), but it would result in gaps on the shop floor or only partially complete ranges, which would not provide a clear or attractive offering to the consumer.
- *Hidden costs* – although the cost of manufacturing is cheaper, there are several hidden costs involved in global sourcing, which makes it not as cheap as it first appears to be. These hidden costs could be in the form of lost inventory – as items have so far to travel and so many different processes to go through before they reach the shop floor, there is a higher probability of some items being misplaced. Furthermore, sending buying teams across the world is not very cost-effective; it is much cheaper and quicker for buyers to visit suppliers in the domestic or European market. Moreover, as negotiations are often done in different currencies, the retailer

is at the mercy of the exchange rate. What may have originally been a favourable exchange rate and good deal for the buyer can change quickly due to the volatility of financial markets, making it much more expensive.

The cost of shipping needs to be taken into account when sourcing items from across the globe. Most fast-fashion retailers get their items transported by ship as it is considerably cheaper, but if speed is of the upmost importance then some may choose to get it delivered via air freight, in which case the delivery cost is high.

Another hidden cost is the additional charge of duty or customs tariffs. When importing products from abroad the retailer must be aware of the extra charges that it has to pay before they are allowed in the country. The charges vary from item to item – for instance, a 'T-shirt' will be in a different category to a 'blouse' – and so buyers and merchandisers need to familiarise themselves with all of the extra charges involved in order not to be caught out. Rather than just calculating the cost price of the garment, buyers and merchandisers need to calculate the *landed cost* for each garment, taking all the hidden costs into consideration and weighing up whether it is actually cheaper to have the product manufactured abroad.

- *Large order quantities and money tied up* – sourcing from domestic suppliers often means buyers are able to order smaller quantities (Carr & Hopkins Newell, 2014). Sourcing globally, however, often means orders are placed in bulk to make it worthwhile for the manufacturer in terms of the cost of production. This is often in excess of 1,000 pieces per style (Goworek, 2007). Manufacturers have minimum order quantities, because it is not financially viable to produce small quantities as machinists are not able to achieve an economical speed of production with a relatively small run, and the cost of overheads will be too high if spread over a small number of garments (Goworek, 2007). This is a gamble for the retailer as it needs to forecast that the product will sell well. However, this can backfire if the product does not sell well as the retailer could be left with a lot of left-over stock, which will have to go to markdown, thereby eating into the profit margins. This could also result in the product having to go to landfill, contributing to negative environmental impacts that the fast-fashion industry already has.

  Furthermore, many suppliers request at least partial payment for the order up front, and as the orders are usually large this is very expensive. Due to the long lead time from production to shop floor, this means that retailers have a lot of capital tied up and no ability to make that money back until months down the line. This can put a strain on retailers' finances and is particularly tough for smaller retailers.

- *Language, cultural, and time-zone challenges* – working with a supplier who is in a different time zone can be very challenging as the working hours are completely different. The buyer must be prepared to have phone or Skype meetings during unsociable hours. Furthermore, speaking different languages can result in communication issues and misunderstandings.

- *Negative environmental impact* – sourcing items on the other side of the world is not very environmentally friendly. The carbon footprint is very high for both the buyers' trips to suppliers as well as the products themselves in transit. Retailers are now under increasing pressure to reduce their carbon footprint and be more environmentally responsible.

- *Ethical issues* – cheaper manufacturing prices are only possible due to the low wages paid to the factory workers. Unlike other industries, many aspects involved in clothing manufacturing are irreplaceable by machine and so must be done by hand.

This has resulted in retailers searching for nations that can manufacture their garments for the cheapest price, which is only attainable by paying garment workers exceptionally low wages and often in poor working conditions. When exposed through the media, ethical issues can be hugely damaging to a brand's reputation. Brands are now under increasing pressure to have full transparency in their supply chains to show that high ethical standards are being upheld. However, this is difficult to enforce when the supplier is on the other side of the world, and visits to factories can be deceptive and not give a realistic portrayal of workers' everyday lives.

The future: back from global to local sourcing?

The process of increasing global sourcing was known as *off-shoring*, a concept that became a buzzword in retail in the 1980s. However, we are now starting to see an increasing trend back to *near-shoring* or even *re-shoring*, bringing sourcing back to Europe or even the UK, by UK retailers. Fast-fashion and super-fast-fashion retailers are now tightly streamlining their supply chains as much as possible in order to minimise lead times and get the product from idea to online as quick as possible. As such, they are using a multimodal sourcing strategy, whereby garments are produced both in low-cost countries off-shoring and those situated closer to the headquarters (near-shoring).

Off-shoring

- Processes, such as production, are moved to countries overseas;
- For example, H&M (a Swedish brand/retailer) getting its garments manufactured in Bangladesh.

Near-shoring

- Processes, such as production, are moved to nearby countries;
- For example, Zara (a Spanish brand/retailer) getting its garments manufactured in Portugal.

Re-shoring

- Processes, such as production, are done in a retailer's own country;
- For example, Boohoo (a UK pureplay retailer) getting its garments manufactured in Leicester, UK.

It is part of the buyer's responsibility to not only source products, but also to ensure that the product in itself is profitable. In the future, near-shoring will be even more profitable with Industry 4.0 promising more automation of processes, which could cut down on costs by increasing labour efficiency and flexibility within the supply chain (Anderson

Figure 8.1   **Simplified production cycle**

et al., 2018). Technological innovations have further revolutionised twenty-first-century fashion retailing, which makes idea exchanges easier and communication processes faster than ever before. Figure 8.1 is a simplified version of a production cycle.

According to Coresight Research (2017), lead times across the industry have changed, with different fashion retailers having been able to optimise their production cycle, thereby dramatically reducing their turnaround times. Figure 8.2 illustrates that the traditional fashion cycle was 26 months, which corresponds to the spring/summer and autumn/winter collection releases. It has to be highlighted that Figure 8.1 is a simplification of what is currently going on in the industry, but can be used for illustrative purposes in that some fashion organisations have almost moved away from the traditional two to four collections per year to producing two to three collections per season (spring, summer, autumn, winter). This, as indicated previously, is largely dependent on product categories – not all products have short lead times, nor is this necessarily the goal of an organisation. Items with longer lead times fall within the 'basics' collections, which is less trend-led, whilst items that are *in season* will be manufactured closer to the headquarters and thus have reduced lead times. In cases of super-fast-fashion companies this process has been taken to the next level. Unlike fast-fashion companies, which face challenges such as product shortages and excessive inventory, super-fast-fashion companies

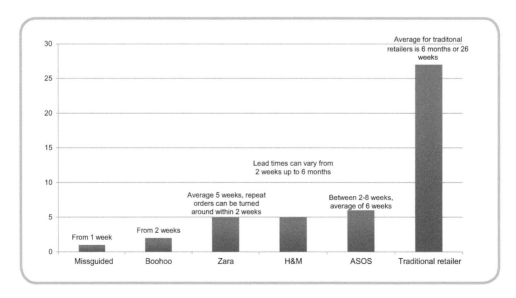

Figure 8.2   **Example of lead times in the fashion industry (adapted from Coresight Research, 2017)**

trial designs in smaller batch sizes, in case these products are successful (e.g. selling fast), and more can be produced within a short time period (e.g. a one-week turnaround). Therefore, both buyers and merchandisers need to be able to effectively communicate and react quickly to changes in consumer demand and taste. This implies that initial orders of products may be smaller, yet if they are selling, it needs to be guaranteed that these can be delivered to stores within almost one week (e.g. Coresight Research, 2017).

Where to source from?

When considering where to source from, retailers will consider the type of product that they need manufacturing and that country/region's expertise, as well as the cost of manufacturing and the risks of sourcing from that country in terms of natural disasters and political unrest. The biggest garment-manufacturing countries include China, India, the European Union (EU), Turkey, Vietnam, and Bangladesh (O'Connell, 2019; Sutherland, 2019). Over the past couple of decades fashion production has shifted from developed to developing countries. The often-referred-to Asian Tigers (South Korea, Hong Kong, Singapore, and Taiwan) were key suppliers of textiles and garments in the 1980s/1990s, yet with increasing labour costs production has shifted to less-developed countries. Today, the biggest clothing manufacturers include China, the EU, Bangladesh, Vietnam, India, and Turkey (WTO, 2019). Figure 8.3 illustrates the annual growth rates of the fashion industry in four of the leading textile- and garment-exporting manufacturing countries (based on data retrieved from Statista; see O'Connell, 2019).

The decrease in China's annual growth rate can be explained as being due to the fact that China is becoming increasingly industrialised, implying that the average wage of workers in going up. In turn, increasing wages suggests that prices for products will go up, in order to keep the profit margins high for producers/manufactures. The more wages

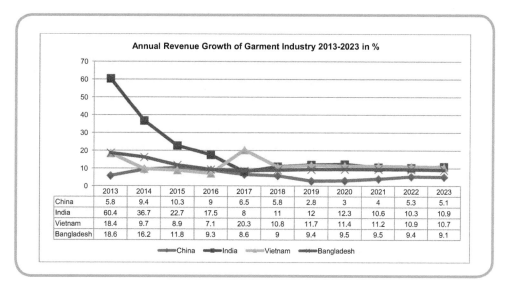

	2013	2014	2015	2016	2017	2018	2019	2020	2021	2022	2023
China	5.8	9.4	10.3	9	6.5	5.8	2.8	3	4	5.3	5.1
India	60.4	36.7	22.7	17.5	8	11	12	12.3	10.6	10.3	10.9
Vietnam	18.4	9.7	8.9	7.1	20.3	10.8	11.7	11.4	11.2	10.9	10.7
Bangladesh	18.6	16.2	11.8	9.3	8.6	9	9.4	9.5	9.5	9.4	9.1

Figure 8.3 Annual revenue growth of garment industry 2013–2023 as percentages (data retrieved from Statista, 2019)

increase, the likelier it is that production is outsourced into countries that are less developed, and thus have lower wages. Thus, with production costs rising in many of these countries (production costs rose by almost 50 per cent in Bangladesh between 2005–2017 and by 33 per cent in China during the same period), retailers have expanded their sourcing base further to Southeast Asian countries and Africa (Sutherland, 2019). With speed-to-market being increasingly important, many retailers are now moving their sourcing strategies closer to home in order to reduce lead times.

Key sourcing countries/regions for UK brands/retailers are discussed below.

Asia

China

China is the world's biggest garment exporter and has been the chief beneficiary of global sourcing strategies for the last three decades (Varley & Pickard, 2019). China is also the world's biggest producer of silk and so is popular for luxury brands as well as fashion retailers. Clothes, clothing accessories, and textiles are amongst the top export goods from China, with the country's total textile exports valued at approximately 119 billion US dollars in 2018, 37.6 per cent of the global market share (O'Connell, 2019).

Chinese manufacturers have become leaner, more technologically advanced, and innovative (Twigg, 2019). As a result, China now has some of the world's most developed and high-tech garment factories, providing more specialised offerings. Investing in high-tech upgrades rather than economies of scale, Chinese factories have adapted to produce fewer units, but at higher profit margins (Twigg, 2019). The technological advancement of the machinery is avant-garde and, combined with support from factory workers, who are experienced and have great expertise, buyers can build long-lasting relationships. It is this high level of competence that will continue to ensure China's staying power as a leading garment manufacturer around the world. The increasingly digitised supply chain will enable Chinese manufacturers to streamline their costs, and automation will suit the needs of their increasingly skilled but ageing workforce (Twigg, 2017). Thus, going forward Chinese factories are likely to employ fewer, but more highly skilled and higher paid technicians (Twigg, 2017). China's economic prosperity has improved and wages have increased, making it not the cheapest option to source from anymore. Therefore, many retailers have explored other areas around the world for fast-fashion garment sourcing, such as Vietnam and Cambodia, in order to keep their manufacturing costs to a minimum. However, many other countries that have cheaper labour costs do not have the capacity or expertise to produce such large volumes of garments so quickly and effectively.

Bangladesh

Brands source basic items, sweaters, jeans, shoes, as well as specialised techniques that can be done on cotton or denim, such as stone-washing and sand-blasting, from Bangladesh. Global clothing exports reached $36.9 billion for Bangladesh in 2018 (Twigg, 2019). However, Bangladesh has been tainted in recent years due to the negative media attention honing in on problems related to labour laws and health and safety issues. In 2010, 21 people lost their lives in a tragic fire in a factory in Gazipur, Bangladesh

(Hickman, 2010). Organisations such as War on Want had previously highlighted that safety standards in six factories supplying budget retailers were lacking, and had pushed for measures to be implemented. Only three years later, in 2013, there was large-scale media reporting of one of the worst factory accidents of all time: the Rana Plaza tragedy, when a garment factory in Dhaka collapsed, killing 1,134 people. As a result, the German government sponsored a meeting of retailers to create an agreement. Numerous retailers signed up and a new Accord on Factory and Building Safety in Bangladesh was created, covering over 1,000 Bangladeshi garment factories. This led to regular building inspections and enforcement of fire and safety standards in garment factories. Organisations such as Fashion Revolution and the Bangladesh Accord on Fire and Building Safety sought to not only force retailers to reveal '#WhoMadeMyClothes', but also have them engage in providing safe working conditions for garment-factory workers (Accord, 2018; Fashion Revolution, 2018). Retailers agreed to continue to support the Bangladesh textile industry despite possible higher costs. Since the Rana Plaza factory collapse, the Bangladeshi government, worker representatives, and international fashion brands and buyers have worked together to make the garment-manufacturing industry in Bangladesh safer (Uddin, 2019). To date, upwards of 3,800 export-orientated garment factories have been checked for building, fire, and electrical safety, and repairs have been carried out accordingly (Uddin, 2019). The Accord finished its operations at the end of 2018, but the work has been continued by the Bangladeshi government, with suppliers investing millions of dollars in safety upgrades to their factories (Uddin, 2019). Bangladesh has made considerable improvements in the quality of its output by importing expensive machinery, such as the laser technology needed to produce high-quality jeans, as well as providing improved training for factory workers (Twigg, 2019).

Although there has been a concerted effort and improvement in workers' rights in Bangladesh since the Rana Plaza disaster, there is still a long way to go (Twigg, 2019). As a result of the increase in utility prices and a rise in the minimum wage for factory workers, the cost of production in Bangladesh has gone up, and the factories are struggling to attract buyers to work with, because they do not want to pay more for the manufacturing of garments (Uddin, 2019). This is concerning for Bangladeshi suppliers as it will be difficult for them to maintain safety standards in future if they do not receive adequate prices from retailers (Uddin, 2019). Additionally, exporting out of Bangladesh does require a longer lead time than Vietnam, and getting raw materials from China to Bangladesh takes a considerable amount of time (although the country is working on developing local raw materials), which is off-putting for brands, which prioritise speed-to-market (Twigg, 2019). Bangladesh has also seen considerable political unrest in recent years and is now considered as a high-risk environment for buyers to visit and retailers to source from (Geoghagan, 2017). These factors have resulted in a recent decline in UK buyers sourcing from Bangladesh.

India

Brands mainly source natural silk and, most famously, natural cotton from India. It is the world's leading cotton-producing country (O'Connell, 2019). India is one of the top textile-producing countries in the world, with exports of 18 billion US dollars in 2018 (O'Connell, 2019). Buyers also source techniques, such as tie-dye and hand-dyed products, as well as hand beading, embellishments, and embroidery. Going forward, sourcing from India is set to increase further, and therefore India's textile and apparel exports are set to accelerate in terms of growth (BoF, 2019). This is primarily because India's average labour cost is significantly lower than China's and comparable with Vietnam's, and there is a high availability of raw materials (e.g. cotton, wool, silk, and jute), which enables participation in the entire fashion value chain (BoF, 2019).

Thailand, Vietnam, Cambodia, and Myanmar

As rising costs and political concerns are forcing retailers to discover other options to China and Bangladesh, countries such as Myanmar and Vietnam are vying to increase their garment production and become an attractive alternative. Thailand, Vietnam, Cambodia, and more recently Myanmar are all used by retailers to source fashion items from as it is more cost-effective to source from these countries than from China. Myanmar in particular pays workers very low wages and so has been seen as an increasingly attractive option for fast-fashion retailers. However, the infrastructure simply is not yet sophisticated enough to compete with larger rivals on a grand scale (Twigg, 2019).

Vietnam dominates footwear sourcing, producing more footwear than any other Southeast Asian market; Nike and Adidas have been sourcing trainers from Vietnam for a decade now (Twigg, 2019). Out of all these countries, Vietnam's industry is the most developed in terms of garment manufacturing. Workers are skilled and whilst wages are higher than in neighbouring countries (at $216 a month), they are less than half of China's. Electricity is also cheap due to government subsidies, and Vietnam also has free trade with end-market countries including those within the EU, Australia, Canada, Japan, Mexico, New Zealand, and Singapore. (Twigg, 2019). Vietnam can now produce apparel goods to a similar standard as China, which speeds up production time when raw materials need to be imported (Twigg, 2019).

Cambodia is used to source garments such as shirts, women's lingerie, trousers, and denim. Cambodia's apparel industry is extremely important to the country as it employs more people than any other and represents 80 per cent of national export earnings (Twigg, 2019). As a result, the Cambodian government has put sourcing-friendly policies in place in order to maximise the potential of this industry, such as allowing 100 per cent foreign-equity ownership and an exemption from import duty on machinery and equipment. Cambodia's workforce is less skilled than Vietnam's, but the average wages paid are slightly less at $182 a month, meaning that items such as woven shirts, T-shirts, and polo shirts have been migrating from China to Vietnam to Cambodia, as skills grow and space opens up (Twigg, 2019). Cambodia is growing the most rapidly in terms of garment sourcing out of all the Southeast Asian countries, because as well as being low-cost it also shares a port with Vietnam, making transport easier, and is close to China and so can obtain raw materials quickly (Twigg, 2019). Gap and H&M have been increasingly sourcing from Cambodia (Twigg, 2019). Yet, Cambodia still remains riskier than Vietnam, because it is a new (sourcing) country and there have been stories in the media of unethical practices. For instance, although Cambodia was a beneficiary of the EU's Everything but Arms scheme, which allows developing countries duty-free access to the EU market for export goods, in 2018 Brussels announced that Cambodia had one year to improve its allegedly poor human rights records or its membership would be suspended (Twigg, 2019).

Although countries such as Vietnam, Cambodia, and Myanmar are cheaper to source from than China, the infrastructure in these countries is not as developed as the factories in China, meaning that they are not as flexible in what and how they are able to produce (Twigg, 2019).

Africa and Europe

Despite the advantages of sourcing from Asia highlighted above, the fact remains that these countries are far away from the UK and it can take approximately six weeks to ship products over. Due to the long lead times, the ability to reorder items that are selling well within that season is only possible if air freight is used. Air freight is very expensive, so will severely eat into the retailer's profit margin, yet retailers may decide that it is worth the lower margin if the product is a guaranteed bestseller. More often than not, retailers are using suppliers closer to home, in either Europe or North Africa, due to their proximity and ease of reordering. Retailers can reorder items that were originally produced in China from factories in Turkey or North Africa with a dual-sourcing strategy, and although the production of the garment will be more expensive from these factories, the delivery is considerably quicker and cheaper than the air freight that would be necessary if reordered from China The buyer needs to work closely with the merchandiser to ensure that the timing of the reorder placement is perfect, as the Turkish factory will need time to develop the pattern and samples as well as manufacture them as it was not the original manufacturer. Thus, the buyer and merchandiser must analyse the sales figures closely and ensure that they reorder potential bestsellers when they are still rising in popularity in the growth stage of the product lifecycle; otherwise there will be too many items and they will have to go into markdown, reducing profits for the retailer.

Africa

Retailers are using factories based in North Africa due to their relative proximity to the UK and flexible manufacturing capabilities (Varley & Pickard, 2019). Morocco, Algeria, and Tunisia are very popular garment-producing nations, and are particularly effective at producing summer cottons. Zara has had a well-established manufacturing base in Morocco for years, and George at Asda also sources from there alongside Tunisia, whilst Primark sources from Tanzania (Sutherland, 2019). There has been a steadily increasing interest in sourcing garments from Africa over the last decade. Morocco and Ethiopia are two of the fastest-growing garment-manufacturing areas, and Kenya, Uganda, and Tanzania are also expected to see growth in the near future (Sutherland, 2019). African sourcing is best suited to large volumes of basic products as opposed to China, which has invested more in innovation and product development and so can manufacture more complex and design-led garments (Sutherland, 2019). However, this will change over time as the African countries become more established and gain more experience in garment manufacturing.

Morocco is relatively close to the UK, with a flight time of three and a half hours, and offers low labour costs, making it a very attractive sourcing option (Sutherland, 2017). Morocco prides itself on speed-to-market and so can serve the European fast-fashion industry well, and has expertise in denim, wovens, and knitwear (Sutherland, 2017). Morocco's garment industry employs 183,000 people, representing 26 per cent of the country's industrial jobs, and produces 1.1 billion garments every year (Sutherland, 2017). Many brands are choosing to source from Morocco in a proximity-sourcing strategy in order to keep up with the competition and order the right quantities of the right product just in time (Sutherland, 2017). However, the country also needs to offer high-quality products to rival the sector's leaders (Sutherland, 2017).

Ethiopia also has ambitious plans for its textile industry with its large workforce, promising land for cotton cultivation, competitive wages, and duty-free access to the EU. The government is investing in industrial parks to help boost manufacturing (Sutherland, 2019). It takes approximately 15–20 days to get items shipped from West Africa to Europe, which is relatively fast compared to how long it would take from Asia (Sutherland, 2019).

Although sourcing from Africa offers the attraction of close geographical proximity, meaning shorter lead times, as well as low costs, brands need to be cautious of the risks of sourcing here due to it its underdeveloped manufacturing industry and lack of specialisation compared to other more established garment-manufacturing countries (Sutherland, 2019). Whilst countries like Ethiopia continue to attract fashion brands due to very low labour costs, the infrastructure is not sophisticated enough to compete with more established garment-manufacturing countries (Twigg, 2019). Furthermore, vertical supply chains are not yet fully in place, meaning that retailers will need to import aspects such as fabric and trims, which may take more time and add further complexity to the buying cycle. Political volatility in recent years has also caused issues for retailers sourcing from these countries, particularly in terms of delivery reliability (Carr & Hopkins Newell, 2014). Retailers need to be careful not to solely base their sourcing decisions on low costs as the product design and quality could suffer. Simply chasing the lowest wages could also be seen as exploitative, an aspect that retailers need to be keenly aware of in a climate where consumers are becoming increasingly aware of ethical issues and sustainability, and intolerant of unethical or non-sustainable manufacturers. If buyers choose to source from the developing African nations then they should ensure that they are supporting workers and training them to help develop their skills.

Europe

As of 2016, the EU accounted for 23.5 per cent of the global market share with an export value of 74 billion US dollars, making it the second largest textile-exporting region in the world (O'Connell, 2019). Sourcing from Western Europe in general equates to high labour costs and so higher manufacturing costs overall for retailers. Therefore, retailers that source from Western Europe do so in order to obtain high-quality and high-end designs or luxury products. Italy is used for its superior-quality soft leather and thus manufactures luxury handbags or premium leather jackets. Italy is also used for knitwear and well-tailored suits. However, manufacturing prices for Eastern Europe are more competitive, and countries such as Poland have grown significantly over the last decade in terms of their garment-manufacturing exports, mainly as an alternative to China for many UK retailers. Cyprus, Hungary, Romania, and Bulgaria are also used to source garments from.

Turkey

Turkey is heavily dependent on garment manufacturing (Bearne, 2017) and predominantly used to source denim, jerseys, and knitwear products as well as swimwear and underwear. Turkey has specialist washing, embellishment, and printing capabilities that also makes it attractive to fashion retailers. Despite not offering cheap labour costs,

Turkish factories have high capacity and can produce high-quality goods and deliver items to the UK quickly via road or rail (Berg & Hedrich, 2014). Its popularity as a garment-sourcing region for UK retailers is mainly due to its ability to offer faster delivery times than Asian countries, and the ability to repeat orders if they are selling well (Clark, 2018). Despite being more expensive than Asia, having garments manufactured in Turkey means shorter lead times, which is particularly attractive for fast-fashion retailers, who need to react to consumer demand as quick as possible in order to gain a competitive edge in the market. It is often used for fast fashion or replenishment as it enables buyers to be much more flexible, mainly due to its relative proximity to the UK and flexible manufacturing capabilities (Varley & Pickard, 2019).

However, there has been a decline in recent years from buyers sourcing from Turkey due to the political and economic turmoil faced by the country, making it too risky as factories could potentially go bust when manufacturing a product range (Clark, 2018). Due to this political and economic uncertainty, the Turkish lira is currently experiencing a slump, prompting concerns from retailers about how suppliers are keeping their factories afloat and funding their machinery (Clark, 2018). Thus, Turkey was once the near-sourcing market of choice for many British retailers, due to its abundance of raw materials, short lead times, and expertise, but political instability in the country has led to some retailers cancelling sourcing trips because of safety concerns, which has resulted in many turning to Morocco instead (Sutherland, 2017).

The UK

The UK manufacturing industry has experienced significant decline since the 1980s, and the factories that still exist have had to change their offering significantly. Whereas international suppliers are mainly chosen based on cost, UK suppliers are chosen based on service considerations, a fast turnaround of products, and superior quality or design (Goworek, 2007). Domestic sourcing is usually associated with higher quality and enables buyers to maintain control and communicate easily and regularly with their suppliers as they are much closer geographically (Carr & Hopkins Newell, 2014). Sourcing domestically also often provides buyers with the opportunity to order in smaller quantities, which is particularly advantageous if the product is untested or of higher risk. However, the smaller order quantities are often produced at a higher cost, which will reduce profit margins for the retailer (Carr & Hopkins Newell, 2014).

Clothing manufacturing in the UK has increased in recent years in a modest return to its roots. A report from the UK Fashion and Textile Association found that there were 7.6 per cent more companies producing textiles and clothing in the UK in 2015 than in the previous year (Bearne, 2018). The report found that the number of people employed in textile and clothing manufacturing was at its highest since 2006, at about 132,000 (Bearne, 2018). The growth was attributed to the rising cost of overseas production, increasing need for control of the supply chain due to ethical scandals, and the need for flexibility, as well as a growing demand for UK-produced clothing (Bearne, 2018). There are higher ethical standards guidelines in the UK, with laws on minimum wage and working conditions. However, this comes at a cost as the higher wages and more reasonable working hours result in UK manufacturing being more expensive. As a result, it is generally more premium retailers that are manufacturing in the UK as they can pass the cost prices on to the customer with their higher price points. Nowadays, the UK is generally used to manufacture wool and tailoring. 'Made in the UK' clothing labels have become increasingly desirable as British heritage brands and UK-made goods have a reputation for being luxurious and high-quality. The British Fashion Council is driving growth in high-end, designer clothing, exemplified by both Mulberry and Burberry manufacturing in the UK still (Somerset and Leeds respectively). Manufacturing in the UK is often advantageous for branding and marketing purposes as a result, as people tend to view this favourably.

Sourcing from the UK provides retailers with the advantage of much shorter lead times, enabling faster buying cycles. This also makes it a more sustainable way to produce garments as they travel much less, diminishing the amount of CO_2 emissions that arise from transporting clothing across the globe. There is a considerable fast-fashion hub in Leicester, which pureplay retailers such as Boohoo, Pretty Little Thing, and Missguided source from for the purposes of speed. These pureplay super-fast-fashion brands can have samples of celebrity-inspired styles in the head office within 24 hours (Brown, 2019). The buyer sends images of an item on social media to their UK supplier, who produces the first sample and can send them to the head office the following day. If the first sample does not need any fit or styling adjustments, the item could be shot on a model and uploaded to the website for pre-orders the same day and customers could receive it within a week (Brown, 2019). Once an item has gone live, the brand operates a 'buy, test, repeat' model, initially ordering a small number – often 15 to 20 styles – and upping this depending on customer demand (Brown, 2019). This speed builds customer loyalty and taps into demand; thus, despite higher costs, retailers are seeing return on investment when they develop rapid-response production cycles (Brown, 2019).

However, there are concerns of a skills shortage in the UK, with a lack of people who are trained and able to manufacture garments. In a survey of textiles employers for a report published by the Alliance Project in 2015, 37 per cent of companies said that skills shortages were a barrier to growth, and half said that their recruitment problems in the past two years were due to the small numbers of applicants with the experience and qualifications required (Bearne, 2018). The age profile of the workforce is another limitation. The majority of the skilled garment-factory workers are now over 40, and attracting new talent has proved very challenging (Bearne, 2018). Roles such as pattern-cutter, sample machinist, and garment technologist are very much in demand, and essential to supporting the UK textile industry going forward, but there are not enough young people in the UK that are interested in working in these kind of jobs (Bearne, 2018). Despite investment and support through schemes such as the Regional Growth Fund and Reshore UK, there are calls for the government to do more to boost skills-training opportunities in the UK.

Outsourcing by manufacturers

As wage levels of Eastern Asian manufacturers have increased, based on their experience in the industry and high skill level, they have developed their own supply networks in order to seek low costs of production elsewhere, so they can pay higher wages but still maintain low prices to keep retailers' business. It is not just retailers that are outsourcing their manufacturing, but the manufacturers themselves now, particularly if they have large orders and tight deadlines. The issue with outsourcing is that although it can save on costs, it results in a loss of control over the production. This can cause quality issues and unethical practices, such as poor working conditions or child labour, to be included in the supply chain unknowingly or unwittingly. This has happened when factories that retailers are working with have outsourced part of the manufacturing to other factories who have not been checked for ethical standards.

Selecting suppliers

Retailers may need to find a new supplier for a number of reasons. They may wish to increase the volumes that can be produced on certain products and their current supplier does not have the capacity to do so. It may be that they want to source a different type of product or a new fabric that the present supplier(s) do not manufacture, or that other suppliers manufacture to a superior standard. This is particularly relevant in the current climate where buyers are looking to incorporate more sustainable materials into their product lines and so are searching for suppliers that specialise in these new materials. It may also be for reasons such as alternative suppliers offering better prices for the same manufacturing order, or faster lead times, which again is becoming an increasingly popular reason.

Buyers can find suppliers from various different sources, namely trade shows, trade publications, or specific platforms on the internet. Buyers will often speak to buyers from other companies and ask them for their feedback on particular suppliers. When selecting a supplier, buyers look for the best value for money in terms of quality of the product, cost of production, and speed of production. Buyers should consider a few different suppliers and compare and contrast them against each other. Although price is an important factor, it should not be the sole consideration when selecting a supplier; quality assurance and ethical conditions should be valued just as highly in order to achieve success in the long term (Carr & Hopkins Newell, 2014). There is an abundance of garment suppliers available to fashion retailers across the world, so selecting the right one can be time-consuming and just as important as selecting the right trend to incorporate. In order to assess whether a new supplier is suitable or a previous/current supplier is still the best option, buyers will appraise them using the following criteria:

1. *Past performance and experience in manufacturing fashion garments* –if the buyer has worked with that supplier previously, they can assess how reliable they were and whether they produced a garment of good quality and to the timeline agreed. Buyers will assess whether the supplier stuck to the agreed deadlines, an aspect which is particularly important for fast-fashion retailers, who prioritise speed-to-market. Any suppliers that repeatedly incurred late deliveries may be replaced by more reliable ones. The buyer will consider the amount of items that were sold at full price vs the ones that had to go into markdown. They will also assess how many product returns they received from items produced by that supplier and what the reasons were – particularly if it was quality or fit. If the buyer has not worked with that supplier before then they will consider their experience in delivering fashion garments and ask other buyers in the industry how reliable they are. The more experienced at manufacturing fashion garments the better, as the supplier will understand the acceptable quality

levels and the time-pressured nature of the industry. The reputation of the supplier in terms of their efficiency and performance will be investigated. Buyers will also ascertain whether the supplier will provide any returns or exchange privileges if they are not 100 per cent satisfied with the product or if it does not sell well.

2. *Suitability of factory size, equipment, and machinery* – the supplier must have an efficient factory and good working machinery in order to produce the garments required. With new innovations in technology being brought out continuously, the supplier should be up to date with the latest equipment and show that they are willing to invest in innovation. The factory must also be big enough to be able to produce the right volumes required by the buyer. The buyer will ascertain what the minimum and maximum order quantities of the factory are and see how compatible they are with their business objectives. Some buyers may also wish to find suppliers that will offer them exclusivity, a practice where the supplier only sells to one retailer in that market. This ensures that the products will be more unique and that competitors will not be able to sell the same items.

3. *Supplier's reputation and financial stability* – a supplier's credit rating is often checked in order to ensure that they are a financially viable business. If a supplier is in trouble financially then a buyer will be wary of working with them as there is a risk that they could go bust and be unable to fulfil the order. The buyer will ascertain their reputation for aspects such as late deliveries, handling complaints, adjustments, and quality (Clodfelter, 2012), as well as ethical standards, before deciding whether to work with them.

4. *Speed of production* – the speed at which the supplier can manufacture large orders is carefully considered, particularly by fast-fashion brands. Receiving the items on time and as fast as possible is an attractive offer for buyers and will often be the determining factor for choosing to work with that supplier over others. They may also ask to get exclusivity with that supplier if they can provide a large enough order so that they are not 'distracted' by other clients' orders and can solely focus on the buyer's.

5. *Cost of production* – the cost of production is one of the driving forces behind selecting a particular supplier. The lower the cost of production, the higher the profit margins for a brand. Buyers will also be looking for value for money, whereby the quality of the garments and speed of production will be weighed up against the cost. Buyers will consider the payment structure and how far in advance they need to pay for the goods before they reach the shop floor. The further in advance that the brand has to pay for the goods, the less attractive the offer is as it will be longer before it can recoup that money back in terms of sales – leading to money being tied up, as discussed earlier.

6. *Quality of garments produced* – the brand will want to adhere to a set of acceptable quality levels for garments in order to maintain its reputation. Therefore, any new suppliers must be able to meet the acceptable quality level when producing garments. This is usually assessed through the samples produced by the supplier for inspection. This is important because if poor-quality garments are produced then this will have a negative impact on the brand's image. The buyer will also look for suppliers that can produce a variety of different products or techniques, as well as innovative and distinguished techniques so that the products will be set apart from competitors (Clodfelter, 2012).

7. *Ethical standards* – brands/retailers will conduct an audit of any supplier before agreeing to work with them to check that they are complying with ethical standards.

Suppliers are under more scrutiny now than ever before when it comes to upholding high ethical standards. This is a result of brands now being under more pressure to ensure that their whole supply chain is adhering to ethical trading standards, and the widespread media reporting that occurs when this is not the case. Any suppliers found to be implementing poor ethical practices such as very long working hours, poor working conditions, or child labour will be dropped by brands because if this is exposed in the media then it will damage their reputation, resulting in them suffering a loss of customers and profits.

Minimising the risks of global sourcing

Buyers must take the supplier-appraisal process seriously in order to minimise the risks to their business. Buyers have target profit margins and are always trying to negotiate the best cost price for each item; however, chasing the lowest price alone is a dangerous strategy and can lead to the development of a mediocre range. This strategy has also been heavily criticised due to the ethical implications that it has. Buyers need to thoroughly vet the suppliers that they work with, and ensure that they are maintaining rigorous standards when it comes to ethical issues. Buyers must visit factories themselves in order to check the working conditions and educate or train the factory managers on the importance of ethical standards. However, inspecting the factories takes time, which may mean longer lead times and ultimately the brand missing out on the peak of consumer demand. Nevertheless, negotiation can no longer be focused on getting the lowest price and fastest lead time possible as this can push suppliers to work unethically, forcing employees to work long hours in poor conditions with few or no breaks, for very little pay. Buyers must discuss realistic deadlines with suppliers to ensure that workers are not pushed too hard, and be prepared to pay higher prices to ensure that workers are paid a fair wage; however, this could lead to lower profit margins for the brand. An alternative could be to pass the higher price point onto customers, which means increasing the selling price. Yet, this could undermine brand positioning and diminish the brand's competitive advantage. On the other hand, buyers could do everything right but it is hard to know if the supplier is subcontracting to another unethical factory. Outsourcing is common practice amongst suppliers, especially if they do not possess the required raw materials or skills, or when they are trying to fulfil a large order on a tight deadline. Buyers must also be more involved with the supplier once the order has been placed, building up a strong relationship and taking more responsibility than has previously been the case to ensure that they are abiding by ethical practices. However, this is not as simple as it sounds. There is no set standard or legal requirement across countries and so it is not easy to impose. Similarly, when the retailer does an audit the supplier can cheat to appear more ethical than they are. Instances have been known where suppliers have played a certain song on a radio which signals for any children working there to hide in the back room. It is also common for factory managers to brief workers about what to say to buyers, and tell them they are not allowed to say anything negative. As the garment workers fear losing their jobs they will often stay silent. Therefore, ultimately it is very difficult for the buyer to know what the true working conditions are like, which is why educating suppliers is the best form of action.

Buyers must also ensure that they are aware of all the hidden costs ahead of placing the order so that there are no nasty surprises and the profit-margin projections are clear and accurate. If the supplier is located in an area prone to natural disasters or there are political tensions in that surrounding area, then buyers must seriously consider the risks and potentially avoid that area in the foreseeable future. Once underway, the buyer cannot change an order, so they need to have a contingency plan in place and react quickly and effectively. Worst-case scenarios should be planned for and anticipated in advance. Buyers need to use the critical path effectively to ensure that they account for any late deliveries, and put in buffer zones to absorb this time and not have a knock-on effect on the time it reaches the shop floor.

Many brands/retailers use a combination of manufacturers in order to minimise the risks of global sourcing (Birtwistle et al., 2004). This allows them to ensure that they are not too reliant on one supplier if anything does go wrong. It can also help to balance the lead times vs the costs, by manufacturing certain items such as basics that can have long lead times in the Far East, fashion items with shorter lead times in North Africa or Turkey, and items that will definitely need to be reordered from the UK. This is known as a combination of near-shoring (or proximity sourcing) and off-shoring.

Finally, buyers must work closely with suppliers in order to minimise the risks. Buyers can invest in new technology in order to ensure frequent and clear communication with the supplier and also track the production of orders in more detail. This highlights the importance of the buyer–supplier relationship.

The buyer–supplier relationship

Once the buyer has selected a supplier to work with, it is very important that they build up a relationship with them. Mutual respect, trust, and cooperation between the buyer and supplier are imperative to ensure a strong relationship and long-term profitability for both parties (Diamond & Pintel, 2014). As in any relationship, it takes time to strengthen it, so buyers should be cautious changing suppliers regularly as they will be unable to have as much of an effective relationship. Getting the right suppliers and having a trusting relationship is the key to success of fashion businesses (Grose, 2012). This is because long-term stable relationships will cut costs and lead times; e.g. paying on time. Having a good relationship between the buyer and supplier will reduce risks as suppliers are likely to be more flexible and more reliable, and implementing processes or agreements will be much simpler. The buyer and the supplier must become partners, working together in order to achieve a common goal of both being profitable businesses. Yet, the relationship should always remain professional and not cross the line in terms of friendship as buyers need to remain objective when appraising suppliers. As such, buyers should not accept any large gifts from suppliers, because this could be seen as bribery and the business may appear to be corrupt.

Nowadays, buyers and suppliers are being much more open with each other than in the past. The supplier has to make a profit in order to sustain their business and so being open and honest about their bottom line will prevent the buyer from trying to push them too hard on price. Similarly, buyers need to be upfront about the likely selling price of the garment based on past sales and the current market, explaining their desired margin and profit. This less cagey way of negotiation will result in less of a strain on the relationship and allow buyers and suppliers to have a mutual understanding and respect of one another's businesses.

Buyers can build strong relationships with suppliers by following these principles:

1. *Effective communication* – it is important that the buyer communicates their needs and priorities with the supplier from the outset. If speed is the main priority then this needs to be made clear; likewise if quality is the most important aspect. Setting clear objectives and deadlines in place at the beginning of the contract results in less confusion and fewer potential issues further down the line. Likewise, the buyer must be prepared to listen to the supplier's needs and be flexible where possible. Rather than being adversaries, the buyer and the supplier should work together as a partnership and look to help each other achieve their targets. However, as discussed earlier, when suppliers are located halfway across the world communication is not easy, with language and time-zone barriers. Nevertheless, with new technology developing constantly, communication with people in different countries is easier than it has ever been and buyers must take advantage of instant messaging and videocall facilities and be prepared to talk to their suppliers during less sociable hours in order to maintain an effective relationship. Buyers should also consider if the supplier's working week is different to theirs and respect the days of the week that they do not work by not contacting them. Buyers need to communicate with their suppliers obtaining progress updates weekly. Furthermore, they should use diagrams to help illustrate what they want, making it clear what they want, especially in terms of the sampling stages, when English is not the supplier's first language.
2. *Listen to and respect the supplier's needs* – in the past, focus has always been on getting the most out of the supplier and praising the buyer for having an almost bully-like role, forcing the supplier to manufacture products as quickly as possible at the lowest cost possible. Whilst this is, of course, the desired outcome for the buyer and the brand, it is not always feasible and has caused huge ethical implications as a result, not to mention having a hugely detrimental effect on the buyer–supplier relationship. Buyers need to listen the supplier and their requirements. If a supplier states that a certain garment will take 'x' number of days to manufacture then the buyer should not expect it to be done sooner or push for it to be so as this could result in poor ethical practices. The supplier will often have multiple orders from different businesses, all with tight deadlines, and so managing them all and ensuring that they are on time is challenging. Thus, the supplier often prioritises larger retailers or long-standing relationships as they are the most important in terms of long-term profits and business, much to the detriment of smaller, independent retailers. Buyers need to be flexible and come up with compromises that suit both parties. Buyers should show their respect to suppliers by giving their full attention to their presentations and learning from their advice and input (Clodfelter, 2012).
3. *Meet in person* – being on the other side of the world and possessing the latest communications technology, it is often tempting to save time and money by just communicating with suppliers via phone and email. However, the best negotiations happen and relationships flourish when face-to-face. The buyer should aim to visit the supplier in person to perform the negotiation and, thereafter, meetings should happen regularly. By visiting the factory, buyers will also be able to gain a greater understanding of the realities of garment production and the experience of the supplier, which will foster a positive partnership (Goworek, 2007).

4. *Agree on terms at the outset* – the buyer should be clear on deadlines and the expected ethical standards to be upheld at the outset to ensure that the supplier knows the required expectations. This includes making any late penalties clear so that they do not come as a surprise to the supplier. A contract should be signed and put into place making all these agreements clear and obvious before the manufacturing actually takes place. It is best to take a photograph, drawing, or fabric swatch to the initial meeting to ensure that the supplier is clear on what the final produced garment should look like – this is particularly important in order to help overcome language barriers and prevent any unwanted surprises.

5. *Be fair, professional, and supportive* – just as it is important for buyers to have suppliers that deliver on time, buyers should ensure that they pay for the order on time and according to their agreement. The buyer should always be on time for meetings and reply to emails promptly to show how much they value the relationship and not cause any hold-ups. Promises should be honoured and there should not be any last-minute U-turns or demands from the buyer after the agreement is in place. The buyer should also provide detailed feedback on how the products were received by customers in order to help the supplier understand and improve (Clodfelter, 2012).

Negotiation

Negotiation is the process where interested parties resolve disputes, agree on courses of action, bargain for an advantage, and attempt to achieve an outcome that will serve both parties' mutual interest (Clodfelter, 2012). Negotiating the cost and terms for the manufacturing of products is a huge responsibility of the buyer. As such, brands often provide training courses on negotiation in order to help prepare buyers, as it is their task to negotiate the lowest cost price possible with the supplier in order to achieve a healthy gross margin for the garment and maximise profits for the retailer. However, the supplier also wants to make a profit and have as high a cost price as possible, so both parties must come to an acceptable compromise.

The primary goal of negotiation should be to achieve a mutually acceptable deal, which accomplishes the objectives of the negotiation, without making the other party walk away or damaging a valuable relationship (Clodfelter, 2012). The aim should be for both parties to be happy with the outcome. Buyers must think of the long-term impacts of their negotiation strategies and not just try to get a 'quick win' by driving the supplier down on price. The way they negotiate in the first instance will affect all future negotiations and set the precedent for either a good or bad working relationship.

The following aspects can be negotiated between the buyer and the supplier:

- Price;
- Quality;
- Quantity;
- Delivery time;
- Delivery terms;
- Returns privileges;
- Number of sizes/colours produced.

Negotiation is a complex art that involves strategic planning, arithmetic ability, commercial creativity, and high levels of interactive skills. It should be carried out assertively, yet professionally (Clodfelter, 2012). There are generally four stages that occur in the planning, preparation, and execution of a successful negotiation:

1. *Research and planning* – the buyer must research their customers and the current market so that they know exactly what they want to achieve in the negotiation. Once the buyer has the initial plan they will usually discuss it with the buying and merchandising teams in order to gain additional insights and advice.

   Buyers also need to research the supplier and compare them to other suppliers, as well as gaining a sound knowledge and awareness of that supplier's country and culture. Cultural differences are particularly important to be aware of as the buyer needs to ensure that they do not offend the supplier. Some subjects should never be talked about, such as sensitive political situations, as the buyer should remain professional and neutral (Diamond & Pintel, 2014). Furthermore, buyers must be respectful of certain customs and ways of dress.

   Buyers should analyse past negotiations and cost prices vs lead times of products in order to prepare and know what to expect. It is important that buyers have some knowledge about the garment's properties and, although they are not expected to be experts in the technical aspects of materials, an understanding about the appearance and make-up of different fabrics will be very useful in aiding with decision-making, especially as buyers are responsible for placing such large orders (Goworek, 2007). Buyers need to research the technical aspects of the product and understand the design and manufacturing process in order to show the supplier that they are knowledgeable in these areas, and also understand how long that process will realistically take so as not to push the supplier too hard (Clodfelter, 2012). This is also true for researching the cost of production so that the buyer knows whether the supplier's price is reasonable or not.

   Prior to the negotiation process, the buyer must know what their desired outcome and goals are, what their priorities are and which aspects they may be prepared to concede on. The buyer also needs to plan out their ideal price and the highest that they would be prepared to go in order to achieve a good profit margin. This involves identifying their maximums and minimums in terms of price, quantity, and lead time. They should plan out their strategy with the realistic cost that they would expect to pay based on experience and what their opening offer will be. From this the buyer could plan out what the supplier's potential reply might be and how they could respond to it. Buyers must also plan what they want the overall objective of the negotiation to be – a lower price for a product, faster delivery, bigger discounts, better quality, or an improved relationship? The buyer must think about what they can trade, what they can bargain for, and what they will not budge on. Aspects that they could trade could be higher order quantities, longer lead times, repeat orders, future orders, and payment terms.

2. *Offer* – buyers should build up a rapport with the supplier to keep the negotiation friendly and respectful. Both the buyer and supplier make their initial offers and establish the boundaries for the negotiation. It is important for the buyer not to make an offer that is too extreme so that they do not offend the supplier as this can sour the negotiation from the outset and be detrimental to the buyer–supplier relationship. These initial offers are very rarely accepted and so the buyer needs to

ensure that they leave room for manoeuvre. It is unwise to accept the first offer in a negotiation because doing so does not test the other person's position; thus, quick concessions should be avoided (Clodfelter, 2012). A good tip is to let the supplier make the first offer as the buyer is much more likely to achieve favourable terms. It is also wise not to start with high-priority issues in order to facilitate some easy 'quick wins' or agreements to get the negotiation process started.

3. *Discussion and bargaining* – in this phase the negotiation begins to get serious as both parties start to put forward their realistic offers. Both sides will be exploring possible areas of compromise, seeing where ground could be conceded if necessary and where they can reach an agreement. The buyer should remain friendly in order to avoid a hostile or pressured atmosphere, saying a firm but polite no to extreme offers. It is unwise to employ 'tough guy' tactics and bully suppliers. It may work for that negotiation, but it will not lead to an effective buyer–supplier relationship as the supplier will resent the buyer and may not want to do business again in the future. Instead, there are many different styles of negotiating outlined by Clodfelter (2012):

   - *Take it or leave it* – used when there is a deadlock or no time for further negotiation. There is a risk that no agreement will be reached and the other side may leave it. This tactic produces resentment if not handled carefully.
   - *Limited authority* – requires the buyer to say that he/she is authorised to pay up to, say, £20 for an item and higher prices would require the approval of the merchandising manager.
   - *But you can do a little better* – challenges the supplier to do a little better to finalise the deal.
   - *What if?* – uses questions such as 'What if I increase the purchase quantity?' or 'What if I pay the invoice in ten days instead of 30 days?'
   - *Let's split the difference* – both the buyer and supplier relinquish an equal amount of disputed difference. This tactic is usually employed when the difference is small and the end of the negotiation is near.
   - *Time pressure* – used frequently by suppliers and buyers. Designed to make the other person give up something, pressurising the other side into making a quick rather that correct decision.
     - Suppliers: 'The price will increase next month', 'The offer is good for only ten days', 'There is only a limited inventory available.'
     - Buyers: 'I'm returning home tomorrow.'

   Ultimatums should be avoided; they are one of the most common but least effective negotiating tactics because even if the supplier gives in, he or she will resent the buyer (Clodfelter, 2012). A good approach is to use probing techniques, asking the supplier how they have arrived at that price in order to try to establish what the other is thinking (Clodfelter, 2012). The last 20 per cent of negotiating time is when most concessions are made and when the cost price is finally decided upon (Clodfelter, 2012). Compromise is usually arrived at during the normal course of negotiation; however, the sole intent of negotiation should not be to compromise, and the buyer should only make concessions if they are receiving them in return (Clodfelter, 2012).

4. *Outcome* – elements of the negotiation such as quantity, product detail, cost, and lead times need to be finalised and an agreement made. It is important to note that it is still possible for the negotiation to break down at this stage. The reasons for this are usually because one of the parties might introduce a completely new set of

conditions that is seen as unreasonable by the other party. Or it might just be that the buyer and the supplier are too far apart with their desired outcomes and neither wants to concede.

The final agreement needs to be comprehensive, unambiguous, and clearly understood by each party. This should be put in writing and should clearly state who is responsible for what, and list timescales. So much is discussed that small points can be forgotten; a record of agreement addresses this and shows how the deal was constructed should there be an issue later.

The outcome of the negotiation must hold benefits for all parties. There are two types of outcomes:

1. Tangible: price, delivery, quality, guarantees;
2. Intangible: making the other person happy, both 'winning', being fair, preserving your reputation/integrity.

If both parties believe that they have won, they can acquire a relationship based on mutual respect (Clodfelter, 2012).

CHAPTER SUMMARY AND THE FUTURE OF SOURCING

As the cost of labour is increasing in traditional garment-manufacturing nations such as China, brands/retailers are now looking to Africa for sourcing opportunities, again chasing the cheapest wage. However, ethical issues are now higher on the agenda than ever, and so brands need to be careful implementing this strategy. Despite an increase in awareness of ethical issues that are occurring throughout the fashion supply chain, there is still a very long way to go before we see a global set of ethical standards being adhered to. In 2019 a report by Labour Behind the Label found that no major clothing brand (and it surveyed the leading 32 fashion brands in the world) was able to show that garment workers that it employed in Asia, Africa, Central America, or Eastern Europe were paid enough to escape poverty (Imms, 2019). As speed-to-market is becoming an increasing priority to meet consumer demand and beat the competition to be the first to sell desired products, brands are moving their sourcing closer to home in a process known as near-shoring or re-shoring. As a result, it could be argued that sourcing strategies are now coming full circle.

Finally, buyers may need to consider sourcing products made from different materials in the future. Shortages of raw materials such as cotton are causing fabric prices to rise. The increased awareness of sustainability and the damage done to the environment by certain non-biodegradable fabrics often used in the production of fast-fashion garments, such as polyester, are putting pressure on brands to produce items made from more sustainable materials. This may mean recruiting new suppliers and having to build up long-term relationships with them from scratch. It will also be challenging working with different types of fabric, such as lyocell and bamboo, and production times and processes may change, meaning that buyers will need to learn this and adapt accordingly.

References

Accord. (2018). 'Safe workplaces', n.d., available at: https://bangladeshaccord.org

Anderson, J., Berg, A., Hedrich, S., Ibanez, P., Janmark, J., and Magnus, K. (2018). 'Is apparel manufacturing comng home? Nearshoring, automation, and sustainability: Establishing a demand-focused apparel value chain', McKinsey Apparel, Fashion & Luxury Group, October, available at: www.mckinsey.com/~/media/mckinsey/industries/retail/our%20insights/is%20apparel%20manufacturing%20coming%20home/is-apparel-manufacturing-coming-home_vf.ashx

Bearne, S. (2017). 'Buying and sourcing in Turkey', 8 February, Drapers, available at: www.drapersonline.com/business-operations/supply-chain/buying-and-sourcing-in-turkey/7018069.article.

Bearne, S. (2018). 'Manufacturing a new UK clothing industry', 28 August, Drapers, available at: www.drapersonline.com/7031835.article.

Berg, A., & Hedrich, S. (2014). 'What's next in sourcing?', May, McKinsey, available at: www.mckinsey.com/industries/retail/our-insights/whats-next-in-apparel-sourcing.

Birtwistle, G., Bruce, M., & Moore, C. (2004). *International Retail Marketing: A Case Study Approach*. Waltham, MA: Butterworth Heinemann.

BoF (Business of Fashion). (2019). 'The year ahead: All eyes on India's Ascent', 4 January, available at: www.businessoffashion.com/articles/intelligence/the-year-ahead-all-eyes-on-indias-ascent.

Brown, H. (2019). 'Super-fast fashion: From screen to store in seven days', Drapers, available at: www.drapersonline.com/7034964.article.

Carr, M.G., & Hopkins Newell, L. (2014). *Guide to Fashion Entrepreneurship: The Plan, the Product, the Process*. New York, NY: Fairchild Books/Bloomsbury.

Clark, T. (2018). 'Is Turkey's supply chain unravelling?', 24 August, Drapers, available at: www.drapersonline.com/news/is-turkeys-supply-chain-unravelling/7031870.article.

Clodfelter, R. (2012). *Retail Buying: From Basics to Fashion*. 4th ed. New York, NY: Fairchild.

Coresight Research (2017). 'Fast fashion speeding toward ultrafast fashion', 19 May, available at: https://coresight.com/research/.fast-fashion-speeding-toward-ultrafast-fashion/

Diamond, J., & Pintel, G. (2014). *Retail Buying*. Pearson New International ed., 9th ed. Harlow: Pearson Education.

Fashion Revolution. (2018). '2018 impact', n.d., available at: www.fashionrevolution.org/2018-impact/.

Geoghagan, J. (2017). 'Bangladesh terror threat still a concern for fashion industry, says report', 15 February, Drapers, available at: www.drapersonline.com/news/bangladesh-terror-threat-still-a-concern-for-fashion-industry/7018594.article.

Goworek, H. (2007). *Fashion Buying*. 2nd ed.. Hoboken, NJ: Blackwell.

Grose, V. (2012). *Fashion Merchandising*. New York, NY: Bloomsbury.

Hickman, M. (2010). '21 workers die in fire at H&M factory', 2 March, *The Independent*, available at: www.independent.co.uk/life-style/fashion/news/21-workers-die-in-fire-at-hm-factory-1914292.html.

Holweg, M., Reichhart, A., & Hong, E. (2011). 'On risk and cost in global sourcing', *International Journal of Production Economics*, 131(1): 333–341.

Imms, K. (2019). 'Fashion brands fail to pay supply chain workers living wage', 7 June 2019, Drapers, available at: www.drapersonline.com/7036146.article.

O'Connell, L. (2019). 'Value of the leading 10 textile exporters worldwide in 2018, by country', 1 August, Statista, available at: www.statista.com/statistics/236397/value-of-the-leading-global-textile-exporters-by-country/.

Shaw, D., & Koumbis, D. (2014). *Fashion Buying*. New York, NY: Fairchild.

Sutherland, E. (2017). 'Morocco's race to be a fast fashion sourcing destination', 7 November 2017, Drapers, available at: www.drapersonline.com/7027166.article.

Sutherland, E. (2019). 'Out of Africa: the new sourcing hub', 7 June 2019, Drapers, available at: www.drapersonline.com/business-operations/out-of-africa-the-new-sourcing-hub/7035964.article.

Twigg, M. (2017). 'Is the old sourcing model dead?', 14 September, Business of Fashion, available at: www.businessoffashion.com/articles/global-currents/is-the-old-sourcing-model-dead.

Twigg, M. (2019). 'What's your "Plan B" for "made in China"?', 28 June, Business of Fashion, available at: www.businessoffashion.com/articles/professional/whats-the-plan-b-for-made-in-china.

Uddin, M. (2019). 'Comment: Safety in Bangladesh is a joint responsibility', 24 April, Drapers, available at: www.drapersonline.com/7035209.article.

Varley, R., & Pickard, H. (2019). 'Fashion Supply Chain Management', in Varley, R., Roncha, A., Radclyffe-Thomas, N., & Gee, L. (eds), *Fashion Management: A Strategic Approach*. New York, NY: Red Globe Press, pp. 175–193.

World Trade Organization. (2019). World Trade Organization Statistical Report 2019, available at: www.wto.org/english/res_e/statis_e/wts2019_e/wts2019_e.pdf.

CHAPTER 9

Range finalisation

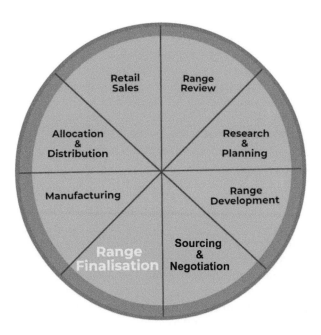

Introduction

Once the initial range plan has been completed the buyer must ensure that the first samples and key information are developed in order to discuss the range at the pre-selection meeting. This chapter will outline the steps that buyers and merchandisers take in order to finalise a product range. A discussion of both the pre-selection meeting and the final selection meeting will take place, as well as a thorough analysis of the sampling, fitting, and fabric-testing stages.

Learning outcomes

After reading this chapter you will be able to:

- Explain the purpose of the pre-selection meeting and final selection meetings;
- Identify the three stages of sampling and outline what occurs during each one;
- Discuss fabric testing;

- Discuss the importance of garment fitting;
- Discuss the importance of quality control.

Preparation for the pre-selection meeting

A lot of time, research, and effort has gone into the development of the product range, but it is only when a sample is produced in the key fabrics by the supplier with accurate pricing details that it is possible to ascertain whether the ideas can actually be realised. Working closely with suppliers regarding the products is key to success for buyers and merchandisers. Buyers and merchandisers discuss the initial ideas for products with suppliers either in person or via email in order to start the development of the range from 2D images to actual garments. Having actual samples in the correct or similar fabrics with price, quantity, and lead time information enables accurate decisions to be made for the range. All samples need to be ready for the *pre-selection meeting* where key discussions take place regarding each of the products and ranges.

The pre-selection meeting

The pre-selection meeting is a crucial meeting that takes place in which all the buying team for that category or department meet with the more senior team to present the products and ranges that are in development. The meeting allows the senior team to see what the junior buyers are developing, make sure that there are not any overlaps or similarities between departments, check that the key looks for the season are covered, and make sure that the ranges being developed are following the key vision that the brand is intending to follow. The purpose of the meeting is to assess how the products work together as a whole, and check that they have a workable price architecture and that there is sufficient variety for customers, alongside the supplier details and delivery dates (Goworek & McGoldrick, 2015). Samples of the garments are 'racked up' around the room and the buyers and merchandisers will discuss the garments, colourways, and prints potentially available, initial cost prices, and selling price with potential margins, and, in some cases, initial quantities may be discussed. During the pre-selection meeting, the first sample, or prototype sample, is analysed thoroughly and many changes are made in order to perfect the item, as it is much more cost-effective to make any modifications earlier rather than later. The costs of the fabric and of producing the garment are carefully considered and discussed. Many garments are discarded at this point due to such reasons as them perceived to be too expensive, too similar to other styles, or potentially too risky to produce. The pre-selection meeting will provide a critique of the range, meaning that new samples may need be requested as a result and the range plan rewritten to include any changes. The garments that are accepted at the pre-selection meeting are all given an individual style number which will be used by buyers, merchandisers, and suppliers to communicate about them throughout the production process.

PRE-SELECTION MEETING

The pre-selection meeting is where all the buying team meet with the more senior team to present the products and ranges that are in development.

Sampling

Once the initial product range has been established, a sample needs to be developed. The samples are often produced in a UK size 12 in womenswear, or size Medium in menswear, in order to test the style, fit, and quality of the product. Sampling needs to be done as accurately and as quickly as possible in order to ensure that the intended deadlines are achieved. It can be very risky to sign off a product without an accurate sample, as, whilst product ideas may look great in 2D CAD (computer-aided design) form, this may not be the case once the idea is converted into a 3D product. The sample is also a way for the supplier to accurately cost the garment as the exercise itself will identify any issues with fabrics, fit, and time allocation that will appear during the bulk manufacturing stage. Making samples is an expensive and laborious process and each sample will take far longer to make than its final mass-produced version. This is why the range-planning process is so crucial: it is far cheaper and more efficient for retailers and their suppliers to develop mood boards and sketches than excessive sampling of garments.

Suppliers produce samples at different stages in the buying process with various approvals required before manufacturing can begin, with the three main stages being (Jackson & Shaw, 2001):

1. Fit sample;
2. Pre-production sample;
3. Sealed sample.

Fit sample

The manufacturer's first attempt at producing a garment from a 2D specification sheet is called a 'fit sample'. This first sample will be developed from the CAD image provided from the buying team to the supplier, or it can be developed from previous styles or even images from other brands. In some cases when there is a fast turnaround required and suppliers may be located in other parts of the world, the fit sample may not be created in the correct colour or fabric but in as close a match to the real fabric as possible in order to save time and money. Obviously, if the sample is produced in the correct fabric then it will be more accurate. The main purpose of the initial sample is to test the concept (Carr & Hopkins Newell, 2014). Once completed, the fit sample is sent to the buyers and garment technologists for approval, where it is tried on a model to assess the fit. It is normal at this stage for samples to require some amendment. After all the adjustments are made a second sample is developed.

Pre-production sample

The pre-production sample is the final garment in terms of the correct colour and trims but without all the care labels and tickets (Jackson & Shaw, 2001). This sample will be checked to ensure that all the requested changes from the initial fit sample have been addressed, and discussions will take place about their accuracy.

(Final) sealed sample

When a buyer is satisfied with a garment sample, it is 'signed off and sealed'. This sealed sample is used as a benchmark in the inspection of the completed mass-produced garment order. Sealing samples ensures that if any product-quality, sizing, technical, or other disputes arise then both parties can refer back to these agreed samples to check what was ordered (Shaw & Koumbis, 2014). Hence, two identical samples are checked and sealed, one of which is returned to the manufacturer and one which is kept for reference by the retailer. The final production sample is graded into different sizes according to the buyer's specifications and it is essential that the final production sample is produced on the same machines as the bulk-manufactured garments in order to ensure that they are identical (Carr & Hopkins Newell, 2014).

Sample management

Sampling is key to the accuracy in product development, but it is also a very costly and time-consuming aspect, as well as a challenge to sustainability. With so many different types of samples moving in and out of fashion buying offices, the benefits of good sample management become apparent (Shaw & Koumbis, 2014). Keeping track of samples and their location is often the role of the assistant buyer and/or buyer's admin assistant (BAA). Sample rails and sample rooms need to be constantly tidied and rearranged to ensure that samples can be located quickly (Shaw & Koumbis, 2014). In many cases samples can be loaned to other departments, such as marketing for promotional campaigns, the studio for the photography in order to put them on the website, and even externally for press and media coverage. Again, it is the role of the assistant buyer and BAA to keep track and chase up the return of the sample. As retailers produce thousands of different styles per season, sample management can be a challenging and exhausting activity.

Fabric and garment testing

Most fashion retailers require fabrics to be tested to check that the quality meets the company's requirements, and to supply appropriate washing instructions on the garment label (Goworek, 2007). Some garments will require additional testing than standard garments, such as items claiming to be flame- or water-resistant, or fabrics used for sports that need to be fit for purpose. Furthermore, products that may cause a hazard, such as a fire risk, must carry labels with flammability warnings. All products developed must pass performance-testing requirements and it is the responsibility of the supplier to ensure that all products meet, or exceed, the standards required by the retailer. The garment manufacturer has to have the sample fabric tested at an approved laboratory. Final bulk testing is completed before bulk production of the garments commence, and accurate records are kept by the manufacturer and retailer in case of any faults or customer complaints.

Fabric and trims approval

The buyer will probably request that the garment be dyed a specific colour, so the fabric manufacturer must dye the swatch that shade. This swatch is known as a *lab dip*. The lab dip is compared to the original colour swatch that the buyer requested the colour to be matched to, and then the buyer either approves or rejects it. The buyer looks at the lab dye in a 'light box', which is a small booth containing the same light bulbs used in the retailer's stores to demonstrate how the colour will appear to the customer when making the purchase, as well as in daylight (Jackson & Shaw, 2001). It is important to do this because different types of fabrics, such as Lycra, cotton, or polyester, can be dyed using the exact same Pantone colour reference but will all look very different due to the fabric construction and properties of its raw materials. Lab dips enable buyers to double-check the consistency and make sure that the colours being dyed are as accurate as possible when developing a coordinated range. Each lab dip is given a reference number which is a record of the exact recipe used to make the shade. This information is then shared across the different suppliers. This is vital as the buyer might be having the trousers produced in Turkey and the top produced in China, so they need to have the exact same shade made up to support a fully coordinated range. This time-consuming process is vital for accurate product development, and buyers need to take into account the lead times involved in both the process and the sourcing from many different global suppliers (Jackson & Shaw, 2001).

Garment fitting

Garments must be fitted in order to ensure that they are consistent in terms of sizing for all the product ranges. Getting the accurate size and fit is very important as, if they are wrong, it can lead to product returns by consumers, which are very costly for the retailer. Indeed, Brownbridge et al. (2018) found that women identify with their clothes' size and when this link is disrupted it causes discomfort and body dissatisfaction, which, in turn, contributes to the rejection of the garment, increasing the potential for the creation of waste.

As a vast number of products are developed by different suppliers all over the world, it is crucial that there is consistency in sizing. During the garment-fitting stage, the size of the garment is reviewed as well as how the product looks when it is worn, including an assessment of the practicalities, such as whether or not it is easy to take on and off and easy to walk around in, ultimately checking that the product is fit for purpose (Goworek, 2007). In order to speed up the communication process, some retailers' fittings are attended by a representative from the manufacturer alongside the buyer, garment technologist (quality assurance or quality control), and designer in order to minimise the number of fitting sessions before approval of a style (Goworek, 2007).

Quality control

Quality assurance (QA) refers to the activities that are involved in seeking to guarantee the quality of the garment (Carr & Hopkins Newell, 2014). Before signing an agreement it is important the supplier understands and agrees to the quality standards requirements of the retailer. It is the responsibility of the supplier to ensure that all products meet, or exceed, the standards required by the retailer. Quality control (QC) staff will often travel to inspect the manufacturer's standards and execution of the style, and samples may be checked at random in the factory. Thus, although suppliers usually conduct their own QC, buyers must also do their own inspection (Carr & Hopkins Newell, 2014). Retailers also do surprise testing of garments in stores in order to discourage suppliers from submitting garments in bulk that do not match up to the quality approved for final production in the sealed sample. Moreover, in the case of some textile products (e.g. those used in extreme sports) fitness for purpose and quality of manufacture can be a matter of life or death, so this process must be taken seriously.

Financial and product information

Once the samples are accurately developed and the costing and product information is finalised, all this information is collected within the range plan spreadsheet. The range plan spreadsheet is a key document for all buyers and merchandisers and, although what is included on it varies from retailer to retailer, Figure 9.1 shows a typical range plan.

Figure 9.1 illustrates the range plan in a spreadsheet, used to collate and illustrate the information in a readable and comparable format. Some of the information is used to help identify products and their width and depth, whereas some of the information supports their fabric composition and COO (country of origin) or supplier. However, the majority of the information supports the financial elements of the range, such as the cost price, RRP (recommended retail price), margin, volume, overall cost, and profit. This information is used as a basis for merchandisers to ensure allocation, replenishment, and weekly forecasting are accurate, and it informs the critical path with key information to support the tracking of progress once the product is being manufactured.

Here is the key for each of the columns for a typical range plan:

Style – code reference for each style. Each style needs to be identified via its own unique code to make sure that there are no mix-ups or mistakes when dealing with hundreds of products at a time;

Sketch – the CAD image is used for identification purposes to support the Style number reference;

Fabric – breakdown of fabric compositions of all the fabrics used to create the garment; for example: 10 per cent Lycra, 90 per cent cotton.

Colour – the different colourways and prints that the product will be available in;

Size – breakdown of the size ratio of all the available sizes that the product will be produced in;

Product classification – classification of the product, such as Basic, Classic, Fashion, Hero, or Fad;

STYLE	SKETCH	FABRIC	COLOUR	SIZE	PRODUCT CLASSIFICATION.	SELLING PRICE	RETAIL MARGIN	RETAIL MARGIN (£)	SINGLE PRODUCT COST	% RANGE	TOTAL RANGE COST	TOTAL RETAIL VALUE
68B01MGRY 68B02MBLK 68B03MYLW		86% Polyester and 14% Elastane		XXS-XL	-Basic product 68B01MGRY (370 units for Class A, 2,000 for Class B, 1,920 units for Class C, 400 units for Class D). -Fashion product 68B02MBLK (200 units for Class A, 1,280 units for Class B, 1,280 units for Class C and 200 units for Class D) -Hero product68B03MYLW (90 units for Class A store, 80 units for Class B store, 70 units for Class C stores.)	£36.00	64% 55% 47%	£23.04 £19.80 £16.92	£12.96 £16.20 £19.08	9.3% Total Quantity 7,890	£113,313.60	£284,040.00
68B04MGRY 68B05MBLK 68B06MYLW		100% Polyester		XXS-XL	-Basic product 68B04MGRY (370 units for Class A, 2,000 units Class B, 1,363 units Class C, 300 units Class D). -Fashion (200 units Class A, 1,280 Class B, 1,173 units Class C and 100 units Class D) -Hero (90 units Class A store, 80 units Class B store, 80 units Class C stores.	£32.00	64% 55% 47%	£20.64 £17.60 £15.04	£11.52 £14.40 £16.96	8.3% Total Quantity 7,036	£90,344.36	£225,152.00
68B07MGRY 68B08MCMO 68B09MBLK		100% Polyester		XS-XXL	-Basic (280 units Class A, 1,900 units Class B, 1,600 units Class C, 350 units Class D). -Fashion product 68B08MCMO (190 units Class A, 700 units Class B, 653 units Class C, 105 units Class D). -Fashion product: 68B09MBLK (190 units Class A, 1,000 units Class E, 690 units Class C, 145 units Class D).	£35.00	64% 55% 55%	£22.40 £19.25 £19.25	£12.60 £15.75 £15.75	9.2% Total Quantity: 7,803	£109,887.75	£273,105.00
68B10MGRY 68B11MYLW 68B12MBLK		70% Polyester and 30% Polyamide		XXS-XXL	Basic product 68B10MGRY (300 units Class A, 1,425 units Class B, 1,500 units Class C, 350 units Class D). Fashion product 68B11MYLW (200 units Class A, 1,310 units Class B, 1,288 units Class C, 200 units Class D). Basic product 68B12MBLK (358 units Class A, 1,825 units Class B, 1,790 units Class C, 500 units Class D).	£30.00	64% 55% 64%	£19.20 £16.50 £19.20	£10.80 £13.50 £10.80	13% Total Quantity 11,046	£127,391.40	£331,380.00
68B13MGRY 68B14MSLV 68B15MBLK		100% Polyesie		XXS-XXL	Fashion product 68B13MGRY (163 units Class A, 750 units Class B, 690 units Class C, 100 units Class D). Basic product 68B14MSLV (362 units Class A, 1,940 units Class B, 1,636 units Class C, 300 units Class D) Fashion product 68B15MBLK (201 units Class A, 1,150 units Class B, 944 units Class C, 210 units Class D).	£55.00	55% 64% 55%	£30.25 £35.20 £30.25	£24.75 £19.80 £24.75	9.9% Total Quantity: 8,436	188,069.40	£463,980.00
68B16MCMO 68B17MYLW 68B18MBLK		90% Cotton, 10% Polyester		XXS-XXL	Fashion product 68B16MCMO (270 units Class A, 1,700 units Class B, 1,600 units Class C 200 units Class D). Hero product 68B17MYLW (122 units Class A, 330 units Class B, 224 units Class C) Basic product 68B18MBLK (400 units Class A, 2,290 units Class B, 2,100 units Class C and 400 units Class D.)	£25.00	55% 47% 64%	£13.75 £11.75 £16.00	£11.25 £13.25 £9.00	11.3% Total Quantity: 9,636	£98,079.50	£240,900.00
68B19MGRY 68B20MSLV 68B21MYLW 68B22MDRK 68B23MBLK		95% Polyester 5% Elastane		XS-XL	Basic 68B19MGRY (250 units Class A, 1,400 units Class B, 1499 units Class C, 200 units Class D). Fashion product 68B20MSLV (190 units Class A, 900 units Class B, 1,070 units Class C, 170 units Class D) Fashion product 68B21MYLW (190 units Class A, 900 units Class B, 1,065 units Class C, 170 units Class D). Fashion product 68B22MDRK (170 units Class A, 600 units Class B, 661 units Class C). Basic product 68B23MBLK (300 units Class A, 1,800 units Class C, 260 units Class D).	£26.00	64% 55% 55% 55% 64%	£16.64 £14.30 £14.30 £14.30 £16.64	£9.36 £11.70 £11.70 £11.70 £9.36	15.9% Total Quantity: 13,495	£14,0554.44	£350,870.00
68B24MGRY 68B25MYLW 68B26MBLK		60% Cotton, 40% Polyester		XXS-XXL	Basic product 68B24MGRY (290 units in Class A, 1,342 units in Class B, 1,231 units in Class C and 210 units in Class D). Fashion product 68B25MYLW (110 units in Class A, 1,000 units in Class B, 900 units in Class C, 100 units Class D). Basic product 68B26MBLK (32e units in Class A, 1,498 units for Class B, 1,793 units for Class C, 290 units for Class D).	£32.00	64% 55% 64%	£20.48 £17.60 £20.48	£11.52 £14.40 £11.52	10.7% Total Quantity: 9,090	£110,793.60	£290,888.00
68B27MSLV 68B28MYLW 68B28MBLK		100% Polyester		XXS-XL	Basic product 68B27MSLV (290 units for Class A, 1,540 units for Class B, 1,593 for Class C, 330 units for Class D). Fashion product 68B28MYLW (205units for Class A, 1,230 units for Class B, 958 units for Class C, 200 units for Class D). Basic product 68B29MBLK (330 units for Class B, 1,790 units for Class C, 370 units for Class D).	£32.00	64% 64%	55%	£20.48 £17.60 £20.48	£11.52 £11.52	£14.40	12.4% Total Quantity: 10536	£128,842.56	£290,888.00

Figure 9.1 Range plan with key product information

Selling price – this is the price of the product for the customer. It is often referred to as the recommended retail price or RRP;

Retail margin (per cent) – this is the profit mark-up that the retailer will make on the garment. The amount is the difference between the cost price and selling price expressed as a percentage;

Retail margin (£) – this is the profit made displayed the monetary terms. The amount is the difference between the cost price and selling price expressed in pounds;

Single product cost – this is the cost price of the product: the amount that the retailer pays the supplier to manufacture it;

Total quantity – this is the total number of all the products in all the variations of colourways, prints and fabrics added together;

Total range cost – this is the total cost of the range; the cost price of one unit multiplied by the total quantity;

Total retail value of range – this is the total amount that the range will generate if all items are sold at the RRP price: the RRP price of one unit multiplied by the total quantity.

KEY TERMS

Cost price – the price that businesses pay manufacturers;

Margin – the business profit;

Recommended retail price (RRP) – the price that customers pay.

Calculating the margin

Many retailers charge customers 2.5 to 3.5 times more than the price that the manufacturer charged them for a garment (Goworek, 2007). This difference in price is not all profit for a business: the majority of it will cover the business overheads, from wages for all staff to rents and tax, as well as many other miscellaneous costs. The margin is the measure used to calculate the amount of profit that retailers make on the products that they sell. Every product will have a margin that it needs to achieve in order to ensure that it is commercially viable. The margin is measured in two ways: (1) as a percentage or (2) as a monetary amount. Calculating the formula will become second nature to a buyer in a very short space of time (Goworek, 2007).

Formula to calculate the margin

Each retailer will have their own target margin and set formula for achieving it (Goworek, 2007). Nevertheless, the formula below is one of the most commonly used:

RRP minus Cost Price (CP) equals Gross Profit (GP)

Then, GP divided by RRP multiplied by 100 equals Retail Margin %

RRP – CP = GP, than GP divided by RRP × 100 = %

For example, if the product is £20 and the cost price from the manufacturer is £4, to calculate the margin the following formula would be used:

£20.00 (RRP) – £4.00 (CP) = £16.00 (GP)

£16.00 (GP) divided by £20.00 (RRP) X 100 = 80% (MARGIN)

Calculating margins can be a highly numerical and mathematical task but it is essential in order to truly understand whether the product range developed is commercially viable. At the end of the product-development process, after all the creative and technical efforts that have gone into the product, it is vital that the product actually makes money. By understanding and planning a financially successful range, buyers can identify which garments are not making enough profit margin and take the opportunity to replace such styles before committing and placing orders with suppliers (Goworek, 2007).

Final selection meeting (sign-off meeting)

The final selection meeting is when the buying team presents the complete range to the head of buying and head of merchandising as well as the whole buying and merchandising teams. The final selection meeting enables the buyer and merchandiser to present the range in its entirety with perfect samples for each style. This is the opportunity to sign off garments for bulk manufacture. At this meeting the senior team of buyers, merchandisers, QA and, in some cases, suppliers will discuss the total budget allocated for the category and the entire range by line. Proposed bestsellers, supplier information, and projected delivery dates are all made clear, as well as the confirmed cost prices and retail selling prices of each garment, quantity of units per line, and size range per line. Each department will have their own sign-off meeting on the final range selection. In some instances, it may be a case of finalising the suggestions and edits discussed during the pre-selection meeting, whereas in others there may be concerns or issues that need addressing. Manufacturing large volumes of products is an extremely costly procedure so it is vital that there are people involved in the process, particularly the senior team members, that are able to review orders and sign off the range plans and products in order to minimise any errors made.

The financial spreadsheet is an important document to use within the final selection meeting, as the document allows the teams to see and compare different products across the ranges from a numerical and financial commitment. This can help highlight which products need to be pushed through for completion in order to launch fully coordinated ranges at the same time. Once signed off during the final selection meeting, the initial orders and *purchase orders* (POs) can be sent to suppliers for manufacture.

Order confirmation – purchase order

Once the range has been finalised and the sealed sample created, as well as all the prices and lead times negotiated between the buyer and the supplier, then signed off in the final selection meeting, a PO form can be created. The PO form acts as a contract between supplier and retailer. It is a legally binding document that authorises the shipment of merchandise and the payment of merchandise. It is critical for buyers and suppliers to be absolutely clear about what needs to be included on the PO form, such as the agreed cost price for each stage; thus, the order contains a wide range of cost-related information (Jackson & Shaw, 2001). In such a fast-paced business environment where buyers and merchandisers are developing many products from a variety of different suppliers at the same time, the PO acts as the main reference document for a product, to keep a reliable record of not only what has been ordered and when it will be delivered, but also of the financial commitment made from the budget allocated.

Aspects that are included on the PO form are:

- Total order quantity;
- Shipment date;
- Cancellation date;
- Cost price;
- Terms and conditions;
- Size assortment;
- Colours;
- All raw-material information;
- Reference to the specification.

Buyers and merchandisers are responsible for managing and tracking the PO. It contains an accurate description of what the distribution centre should expect, the information which will be used to inform the distribution schedule and critical path. Prior to the PO being committed, a pro forma is produced. A pro forma is an initial order in writing, where both the supplier and the buyer can check accuracy and confirm any changes, and then the PO is produced from the pro forma incorporating any amendments or changes. The PO will also include the payment terms, which are extremely complex and subject to company terms and conditions and will also vary from supplier to supplier.

PURCHASE ORDER FORM

A purchase order form acts as a contract between supplier and retailer. It is a legally binding document that authorises the shipment of merchandise and the payment of merchandise.

Although suppliers must adhere to the PO form and faithfully reproduce what was agreed with the buyer, unfortunately this is not always the case. Suppliers may deviate from the PO form agreements for various reasons, such as not having the specific colour that was requested and so substituting it for a similar one, or not having the exact fabric, or enough of it to produce all the garments and so substituting it for a similar one (Diamond & Pintel, 2014). It may also be the case that the production of the order takes longer than the supplier anticipated, causing later deliveries than promised. Buyers must discuss anything that is produced that is not up to specification with the supplier and negotiate a discount if they are unhappy with the finished result.

CHAPTER SUMMARY

This chapter has provided a detailed overview and breakdown of the stages necessary to finalise garment production. As indicated, it is a time-consuming process that needs to be carefully monitored. Rather than simply putting all responsibilities on junior members of the buying and merchandising teams, the final signing off is done by more senior members of staff. This ensures that expertise and experience are incorporated in the process. Buyers and merchandisers need to carefully document everything, as they are working with a variety of suppliers within a global environment; thus, recording costings and clearly outlining agreements is essential. The final stages of getting a garment into production can be lengthy, as sampling, fabric testing, and garment fittings need to be undertaken in order to guarantee that the fashion ranges will have *the look* that was anticipated in the planning phases.

References

Brownbridge, K., Gill, S., Grogan, S., Kilgariff, S., & Whalley, A. (2018). 'Fashion misfit: Women's dissatisfaction and its implications', *Journal of Fashion Marketing and Management*, 22(3): 438–452.

Carr, M.G., & Hopkins Newell, L. (2014). *Guide to Fashion Entrepreneurship: The Plan, the Product, the Process*. New York, NY: Fairchild.

Diamond, J., & Pintel, G. (2014). *Retail Buying*. Pearson New International edition, 9th ed. Harlow: Pearson Education.

Goworek, H. (2007). *Fashion Buying*. 2nd ed. Hoboken, NJ: Blackwell.

Goworek, H., & McGoldrick, P. (2015). *Retail Marketing and Management: Principles and Practice*. Harlow: Pearson.

Jackson, T., & Shaw, D. (2001). *Mastering Fashion Buying and Merchandising Management*. London: Palgrave.

Shaw, D., & Koumbis, D. (2014). *Fashion Buying*. New York, NY: Fairchild.

10 Manufacturing

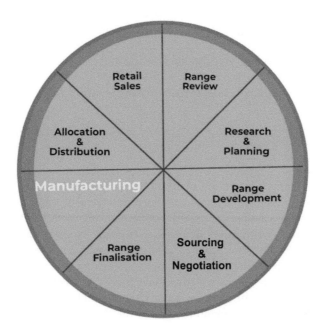

Introduction

Once the negotiation with the chosen supplier is complete, the product range has been signed off at the final selection meeting and the purchase order generated, the mass production of the items can begin. The manufacturing of garments is a time-consuming process that involves multiple stages that all need to be monitored closely by the buyer and merchandiser through the critical path. Buyers and merchandisers have to surrender full control of the range at this stage, an element that brings with it many risks, as they have to trust their supplier to conduct the mass production of garments in a timely and ethical manner.

This chapter focuses on the manufacturing process within the fashion industry and outlines what the mass production of garments entails. The chapter discusses the different production processes available to fashion retailers and illustrates these through different case studies. Finally, this chapter explains the roles of buyers and merchandisers during the manufacturing process and how they monitor it using the critical path.

Learning outcomes

After reading this chapter you will be able to:

- Describe the apparel pipeline and critically evaluate each of the stages;
- Distinguish the different types of production processes;
- Examine key issues that are faced by the industry;
- Map out the manufacturing process with touchpoints for the buyers and merchandisers;
- Describe the use of a WSSI (Weekly, Sales, Stock, and Intake) and identify the key formulas that help in sales forecasting, such as stock turn and week's cover;
- Explain how the critical path is used to monitor the production of garments.

The apparel pipeline and its link to manufacturing

Whether they are high-street or high-end stores, sustainable or luxury, all 'fashion'-producing entities have one thing in common: garments and accessories need to be manufactured and delivered to various different retail outlets in order to make them accessible to the (end-)consumer. Consumers themselves are often unaware of how items come into existence, how they are developed, and what is involved in the fashion-production process. Thus, it is often challenging for them to understand the implications of a price tag on products in terms of the actual cost versus production cost versus worth. In 2013, Ecouterre provided an insightful infographic that highlights the 'true cost' of a simple T-shirt (Figure 10.1). The infographic shows the different considerations and costs encountered along the apparel pipeline, from prices associated with raw materials to paying a living wage. These areas are further touched upon in Chapter 13.

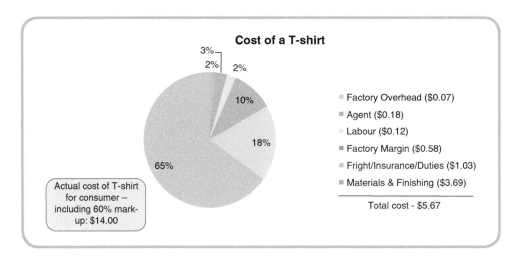

Figure 10.1   Cost of a $14 T-shirt (adapted from Ecouterre, 2013)

Figure 10.1 shows that there is a significant difference between production costs ($5.67) and actual selling price ($14.00) and that the creation of a T-shirt involves a variety of stages, from sourcing raw materials to finding (skilled) labour able to produce the garment, to finishing the item, to transporting it to the retail outlet. Each stage comes with its own costs, and, whether they are direct (e.g. labour) or indirect (e.g. overheads), they need to be carefully calculated in order to be able to create a garment and sell it to the end-consumer at an 'affordable' price. ('Affordable' here is a relative term and depends on whether consumers are price-sensitive or not). Whilst it is assumed that luxury is more expensive than high-street fashion – a question that remains is, how can prices, whether they are high or low, be justified? What is the difference between the production of a high-end garment versus one that is sold on the high street? Partly, the price difference may be justified in the raw materials that are used (e.g. leather or silk versus polyester or nylon); yet it is questionable whether a higher price tag implies higher wages for garment workers, safe working conditions, or more environmentally friendly sourced raw materials. Although we cannot focus in detail on this aspect as this goes beyond the scope of the book, we address it partially, by honing in on the manufacturing process.

Prior to discussing the manufacturing process, it is vital to get a better understanding of what is often referred to as the 'apparel pipeline', defined as 'a series of interrelated activities, which originates with the manufacture of fibre and culminates with the delivery of a product into the hands of the consumer' (Jones, 2006, p. 1). It provides an overview of all the stages that are involved in enabling fashion companies to provide consumers with fashion products and accessories. Generally, there are two different ways of viewing the channels of distribution (apparel pipeline), which are the *soft goods chain* or the *four-groups approach.*

Soft goods chain	Four-groups approach
• Textile segment	• Primary group
• Apparel segment	• Secondary group
• Retail segment	• Tertiary group
	• Auxiliary group

The main difference between the two is the that fact the four-groups approach includes an additional component: the auxiliary group.

The soft goods chain

The creation of a garment seems simple as a concept, yet in reality it is rather complex. Initially, for the buyer, it involves colourful fabric swatches that provide information about the actual material, its feel, thickness, and patterns, as well as the colouration of the product and whether it matches the expectations for the range that was envisioned by them and the designers. Fabric swatches allow buyers and merchandisers to make

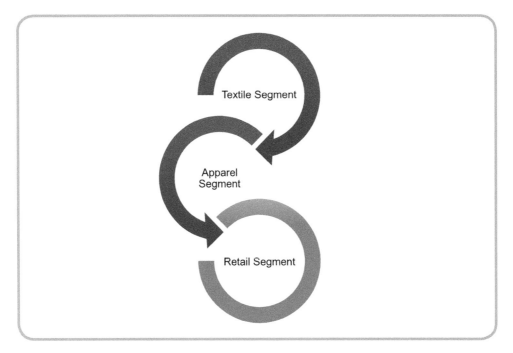

Figure 10.2   **The soft goods chain**

key decisions which have an impact on the manufacturing process, as well as the perfor-mance properties, and potentially the saleability of the fashion range. As such, they are crucial. However, creating fabric swatches takes time, especially when looking at the indi-vidual components needed to create these neat and tidy square pieces that are attached to paper backgrounds. As a result, some fast-fashion retailers are now rushing through this stage with their interest in speed being made a priority.

As indicated, the soft goods chain contains three major elements: the textile, the apparel, and the retail segment (Figure 10.2). The textile segment is predominantly con-cerned with fibre and yarn production, fabric manufacturing, and finishing. Fibres are thin, hair-like strands that can either be naturally grown from plants (e.g. flax, cotton, hemp) or animals (e.g. wool) or synthetically manufactured from regenerated cellulosic fibres (e.g. rayon viscose, bamboo viscose) or synthetic materials (e.g. polyester) (Jones, 2006; Muthu, 2015; Hayes & Venkatraman, 2016). The raw materials can be sourced in different countries; for example, the majority of flax (85 per cent) used for linen produc-tion is grown in Western European countries (e.g. France and Belgium) (Europa, 2016), whilst the largest cotton producers are India and China (Statista, 2018). This indicates that the apparel pipeline is global by nature, which can add complexities in the manu-facturing process, as raw materials have to be transported to factories. Key challenges that need to be taken into considerations can include:

- Political issues, which can impact on quotas and tariffs, or working relationships between counties;
- Economic issues, such as a financial crisis, which may act as a barrier for people to make purchases;

- Sociocultural issues, such as ageing populations;
- Technological issues, which may emerge as technology evolves;
- Environmental issues, such as droughts or floods, which can be linked to climate change, and may affect growth of crops;
- Legal aspects, such as labour law regulations and general working conditions.

PESTEL

A framework that enables marketers to analyse a company's external environment.

The examples provided are not exhaustive, but rather offer a glimpse of the types of issues that can affect the primary stage of the textile segment, as without suppliers being able to gain raw materials, fibres and materials cannot be produced and, ultimately, garments not created. Whilst some of the issues mentioned can be controlled, others – especially environmental issues – cannot. Climate change, in particular, can have an impact on the availability of raw materials. Over the past decade we have seen an increased intensity in severe weather events across the globe, ranging from droughts to floods and changes in precipitation patterns, which can have an impact on the availability of water and thus lead to the loss and the degradation of biodiversity (BSR, 2015; Preuss, 2015). One also needs to keep in mind that not all raw materials are plant-based; some may stem from animals, which can lead to ethical issues (e.g. fur, leather), and others are petroleum-based (e.g. polyester, spandex). The implication here is that crops and livestock could be affected by these severe weather conditions, and thus this could limit the raw materials available for the market in terms of wool, flax, cotton, or bamboo, and/or the quality of the material. Material sourcing is vitally important in the overall manufacturing process as it can determine the quality of the product and subsequently the price that can be achieved (International Trade Centre, 2005). It also has to be highlighted that raw materials in the fashion industry are not only affected by controllable and uncontrollable situations in the external environment, but also each fibre comes with its own challenges and ethical issue, which will be touched upon in Chapter 13.

As mentioned above, once a raw material is identified for the creation of a garment, it is essential to determine whether it is available in both quality and quantity (Rosenau & Wilson, 2006). This can be seen as a key part of the buyer and merchandiser's responsibilities in that they are identifying the most cost-effective supplier of raw materials to ensure that supply can cater for the (predicted) demand. Once the raw material source has successfully been identified, the fibres need to be processed further in order to be able to use them within the fashion industry. The thin, hair-like material, which can be both long or short, is turned into a coherent yarn, which is transformed into actual textiles/fabrics. In order to make the newly created fabrics 'fit for purpose' they have to go through the fabric-finishing process, in which they are bleached, dyed, printed on, and/or receive coatings (e.g. to protect against rain), depending on performance properties required for the finished product.

LEAD TIME

The time that is taken from the initial design of a product until it is produced and ready to be delivered to the target consumer.

Following on from the textile segment, the created fabrics/materials enter the *apparel segment*, which is predominantly concerned with the production of finished garments and accessories. Altogether there are three key stages within this segment: apparel design, manufacturing, and sales. Apparel design, as the name indicates, is concerned with the creation of the actual garment, from sketching an outline of one single item to developing a whole range. The design process can start from scratch in that it is based on new and novel ideas, or it simply updates existing garment ranges in accordance with current market trends (Jones, 2006). Depending on the company the design team can either be in-house or outsourced. Predominantly, design teams are located in developed countries, and designers are usually highly skilled and, overall, rather cost-intensive. Both Zara and Patagonia, for example, have their design teams in-house, which provides them with increased flexibility in adapting to trends and ensuring that these can be realised in relatively short lead times (Ferdows et al., 2003; Patagonia, 2012; Alliance Project, 2017; Fletcher, 2018). A key advantage of having the design team in-house is that buyers and merchandisers are able to communicate with them in a quicker and more efficient manner. Whilst buyers and designers work closely together to establish past and emerging trends that may influence different fashion collections, designers are sketching the actual fashion ranges and developing a vision for what the new season could look like; they create patterns, and develop prototypes of these ranges, which can help buyers in the decision-making process. Buyers, on the other hand, are more involved in trend forecasting, both in terms of what is 'in' and 'out', as well as what the anticipated demand might be, which can in turn impact on stock, as ideally companies will neither over- nor understock garments. It is also at this stage when buyers may request fabric swatches that are used to determine tactile (the feeling of a material) and visual (the look of a material) performance properties of the newly created garments.

Buyers also form strong bonds with suppliers across the manufacturing process, and thus the overall supply chain. Once a range has been designed to the satisfaction of both the buying and merchandising teams, these are forwarded to the apparel manufacturer, where they are produced (Goworek, 2007). Depending on the type of retailer, some garments may be mass-produced, whilst others offer more individually unique pieces; thus, the actual supply chains might be very different. Some supply chains may have multiple tiers of suppliers, such as H&M, which makes it rather complex, whilst independent designers may work with only one or two different companies, and therefore have a relatively simple supply chain.

Different types of manufacturers used

For own-label buyers there are three main types of manufacturer that that they could source from:

1. *A cut-make-trim (CMT)* – this manufacturer will only cut and assemble products from the specifications that are provided for them;
2. *A full-package programme (FPP)* – this manufacturer sources all the materials, develops the patterns according to the retailers' guidelines, and then creates the product;
3. *A contractor* – an independent entity that procures either a set number of products, fabric, equipment, personnel, or services for an agreed price and within an agreed timeframe.

It should be pointed out here that, for smaller own-label retailers, the minimum order levels for manufacturers are often too high and so they source from 'middlemen', known as *wholesalers*, who buy directly from the manufacturers and sell items on to retailers in smaller quantities. Similarly, branded buyers source finished garments (that have already been manufactured) from the brand directly, purchasing items at wholesale prices and then selling them onto the customer for a profit.

When referring to suppliers throughout this book we often equate them to manufacturers. *Suppliers* can be defined in a narrow sense, in that it refers to providers of raw materials (e.g. cotton, polyester) or business necessities (e.g. machinery, additional parts, business services). More broadly speaking, suppliers can also be seen as entities that provide the land on which factories are built, capital to run the business, information, or technology. As such, suppliers can be actual producers of input or intermediaries, implying that they act as a distributor or agent. Within the supply chain, *upstream* and *downstream* suppliers are often distinguished; upstream suppliers convert raw materials into finished products, whilst downstream suppliers focus more on bringing this product to the end-consumer and ideally add value in the process. The more tiers of suppliers are involved with the supply chain, the more complex it becomes. Thus, it is essential that fashion organisations carefully manage their supply chains, which involves careful planning of tasks and implementing control mechanisms that help monitor progress. Figure 10.3 illustrates the relationship between upstream and downstream suppliers.

In terms of manufacturing and progressing through the supply chain, different companies have different production strategies. Garments might be produced close the company's headquarters (HQ) (near-shoring or even re-shoring), whilst others are produced further afield (offshoring), depending on what is required. Patagonia, for example, sources its socks from a family-owned company in North Carolina, which allows it to brand these specific products as 'Made in the USA', which can be a unique selling proposition and an aspect that is of importance to its consumers. However, Patagonia's outerwear is produced in nearby countries, such as Nicaragua; as such it is near-shored. Its sportswear is predominantly produced in Asia, making it off-shored (Patagonia, 2019). Producing closer to the HQ is beneficial as lead times are shortened, transportation costs minimised, and communication flows potentially enhanced, as time differences are less severe than in other countries.

As already indicated, the fashion apparel pipeline is complex. Whilst it may be individual companies that are producing the yarns, creating fibres, applying finishings (e.g. sewing thread, tags, adding features, rips, texture, embroidery), and/or designing garments, they are all part of an organisation's supply chain. With increasing competition and the threat of fashion companies looking for alternative production places, countries have come together to form *regional economic trading agreements* (e.g. ASEAN – Association of Southeast Asian Nations, COMESA) in order to be more competitive and to survive within this volatile market environment (Rugman & Collinson, 2012; USAID, 2005).

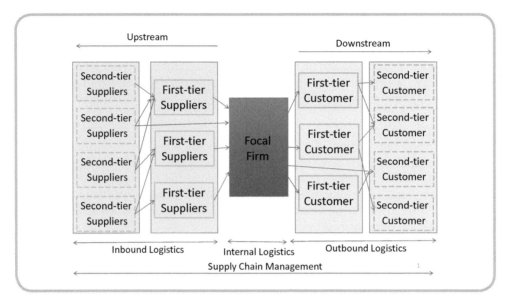

Figure 10.3   Upstream and downstream suppliers

REGIONAL ECONOMIC TRADING AGREEMENTS

A group of countries located within geographical proximity of one another that decide to cooperate for economic benefits.

The majority of these countries are part of the upstream supplier network.

CASE EXAMPLE: COMESA

The apparel pipeline can encompass a variety of countries to grow/produce raw materials, make them into textiles, and send the finished garments to the end-customer. In order to be more competitive in a highly volatile market, various trading agreements have been established to create a competitive advantage across the value supply chain, whilst working together to overcome key barriers associated with legal, technical, social, political, or economic aspects. An example is COMESA, which is the acronym for the Common Market for Eastern and Southern Africa free trading agreement between 21 countries (Burundi, Comoros,

Democratic Republic of the Congo, Djibouti, Egypt, Eswatini, Eritrea, Ethiopia, Kenya, Libya, Madagascar, Malawi, Mauritius, Rwanda, Seychelles, Somalia, Sudan, Tunisia, Uganda, Zambia, and Zimbabwe) (COMESA, 2019). COMESA was designed to promote an integrated and competitive cotton-to-clothing value chain that ultimately fights poverty (UNCTAD, 2009). 'COMESA's current strategy can thus be summed up in the phrase "economic prosperity through regional integration"' (COMESA, 2019). Thus, the fashion industry has provided these countries with an opportunity to diversify their exports and provide job opportunities for semi-skilled workers, especially women (UNCTAD, 2009).

Cotton is not only a water-intensive monoculture, but also rather labour-intensive. Within the COMESA countries both requirements are fulfilled, which implies that it provides work opportunities, especially within rural areas, as well infrastructure development, which is needed to move countries in the direction of development. COMESA provides an opportunity for these 21 countries to work together through the creation of enabling environmental and legal frameworks, which fosters greater industrial productivity and competitiveness (COMESA, 2019). Individual countries can specialise in their area of expertise and/or in accordance with their natural environment, which in turn leads to more rational exploitation of natural resources. Small and medium-sized firms are able to become increasingly competitive, both regionally and globally, thereby promoting economic growth. However, the opportunities provided are not necessarily equally distributed. Depending on the size of the country and its economic powers, individual COMESA countries may be able to influence smaller ones more heavily and push through their own agenda. On the other hand, these free trading agreements provide an opportunity for countries to work together for a greater good and jointly fight poverty. To reiterate this further, working together as part of a larger entity has provided economic benefits (e.g. job creation, infrastructure), as well as enabling individual countries to specialise in one area of the supply chain.

The last stage in the apparel segment is *sales,* which refers to the delivery of finished garments and accessories from the manufacturer to the organisation and its respective retail outlets. Interestingly, ten countries currently dominate the market for apparel sales, which are rapidly developing and developed countries and include the BRIC states (Brazil, Russia, India and China), the US, Japan, Germany, the UK, France, and Italy (CO Data, 2019). A key question that can be asked here is: who is part of the retail segment? The most obvious answer is retailers, who operate across the entire fashion spectrum, from luxury, to high-street, to value. The most common retail formats are *bricks and mortar* stores only, multichannel/omnichannel retailers and *pureplay* retailers.

BRICKS-AND-MORTAR

A company that has a physical store where consumers can go to shop, e.g. Primark.

Previous examples also included mail-order retailers, or catalogue retailers, that peaked in the 1970s/1980s. Mail-order retailing consists of the sale of goods through paper catalogues, where orders are placed through the telephone or via an order form sent in the post and delivered straight to the home via couriers. Mail-order retailing was set up based on a lot of the same principles that online retailing later encompassed, as it comprised a network of customers, sold a wider range of goods than would have been possible to fit into a store, and had a reliance on home delivery (Niemeier et al., 2013). Hence, updated versions of mail-order retailing that are still commonly used today are: TV home shopping channels and websites, as well as m-commerce and s-commerce options. M-commerce emerged with the creation of smartphones, enabling consumers to search for things on the go via mobile sites and apps, whilst more recently s-commerce provides consumers with the ability to purchase products via social media outlets including, but not limited to, Facebook and Instagram (Bürklin et al., 2019). Thus, the retail segment is the link between product manufacturers and (end-)consumers and, as such, is also concerned with marketing the product to the latter.

It is interesting to note that the consumer has the power to make or break a fashion business. If consumers purchase fashion lines and these sell out, this can be classified as a success, whilst the opposite can result in reduced profits as the items will have to go to markdown or, in extreme cases, lead to the failure of the business altogether. Thus, consumers have the power to influence what type of 'fashion' works and what does not. As such, if merchandisers predict consumer demand incorrectly then this can lead to the issue of either under- or over-stocking. The issue of over-stocking has received increased media scrutiny in recent years as some fashion retailers burn '12 tonnes of new, unsold clothing per year' (Hendriksz, 2017), which is also referred to as 'Fashion's Dirty Secret' (Siegle, 2018). In order to overcome the negative press and ensure that organisations are not experiencing any negative monetary influence, super-fast-fashion organisations, such as Missguided and Boohoo, have now established strategies to produce garments in small batches first, with an opportunity to reproduce them within a relatively fast turnaround should these trend-led items sell out quicker than expected. This aspect is also known as *sales forecasting* and is one of the key responsibilities of a merchandiser, which is discussed later in this chapter.

The four-groups approach

As indicated, the apparel pipeline can either be explored as the *soft goods chain* or the *four-groups approach* (Figure 10.4).

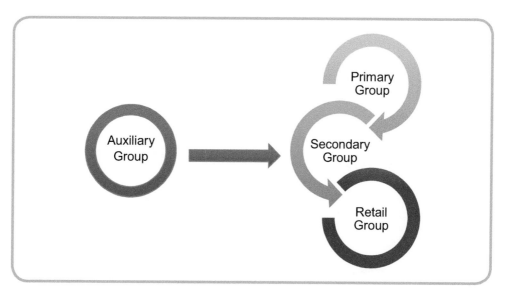

Figure 10.4   The four-groups approach

The main differences between the soft goods chain and the four-groups approach are (1) different names for the different stages, and (2) the addition of the auxiliary group. Within the soft goods chain we refer to the textile, apparel, and retail segments, which in the four-goods approach are listed as the primary, secondary, and retail groups. Although the names are different, they refer to the same stages and aspects. The auxiliary group is seen as a supporting group that provides the other three groupings with vital information through market reports and forecasts as well as trend and colour information. Representatives of this group are consultancy firms and trend-forecasting agencies, as well as trade associations.

Figure 10.5 provides a simplified overview of the various stages that an organisation needs to go through in order to have the end-product (garment and/or accessory). The coloured circles outline the stages that the buyer and/or the merchandiser are involved in the decision-making process.

Sales forecasting

WSSI

Merchandisers are heavily involved with the forecasting of sales, and thus are responsible for predicting the consumer demand of a new fashion range. A key forecasting tool essential for any merchandiser is the *WSSI* (Weekly, Sales, Stock, and Intake).

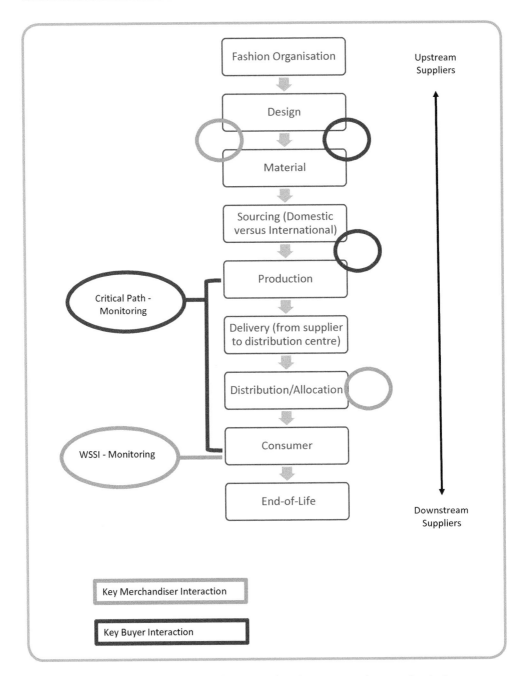

Figure 10.5 Buyer and merchandiser touchpoints across the supply chain

WSSI

- Key sales-forecasting tool;
- Acronym stands for *Weekly, Sales, Stock, and Intake*.

The WSSI is a reporting document that clearly highlights the amount of stock that is available in the business and the amount of stock replenishment coming in at various points during the selling period. As such, the WSSI is used to make decisions about the stock performance, as it provides an indicator of performance against the sales plan in an easy-to-understand manner. Each week the WSSI shows key figures and calculations including the opening stock, the closing stock, the stock cover, sales, and intake.

INTAKE

- New stock that is delivered to the business for distribution to stores;
- Stock quantities and allocation that need to be managed;
- Every store and style will be considered for initial allocation;
- Monitoring sales and intake to ensure that stores are adequately stocked is a priority.

The WSSI starts with various planned activities: (1) forecasting sales, 2) markdowns of unsold garments and accessories, and (3) replenishment intake. Once trading begins, the figures in the WSSI can be updated to include the actual sales figures, which allows merchandisers to see whether their predicted forecasts match the actual figures. If the demand was over- or under-predicted then adjustments can be made. The WSSI is updated on a continual basis, and as such supports key decision-making:

- For the planned delivery of intake;
- For establishing re-buys;
- For understanding whether markdowns are necessary.

COMMITMENT

- Stock that is on order from suppliers that is being manufactured or shipped;
- Remains a responsibility for both retailer and supplier;
- It is important to remember what is on order, especially as it is a commitment to the budget and intake.

Traditionally the WSSI was updated on a weekly basis, predominantly on Mondays, as it marked the beginning of the working week. However, in the past decade we have seen rapid technological advancements, resulting in this traditional tool becoming digitised and, therefore, integrated into specialised software that has complex dashboards that are automatically updated. Retailers now have the opportunity to create customised WSSI software that is linked to the till point systems (ePoS, or electronic point of sale) in-store and e-commerce platforms in order to gain real-time data and more accurate information. As such, the monitoring process is enhanced, with sales monitoring being updated not only in real-time, but also on a daily, if not hourly, basis. Figure 10.6 provides an example of a basic WSSI.

Week	Opening stock	Intake	Forecast sales	Actual sales	Closing stock	Weeks cover
1	26000	0	2166	0	23834	12
2	23834	0	1850	0	21984	13
3	21984	0	2300	0	19684	9.5
4	22184	2500	2500	0	19684	8
5	19684	0	2400	0	17284	8
6	19784	2500	1980	0	17804	10
7	17804	0	2675	0	15129	7
8	15129	0	3225	0	11904	5
9	11904	0	3960	0	7944	3
10	7944	0	3850	0	4094	2
11	4094	0	2300	0	1794	2
12	1794	0	1794	0	0	0

Figure 10.6   An example of a basic WSSI

Stock turn

Stock turn, as indicated by the name, measures how many times a retailer changes their stock over the duration of a year.

CALCULATING STOCK TURN

- Number of weeks in the year divided by the number of weeks of available stock;
- Example: if a retailer changes its stock every eight weeks, stock turn would be calculated as follows:

52 weeks *divided by* 8 = 6.5 stock turns per year

The fast-fashion paradigm sees stock turn over on an almost fortnightly basis, examples being H&M, which offers 12–16 collections per year, and Zara, which produces 24 lines annually (Remy et al., 2016). As such, it can be concluded that H&M is turning over stock every three to four weeks, whilst Zara is turning over stock on average every two weeks.

This is even more frequent for super-fast-fashion retailers such as Boohoo, Missguided, and In the Style. Stock turn can be calculated by the number of weeks in a year divided by the number of weeks that the stock is available. Stock turn in general determines how long retailers have to sell their products before the next product or range will be available for sale. Without regular change and update of stock, a fashion retailer becomes stale and boring, which leads to low sales and ultimately excess stock at the end of the selling season (Jackson & Shaw, 2001).

   This quick stock turnover has led to hyper consumption, in that consumers are expecting to see new things online and in-store every time they visit. As a result, manufacturers need to find ways to satisfy this fashion appetite by producing more garments and fashion lines (Hayes & Venkatraman, 2016; Henninger et al., 2016, 2019; Yan et al., 2019). A key challenge here is to provide both new lines in order to keep customers engaged with new stock, whilst at the same time keeping in-line with seasonal selling periods and trends. Understanding stock turn helps merchandisers when forecasting sales for the WSSI, as the knowledge of how long they have to sell a product for helps to determine exactly how much needs to be sold each week, what promotions are needed to support this, and when the intake needs to be organised.

Weeks cover

The final column of the WSSI contains the Weeks Cover indicator. Weeks Cover is a critical performance indicator for merchandisers. Using the information on stock turn, understanding how long a period of time the product needs to sell for, Weeks Cover provides a numerical figure that can help to understand stock performance. Weeks Cover specifies the number of weeks left for which there is enough stock available if the retailer continues to sell at the current rate (i.e. how many weeks it will take to sell out if sales continue at the current rate). Ideally the Weeks Cover rate will decrease at an acceptable rate as the selling period unfolds. Finishing on a very low number or a zero, which indicates that there is no more stock available, will mean that sales forecasting has been successful against the actual sales and that the merchandiser has been suitably reactive, managing the stock effectively.

   Failure to achieve the planned weeks cover can have a major impact on profit as the planned sales targets will not have been achieved. This, therefore, has negative financial implications coupled with a danger of excess stock carry-over, which causes issues within the retail space. Not having enough space to display the old stock due to the new ranges taking priority can often leave unsold excess stock waiting in stock rooms or distribution centres for the end-of-season sales. This can cause in-season buying with the 'open to buy' budget to be blocked because of issues with space, creating further missed sales opportunities.

OPEN-TO-BUY BUDGET

Available to spend in-season on new orders or re-buys of best sellers.

Using a WSSI

The WSSI is a working document that has live information added to it to calculate the current trading performance. Merchandisers will use the WSSI to action any recommendations or solutions required, dependent on how the products are performing. Figure 10.6 provides a breakdown of the information that is included on a basic WSSI.

Opening stock – how much available stock the retailer has to sell at the beginning of the trading week;

Closing stock – how much available stock the retailer has to sell at the end of the trading week after sales. This then becomes the opening stock for the following week;

Intake – the stock that is planned for replenishments currently stored in the distribution centre;

Forecast sales – the sales figure that the retailer predicts that it will achieve that week;

Actual sales – the actual sales figure that the retailer achieved that week;

Weeks Cover – the number of weeks that the retailer has available for the remainder of the selling period if sales continue at the same rate.

Once the trading information is added there are several formulas to apply to help calculate and review performance, the purpose of this document is to record the current trading situation in an accessible and comparable manner.

Why retailers use the WSSI

The WSSI can be used to:

- *Determine opening stock* – this information comes from the delivery schedule and is confirmed by the staff at the distribution centre once all deliveries have arrived and been checked;
- *Determine intake and forecast sales* – this information is determined by the merchandising team and may be an individual or generic amount. Product styles, consumer sales patterns, and timings, as well as the retail calendar, planned events, and occasions will influence this information;
- *Calculate closing stock* – Opening Stock (+ any Intake) *minus* Weekly Sales = Closing Stock;
- *Calculate weeks cover*: Opening Stock (+ an Intake) *divided by* Weekly Sales = Weeks Cover.

Manufacturing processes

The first part of the chapter provided an overview of the apparel pipeline, which forms a vital part of the manufacturing process from sourcing raw materials, to creating fabrics, to designing products and producing them, and finally selling them to the end-consumer.

The latter half of this chapter provides a brief overview of different production techniques that organisations may incorporate, such as lean, just-in-time (JIT), or sustainable supply chain management.

Lean manufacturing

Lean production implies that an organisation seeks to reduce 'waste', thereby enhancing efficiency, effectiveness, and profitability of the overall manufacturing process, whilst at the same time ensuring that there is no impact on the overall quality (Womack & Jones, 1994; Costa Maia et al., 2019). *Waste* here can refer to a number of different things; for example, discarding of products at any stage of the manufacturing process, such as off-cuts, damaged or faulty raw materials and/or accessories (e.g. zips, buttons), packaging materials, chemicals used in the dyeing process, or the return of unwanted sold stock that was damaged. The Six Sigma concept is often discussed in conjunction with lean manufacturing, which consists of the DMAIC guiding principles that can help an organisation to make its processes leaner:

1. *Define* – what is the source of waste within the manufacturing process?
2. *Measure* – how much of this waste is being produced and how much does it cost the company?
3. *Analyse* – what measures could be taken in order to avoid this waste being created?
4. *Improve* – implement changes based on the analysis.
5. *Control* – ensure that these changes have the effect that was anticipated by the company; waste reduction.

The DMAIC guidelines outlined here are indicative in nature and can be more detailed depending on the company's 'waste' problem. What this should illustrate, however, is that Six Sigma is a continuous process that needs to be carefully monitored and reviewed in order to ensure that the goal of waste reduction, leading towards a lean production process, is achieved.

Just-in-time

Similar to lean manufacturing, JIT seeks to reduce 'waste'. A key difference is that organisations not only seek to reduce waste in terms of overproduction, waiting times, transportation, processing, inventory, motion, and product defects, but also in terms of monetary waste from having less stock inventory. JIT is designed to increase efficiency and decrease waste by carefully calculating when products are needed. This approach further allows for flexibility in that organisations only produce what is demanded by customers. If a fast-fashion company, for example, has set up a system by which raw materials can easily switch between products, it is able to quickly respond to changes in demand. For instance, if a green cashmere jumper was manufactured, yet no longer needed as customer demand stagnated and/or declined, the company has an opportunity to change production and manufacture another product with that material; for example, a scarf. As the company does not have any stock left over in warehouses, this saves on inventory costs and at the same time enables it to respond quickly to changes in consumer demand.

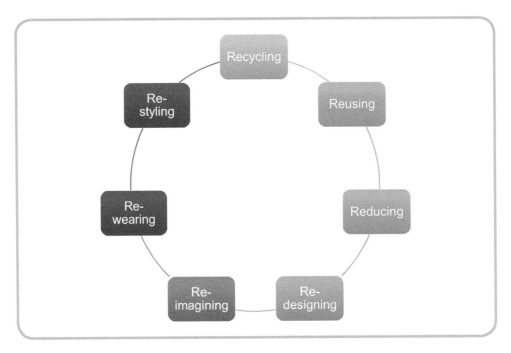

Figure 10.7 **The 7R framework (adapted from Henninger et al., 2015)**

Sustainable supply-chain management

Supply chain management is concerned with the entire the manufacturing process in that it focuses on suppliers all the way to end-users. The aim of supply chain management is to make the supply chain more efficient, which can be done through lean or JIT practices; however, these strategies predominantly centre on economic benefits (Lambert et al., 2006). This is no longer enough, as contemporary retailers should also consider their environmental and ethical impact on the world. Sustainable supply chain management additionally ensures that social and environmental concerns are addressed, which at times can be more expensive, as they require careful monitoring and more financial investment (e.g. paying living wages, purchasing environmentally friendly raw materials). Henninger et al. (2015) developed the 7R model (Figure 10.7), which highlights different aspects that companies can implement in order to reduce their environmental impact.

Critical path monitoring

As discussed in Chapter 4, the critical path is a tool that is used by buyers, merchandisers, and suppliers to map out the key stages of development, production, and delivery of products from the product-development stages to when they are launched onto the shop floor. Thus, the critical path monitors the holistic apparel pipeline. Each item in the product range will have its own critical path with its own key set of dates. This makes the process hard to manage as hundreds of products are being produced at the same

CASE EXAMPLE: THE NORTH FACE

The North Face is an American brand, which is part of the VF Corporation. The company specialises in producing high-performance outdoor apparel, equipment, and footwear and is known for its product's durability, fashionable style, and sustainable sourcing. The North Face has been accredited by the bluesign, which indicates that harmful substances are eliminated within the production process as well as in garments in more general terms, and it sets and controls standards for environmentally friendly and safe production processes (Bluesign, 2017; North Face, 2018). When applying the 7R framework to The North Face, one can see that it is implementing five of the 7Rs, namely: recycling, reducing, re-designing, re-imagining, and re-styling, whilst reusing and re-wearing are only indirectly addressed.

Company commitment

- Recycling – The North Face is part of an initiative that allows its customers to drop off their unwanted garments in order for these to be recycled, preventing them from going into landfill. Customers are motivated to participate by gaining reward points for their next purchase. Similar activities have been introduced by other retailers, such as TK Maxx and H&M (North Face, 2019);
- Reducing – through the bluesign The North Face has reduced the use of chemicals within its manufacturing process, which, as indicated, is carefully monitored;
- Re-designing – the company has redesigned its supply chain in order to be able to 'close the loop' and encourage recycling, as well as conducting more sustainable sourcing (North Face, 2019);
- Re-imagining – the products have been reimagined in that they are made to last by being more durable. As such, the focus has shifted towards longevity rather than the throw-away culture;
- Re-styling – the company is known for its style, and as such it continuously innovates in order to stay true to its image.

Consumer commitment

Without the support of the company's consumers the remaining 2Rs (re-wearing and reusing) cannot be guaranteed. It is up to the consumer base to ensure that items are worn more than just a couple of times, as well as potentially being put into the second-hand cycle, in order to allow the products to be reused.

time, all of which are at different stages with different deadlines, and they all need to end up on the shop floor at the same time. This is what makes fashion buying and merchandising particularly challenging, as critical path monitoring in other industries does not involve such a wide variety and complex set of products. Nevertheless, the fashion buying and merchandising teams use the critical path to monitor each item as it advances through the supply chain. By monitoring the items so closely through the critical path, buyers and merchandisers are able to keep in contact with where the product is up to in the supply chain, thereby minimising the risks as much as possible.

As speed is so important, the critical path enables buyers and merchandisers to see where each item is up to and how long the lead time will be. Buyers will plan out their projected critical path for each item in advance based on past experience with similar products and the same/similar suppliers. This allows them to predict when the items will be ready and the earliest time that they will be available to hit the shop floor/website and go on sale to customers. Thus, the critical path is planned out starting with the product launch date and worked backwards in order to determine by which date the product needs to go into mass production. It is important that the buyers build in some 'buffer zones' on the critical path in order to allow for any delays or issues that occur, so that they can absorb some time and not have an overall impact on the final launch date. However, if too much time is factored in then the buyer is at risk of working too far away from the season, where it is much harder to accurately forecast consumer demand. Therefore, a balance must be sought of working as close to the season (product launch date) as possible in order to have a more accurate indication of consumer demand, and having enough time for manufacturing and the delivery to the distribution centre and then the shop floor, whilst also allowing for any potential hold-ups to be absorbed along the way.

CHAPTER SUMMARY

This chapter has outlined the different manufacturing processes that are available in the fashion industry. Recently, retailers have been looking to incorporate more sustainable supply chain management practices as well as the lean and JIT methods, in order to implement the 7Rs and lessen their negative environmental impact. However, it is important to note that in the majority of cases where the retailer does not actually own its own factories, it is not in actual control of the items at this stage and has to trust that the supplier is conducting the manufacturing process in an ethical manner. Therefore, it is vital that both buyers and merchandisers are work together closely with their suppliers in order to ensure that the manufacturing process goes smoothly and that they carefully monitor the critical path, which can be impacted by a variety of events across the supply chain.

References

Alliance Project. (2017). 'Realising the growth potential of UK fashion and textile manufacturing, UK: National Textiles Growth Programme', May, LTMA, available at: www.ltma.co.uk/wp-content/uploads/2017/05/The-Final-Alliance-Project-Report-Oct-2012-to-May-2017.pdf.

Bluesign. (2017). 'About', n.d., available at: www.bluesign.com/.

BSR. (2015). 'Climate change: Implications and strategies for the luxury fashion sector', n.d., available at: www.bsr.org/reports/BSR_Kering_report_Climate_Change_implications_and_strategies_for_the_luxury_fashion_sector.pdf.

Bürklin, N., Henninger, C.E., & Boardman, R. (2019). 'The Historical Development of Social Commerce', in Boardman, R., Blazquez, M., Henninger, C.E., & Ryding, D. (eds), *Social Commerce: Consumer Behaviour in Online Environments*. London: Palgrave Macmillan, pp. 1–6.

CO Data (Common Objective Data). (2019). 'Volume and consumption: How much does the world buy', n.d., available at: www.commonobjective.co/article/volume-and-consumption-how-much-does-the-world-buy.

COMESA. (2019). 'COMESA members states', n.d., available at: www.comesa.int/comesa-members-states/.

Costa Maia, L., Carvalho Alves, A., & Pinto Leao, C. (2019). 'Implementing Lean Production to Promote Textile and Clothing Industry Sustainability', in Carvalho Alves, A., Kahlen, F.J., Flumerfelt, S., & Siriban-Manalang, A.B. (eds), *Lean Engineering for Global Development*. London: Springer, pp. 319–343.

Ecouterre. (2013). 'What does that $14 shirt from Bangladesh really cost?', n.d., available at: www.ecouterre.com/infographic-how-much-does-that-14-t-shirt-really-cost/.

Europa. (2016). 'Final minutes from the Meeting of the Civil Dialogue Group on Arable Crops 15/4/2016', n.d., available at: https://ec.europa.eu/agriculture/sites/agriculture/files/civil-dialogue-groups/arable-crops/2016-04-15/minutes.pdf.

Ferdows, K., Lewis, M., & Machuca, J.A.D. (2003). 'Zara', *Suppyl Chain Forum: An International Journal*, 4(2): 62–67.

Fletcher, K. (2018). 'The fashion land ethic: Localism, clothing activity, and macclesfield', *Fashion Practice*, 10(2): 139–159.

Goworek, H. (2007). *Fashion Buying*. 2nd ed.. Hoboken, NJ: Wiley-Blackwell.

Hayes, S.G., & Venkatraman, P. (eds). (2016). *Materials and Technology for Sportswear and Performance Apparel*. Boca Raton, FL: CRC Press.

Hendriksz, V. (2017). 'H&M accused of burning 12 tonnes of new, unsold clothing per year', FashionUnited, available at: https://fashionunited.uk/news/fashion/h-m-accused-of-burning-12-tonnes-of-new-unsold-clothing-per-year/2017101726341.

Henninger, C.E., Alevizou, P.J., & Oates, C.J. (2016). 'What is sustainable fashion?', *Journal of Fashion Marketing & Management*, 20(4): 1–19.

Henninger, C.E., Alevizou, P.J., Oates, C.J., & Cheng, R. (2015). 'Sustainable Supply Chain Management in the Slow-Fashion Industry, Chapter 6', in Choi, T.M., & Cheng, T.C.E. (eds), *Sustainable Fashion Supply Chain Management: From Sourcing to Retailing*. Heidelberg: Springer, pp. 83–100.

Henninger, C.E., Bürklin, N., & Niinimäki, K. (2019). 'The clothes swapping phenomenon – When consumers become suppliers', *Journal of Fashion Marketing & Management*, 23(3): 327–344.

International Trade Centre. (2005). 'Source-it: Global material sourcing for the clothing industry', n.d., available at: http://www.intracen.org/uploadedFiles/intracenorg/Content/Publications/prov/22_Source-It%20Global%20Material%20Sourcing%20for%20the%20Clothing%20Industry.pdf

Jackson, T., & Shaw, D. (2001). *Mastering Fashion Buying and Merchandising Management*. London: Palgrave.

Jones, R. (2006). *The Apparel Industry*. 2nd ed. Oxford: Blackwell.

Lambert, D.M., Croxton, K.L., García-Dastugue, S.J., Knemeyer, M., & Rogers, D.S. (2006). *Supply Chain Management Processes, Partnerships, Performance*. 2nd ed. Jacksonville, FL: Hartley Press.

Muthu, S.S. (2015). *Handbook of Life Cycle Assessment (LCA) of Textiles and Clothing*. Cambridge: Woodhead.

Niemeier, S., Zocchi, A., & Catena, M. (2013). *Reshaping Retail*. Chichester: John Wiley and Sons.

North Face. (2018). 'Manufacturing', n.d., available at: www.thenorthface.com/about-us/responsibility/product/manufacturing.html.

North Face. (2019). 'Recycle, reward, renew', n.d., available at: www.thenorthface.co.uk/innovation/sustainability/product/clothes-the-loop.html.

Patagonia. (2012). 'Further 2021: Greetings from Wrangell-St Elias', n.d., available at: www.patagonia.com/blog/2012/04/further-2012-greetings-from-wrangell-st-elias/.

Patagonia. (2019). 'The Footprint Chronicles', n.d., available at: www.patagonia.com/footprint.html.

Preuss, S. (2015). 'How climate change affects the luxury fashion industry', 16 November, FashionUnited, available at: https://fashionunited.uk/news/fashion/how-climate-change-affects-the-luxury-fashion-industry/2015111618343.

Remy, N., Speelman, E., & Swartz, S. (2016). 'Style that's sustainable: A new fast-fashion formula', October, McKinsey, available at: www.mckinsey.com/business-functions/sustainability/our-insights/style-thats-sustainable-a-new-fast-fashion-formula.

Rosenau, J.A., & Wilson, D.L. (2006). *Apparel Merchandising: The Line Starts Here*. 2nd ed. New York, NY: Fairchild.

Rugman, A., & Collinson, S. (2012). *International Business*. 6th ed. Harlow: Pearson.

Siegle, L. (2018). 'Destroying unsold clothes is fashion's dirty secret. And we're complicit', 29 September, *Huffington Post*, available at: www.huffingtonpost.co.uk/entry/burberry-burn-clothes-fashion-industry-waste_n_5bad1ef2e4b09d41eb9f7bb0.

Statista. (2018). 'Cotton production by country worldwide in 2017/2018 (in 1,000 metric tons)', n.d., available at: www.statista.com/statistics/595561/distribution-of-global-cotton-production-by-country/.

UNCTAD. (2009). 'Regional strategy for cotton-to-clothing value chain', June, available at: https://unctad.org/en/PublicationsLibrary/suc2017_Regional_COMESA_Strategy.pdf.

USAID. (2005). 'Integration of the ASEAN textile and apparel industry in the post-quota era', December available at: http://pdf.usaid.gov/pdf_docs/Pnadh136.pdf.

Womack, J.P., & Jones, D.T. (1994). 'From lean production to the lean enterprise', *Harvard Business Review*, 72(29): 93–105.

Yan, S., Jones, C., Henninger, C.E., & McCormick, H. (2019, in press). 'Textile Industry Insights towards Impact of Regenerated Cellulosic and Synthetic Fibres on Microfibre Pollution', in Muthu, S.S., & Gardetti, M.A. (eds), *Sustainability in the Textile and Apparel Industry*. Chams: Springer.

11 Allocation and distribution

Introduction

The allocation and distribution of ranges is a key stage within the buying cycle and crucial to stock management. Making sure that the correct products go to the right stores within the time frame given is the final but key part in the development of a range. As there are high volumes of product lines being manufactured globally, it is important they are tracked accurately during the process using the critical path document. The stock also needs to be managed and organised into a delivery schedule so that there is a transparency of all stock movement. This chapter will outline the distribution and allocation processes and discuss the challenges that merchandisers face when conducting them.

Learning outcomes

After reading this chapter you will be able to:

• Define allocation and its importance within the buying cycle and more generally within buying and merchandising;

- Define distribution and its importance within the buying cycle and more generally within buying and merchandising;
- Explain the concept of store clustering and its effectiveness in merchandise management;
- Analyse the significance of late deliveries and their impact on the buying cycle;
- Discuss the process of replenishment and the importance of sales-reactive replenishment.

Distribution

The distribution of goods is a vitally important task for merchandisers, especially due to the large presence of e-commerce retailers and the simplified shipping processes used in contemporary retailing (Koumbis, 2014). It is vital to consider a variety of elements such as location, automation, size, and online sales, which all can impact on the distribution stage of the buying cycle. Although this is one of the latter parts of the cycle, it is just as important that it runs as smoothly and effectively as the previous stages within the development of products. The efforts made by the merchandising team at this stage supports the logistics of getting the *right product* to the *right place* in the *right quantity*.

Delivery schedule

At the heart of any good fashion merchandise management system is the delivery or commitment schedule (Jackson & Shaw, 2001). The delivery schedule is a document that is regularly updated, showing what is to be delivered into a retailer's distribution centre (DC) or warehouse on a monthly, weekly, and daily basis. The document contains hundreds of garments, as well as highlighting all the global suppliers that the retailer is working with. The purpose of the delivery schedule is to aid the organisation of the distribution and allocation processes and keep track of all of the products holistically in one single place. Using the delivery schedule helps to avoid late deliveries before they happen and promotes communication between the buyer, merchandiser, and supplier regarding agreed delivery dates. Thus, the delivery schedule is critical for ensuring effective stock management. An awareness of what exactly is going to be delivered is also of key interest to the store managers and marketing team so that they can make space and organise visual merchandising in the case of the former, and organise promotional features in the case of the latter. This illustrates that the delivery schedule is key to management of both human and physical resources at different times of the season (Jackson & Shaw, 2001). The document is created, maintained, updated, and distributed via collaborative software in order to reflect the daily, weekly, and monthly deliveries for all stores. The software packages are a helpful tool for creating immediate transparency, yet it is vital to gain input from buyers and merchandisers, as intuition remains vital.

The delivery schedule needs to be flexible and is constantly adapted, as sales data and trading information will impact on the schedule. Hence, the delivery schedule will have a continuous flow of minor changes made to it (Jackson & Shaw, 2001). It is vital that the delivery schedule is flexible in order to allow for opportunities to be taken advantage of, to be reactive to delays and issues. Ultimately any lateness will equate to a loss of profits as the products are not able to fulfil their allocated selling time and may miss the peak consumer demand, as well as not being available for sale for long enough to sell the full quantity as they will need to make way for future ranges planned to reach the store at a fixed time. Fragmented deliveries are also an issue as the range will look unfinished and disjointed on the shop floor, and ultimately result in a loss of profits. Having a partial range of products available, with missing styles, colourways, or sizes, means that the product range will also not be able to reach its full potential in terms of selling. Missing the critical selling time allocated not only causes a loss in profits but also impacts on customer service as the item may not be available in the size/colour that the customer wants. As a result, consumers will purchase similar items that meet their needs/wants from competitors due to the lack of availability from the retailer. Although buyers and merchandisers can ask suppliers for discounts for late stock in order to reduce the financial impact, the real issue is the lack of products on the shop floor.

There are other possible solutions to support late deliveries according to Jackson and Shaw (2001), such as:

- *Bringing forward deliveries on bestsellers* – to fill the space or gaps that a late delivery exposes on a shop floor, buyers and merchandisers can bring forward any deliveries of bestsellers from either the same supplier or others to try and bridge the gap. However, this can be challenging and, in some cases, not always possible.
- *Pushing back deliveries on slow sellers* – this is done in order to allow for more selling time once the delayed delivery has arrived. This provides the products with the full opportunity to reach their selling potential.
- *Cancelling the outstanding balance on slow sellers or changing the style* – this can be done instead of delaying the slow-selling products if there are issues with the potential selling time. Buyers and merchandisers can cancel the order completely to save money or change the style to a more saleable one if possible.

Why are deliveries late?

Late deliveries are very frustrating for buyers and merchandisers as they will have negative financial implications. It is important not to underestimate the impact of poor deliveries (Jackson & Shaw, 2001). As the products have such a restricted window of time to sell, it is vital that lateness is kept to a minimum. As the fashion industry has become so competitive, retailers have developed a late-delivery penalty clause, meaning that suppliers who do not deliver on time are subject to fines (Jackson & Shaw, 2001). Understanding the importance of the critical path and keeping to its deadlines, even very early on in the buying cycle, can support and manage the process and, ideally, ensure that there are no late deliveries. There are many reasons why deliveries can be late, and in many cases it is the fault of several parties rather than one specific person. Below are some of the activities, events, and situations that can cause a late delivery:

- *Product not being manufactured at the planned time* – longer times spent on decision-making and order confirmation can result in a product being late for production. It is vital that decisions made during selection meetings are followed through to the pro forma and then signed purchase-order contracts. Verbal confirmation is no good; there needs to be a written paper trail and clear confirmation on forms, in order to be able to chase any late deliveries. A supplier will not start making an order, or even order the correct raw materials, without official confirmation.

- *Samples not being approved for production* – official approval of samples can cause delays. If buyers are not communicating official approvals it can hold up the manufacturing and ordering process for the production of products.
- *External delivery of fabrics and trims being late* – manufacturing of products cannot begin without raw materials. External factors and suppliers can cause this to happen even if the buyers, merchandisers, and manufacturers are all keeping to schedule.
- *Issues in manufacturing* – this can refer to any issues that occur during the manufacturing process. *Issues* can refer to problems with the work force or environment, or with the machinery used, and they are the responsibility of the supplier. For example, this could involve any sewing machines, cutting equipment, pattern machinery, or any technological elements failing to work.
- *Delays in transporting products and issues at customs* – the logistics of the garments from the suppliers to the DC can be challenged for various reasons. For instance, deliveries can be delayed once they reach customs. Therefore, it is important that communication is frequent and clear and that the critical path is monitored.
- *Weather* – the weather is an element that can never be fully predicted and can have a huge impact upon global supply chains. Deliveries will travel across the world and, regardless of the season, there can be minor or major natural disasters that will inevitably delay travelling.

Allocation

Allocation refers to the planning and managing of stock once it is received at the warehouse from the supplier, and ensuring that it ends up in the correct retail location. The allocator, a junior member of the merchandising team, is usually responsible for this role. The products are held in a central distribution warehouse and subsequently allotted to the right store, at the right time and in the right quantities in order to meet consumer demand and maximise sales for the retailer (Granger, 2015). However, the process does originate much further back through the buying cycle. For instance, Jackson and Shaw (2001) discuss the range-planning documents and how they illustrate allocations to store, and Clark (2015) says that the roots of allocation are much further back in the planning process, ultimately shaping the intellectual direction of physical stock management. Thus, considerations of allocation will initiate within the early activities (the review stages) of the buying cycle. Throughout the entire buying cycle, there will be a focus on how, where, and what garments will be allocated and distributed when retailers have a portfolio of stores. For example, the amount of product needed obviously impacts on the amount of budget required as well as the assortment of varieties that are to fill the space in-store and meet consumer demand. However, there is no 'one size fits all' when it comes to allocation and there are many different variables that will influence the allocation of stock, aspects which will also change from season to season and from range to range.

In particular, Clark (2015) identifies a number of elements that will impact on allocation considerations for product ranges:

- The retailer's business model and brand identity;
- Product type, fashionability, and different options within a range;
- In-store visual merchandising strategies and planned promotional activities;
- Assumptions of sell-through rates and sales forecasts;
- Relationships with and the flexibility of the supplier;
- Planned stock turns and phases of ranges.

When considering stock allocations there are some aspects or rules that need to be applied in order to ensure that the allocations are as accurate as possible. No two stores are the same, so this needs to be considered when allocating products, especially as the difference between the size of the smallest store and the largest in a fashion chain can be immense (Jackson & Shaw, 2001). Space allocation depends upon the relationship between retail space, sales turnover, and profitability (Goworek & McGoldrick, 2015). Furthermore, consumer purchase behaviour and product classifications will also impact on stock allocation:

- *Consumer purchase behaviour* – considerations about the target customer and how they like to shop will influence the amount of products needed within a store. In most cases, consumers will buy more tops than bottoms within a season, and women are likely to purchase more dresses over the Christmas and holiday periods. Thinking about key occasions and events and how these impact on purchase behaviour provides an indication regarding the volume of products required;
- *Product classification* – as discussed in Chapter 7, there are risks associated with certain products, which is why classifying them helps to identify the volumes that should be ordered. For example, hero products are considered risky and therefore it is important to make sure that the allocation of these products is considered in order to manage the risk as effectively as possible. On the other hand, basic and classic items are less risky and easier to measure in terms of customer demand and, therefore, may have a higher volume available per store allocation.

Store clustering

The initial allocation of product ranges is done using the store-grading system, which provides a set initial quantity per store classification. Every retailer will have its own set of specific objectives that influence how it will cluster stores and classify them; the intention is to make the allocation of products as streamlined and as simplified as possible. Dealing with only four or five variations of store classifications is much easier to manage than 150 individual stores, which is why *store clustering* is employed. Store clustering is the grouping of stores based on common store and demographic characteristics. There are two types of store clusters: performance- and non-performance-based.

Performance-based store clusters are grouped according to how they perform. For example, store locations with similar sales performances would be placed in the same store group. *Non-performance-based* clusters consider store characteristics such as climate, store size, and/or store type. Non-performance-based clusters also consider customer demographics such as ethnicity, income level, age group, and fashion preference, if applicable (Donofrio, 2009). However, this latter form of non-performance categorisation may be too complex for initial product allocation. On the other hand, it can be argued that the more you understand the type of consumer that frequents the stores, the better allocation and understanding of stock management there is within a retailer.

Effective store clustering often considers a combination of at least two types of clusters. For example, it is very common to consider both store size and sales volume together as a method of clustering. Not all retail stores are equal; large city locations may generate the greatest volume of sales, but affluent towns may contribute a higher level of profitability. When it comes to the allocation of stock, a hierarchy exists in terms of store importance. The result of good clustering is an improved ability to provide a customer-centric merchandise environment (Donofrio, 2009).

Previously, the most important store for any retailer would have been its main flagship store. This store would have received every product and would have been the priority, not only for the initial allocation of stock, but also for the replenishment of stock. Nowadays, for the majority of retailers, the most important store is the online store. This is because it commands full allocation of stock and replenishment allocations. Furthermore, online stores attract the largest number of customers, making them a priority. Stock availability is critical for the success of an online site in order to maximise sales. Frequent non-availability of product indicates poor customer service levels and is damaging to a retailer's reputation. Therefore, allocation to the online store to ensure stock availability should be a priority for the merchandising team.

The advantage of online and mobile stores is that they can be as big as the retailer wants them to be. The lack of space constraints in online and mobile retailing has created further opportunities for retailers to include more innovative designs and enhance their product mix (Varley & Clark, 2019). However, this still needs to be considered and decisions still need to be made regarding how much and what stock will be featured and how this will impact on the stock constraints in the physical stores. Retailers must offer their customers a seamless experience across all of their channels in order to satisfy them.

Store grading

After the analysis of stores at cluster level is completed, this information influences how the stores can be classified at a grade level. *Store grading* refers to the division of store portfolios into categories in order to support a simpler allocation of stock. Every retailer will use some form of store grading, some being much more complex than others. Retailers will each have their own terminology that will be continually reviewed and updated depending on trading and any changes in the business itself and in the market. Retailers commonly use sales value and store size as the basis for store grading. This allows them to group together similarly performing stores, on the basis that they should have similar ranges assorted to them (PFL, 2019).

Each store grade is dependent upon the number of stores that the retailer has and the differences between them. The grading that a store receives directly determines the amount and variety of products that are allocated to them. Using a grading system reduces the number of decisions that the retailer has to make, simplifying an already

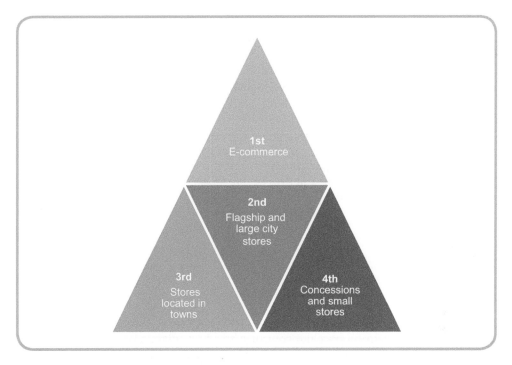

Figure 11.1   **An example of store grading**

complicated job. It allows for retailers to group similarly performing stores together on the basis that they will have the same stock and sell in a similar manner. Figure 11.1 illustrates a basic form of store grading.

Considerations for allocation

Initial allocation and store grading need to be flexible in order to maximise profits and minimise risks at all times. Merchandisers are given freedom to allocate product lines regardless of their classification status using their experience and knowledge of the market and intuition as a guide. It is crucial to exploit market potential and target the differences in consumer demand between similar types of stores. It is also important to note that store grading can change. A store can be re-graded, usually upwards if the store becomes more commercially important, in response to a new market entrant or as the result of a refurbishment, yet stores can also sometimes be downgraded if not performing well.

Size ratios

Inaccurate buying of sizes results in discounted and unsold stock and, subsequently, reduced profit. All stock is ordered and distributed according to the bestselling sizes, previous sales patterns, and target consumers. Using historical sales data helps support and manage the ordering and allocation of products. However, it is not as simple as allocating all the same sizes and amounts of a product to each store. The levels of demand of a product are really important to consider. This will vary from retailer to retailer and product to product and, in some cases, location to location. Retailers will have a standard size ratio and initial allocation quantity to use as a starting point and then consider other aspects, such as:

- *Product classification* – whether the product is a hero, fashion or classic/basic item will impact on the levels of interest and, therefore, change how much to initially allocate per store;
- *Visual merchandising and in-store promotion* – promotional activities can increase levels of interest of a product, and thus initial allocation needs to consider this;
- *Intended rates of sales* – making sure that the initial allocation reflects the forecasted sales to ensure that there is stock available during and after the higher levels of interest.

Distribution centre

Processing time in a retailer's DC is important and needs to be understood and communicated in order to help support and control stock. A DC plays a key role in the supply chain for multiple retailers and it is a vital link in the distribution channel from supplier to retail outlet or online sales. The modern-day DC varies from retailer-owned to outsourced to an external party. Each has its own set of advantages and disadvantages. The DC is highly automated and stock is carried around on conveyor systems for storage and distribution. A central control system monitors and controls the movements of the products and allows large amounts of stock to be delivered, stored, and picked by size and colour for individual branches (Jackson & Shaw, 2001).

The main functions of the DC are:

- Breaking down large bulk orders by organising and storing products ready for distribution to stores or online sales;
- Amalgamating multiple orders from various suppliers and preparing stock ready for store allocation;
- Preparing stock so that it is shop-floor-ready. Preparing stock is a process that needs to take place so that stock can go straight to the shop floor, packaging needs to be removed and products need to be hung and pressed in some cases.

A successful DC must also consider:

- *Location* – how geographically close is the DC to a retailer's outlet? This needs to be considered so that the transfer time of stock orders is as minimal as possible.
- *Technology* – does the infrastructure support the speed at which the business is required to process and deliver stock? Does it have the ability to cope with growth of retail stores and customers?
- *Logistics* – how easy and quickly can the logistics deliver and transfer products effectively?
- *Returns facilities* – are the service levels for an efficient returns facility appropriate?

Good merchandisers realise that stock hanging up in the warehouse equates to 'dead money' (Jackson & Shaw, 2001). Thus, the aim is to get the stock processed through the DC as quickly as possible.

Distribution centres and online sales

The DC is a base to fulfil website orders. Online retailing relies heavily upon the operational effectiveness of the DC and a breakdown in service, logistics, communication, and returns ability can impact on perceived brand image. Hence, stock management becomes central to the service standard of the retailer when considering online sales and, therefore, the DC plays a greater role than ever (Clark, 2015). DCs are designed to deliver within a matter of days but must also now have the ability to support returns processing and updating stock levels to give a true and accurate account of stock levels at all times. Thus, the role of the DC needs a rethink in a digitally influenced retail world. Their function has fundamentally changed because of the multichannel model, and a move towards virtual stock pools where products are procured from the most optimal part of the supply chain is tipped to be the future of stock distribution and allocation (Sillitoe, 2019). This shift will ensure that retailers are able to optimise how fast they react to consumer demand.

Issues with stock

A DC can highlight issues with stock that a merchandiser will need to consider. The merchandiser needs to be aware of these issues as they can impact sales or cause risks in potentially meeting margins. When product ranges start to sell out, naturally this leaves *fragmented stock* behind. This can be in the form of certain sizes and colours left in stores or even in the DC (Jackson & Shaw, 2001). Good stock management ensures that there is an availability of all sizes and colours of a product range where possible. It is poor customer service and can cause a loss of sales if a certain size or colour is unavailable, or only available in different retail locations. In order to combat stock fragmentation, store-to-store transfers to the more popular locations are an effective way to increase sales. Moreover, in some cases, a total stock recall of all the fragmented stock is done, in order for it to be reprocessed in the DC and then redistributed in a more balanced size and colour ratio to specific stores where the product has sold well.

Stock loss

Stock loss has a direct effect on profitability and also causes challenges with stock management and availability, as it provides inaccurate information on stock levels. There are a variety of reasons for stock loss, but the main issues are:

- Human error when accounting for stock when stock-checking;
- Damage to products, which sometimes occurs either on the shop floor or in stock rooms;
- Theft, either by employees or customers.

Replenishment

The problem of allocating inventory from a central warehouse to several locations, satisfying separate demand streams, is considered to be one of the most crucial for buyers and merchandisers, especially for companies that manage an extended network of stores (Martino et al., 2016). DCs hold any excess stock that has been allocated for replenishment. Once the initial stock allocation has been made, it is important to continue to have stock in the right place at the right time. Retailers use technology and user-defined intelligent replenishment algorithms to ensure that stock can be automatically and dynamically moved between DCs and stores. This use of technology makes it a more dependable automated process with a higher level of flexibility than previously. Nowadays a number of automatic replenishment programmes are in use. The most common type includes supplier-managed inventory and continuous replenishment programs (d'Avolio et al., 2015). These automated systems and software are vital to improving full-price sales performance, increasing profits, and providing the best-possible customer experience. Replenishment programmes can be also used in order to reduce merchandise-planning-process errors (Castelli & Brun, 2010). Although automatic replenishment is now standard for retailers with DCs, they will still have regular interventions from merchandisers (Jackson & Shaw, 2001) as the human element of decision-making is crucial for gauging the market and consumer demand.

Retailers usually aim to replenish stock at the rate in which it is sold, either with repeated items or, in some cases, new products (Goworek & McGoldrick, 2015). It is important to have a balance of just the right amount of stock in-store, as too much or too little can limit or distract the customer and the shopping experience, therefore impacting on profitability. Retailers must be able to move stock quickly between different locations, whilst also maintaining healthy warehouse stock for e-commerce orders. There are two popular ways to replenish stock in contemporary fashion retailing: *replenishment-to-pattern* and *sales-reactive replenishment* (Jackson & Shaw, 2001).

Replenishment-to-pattern

A replenishment-to-pattern system (Figure 11.2) works on the basis of a calculation of how much stock needs replenishing as a result of sales forecasts, and thus the initial allocation figure is always established (Jackson & Shaw, 2001). A pattern is programmed to reflect the forecasted sales and can be different for the various store classifications. The pattern will be reviewed each week, and if the actual sales are higher than the forecasted sales then the pattern will be adapted and increased to reflect this. Thus, if a store opens with 200 products then sells 72 across various sizes and colours, a replenishment-to-pattern system will recommend that the same 72 items are replenished, therefore establishing the initial allocation figure.

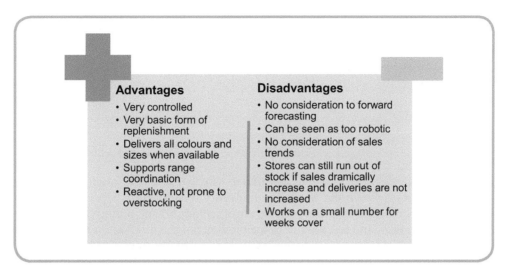

Figure 11.2 Advantages and disadvantages of a replenishment-to-pattern system

Sales-reactive replenishment

A sales-reactive replenishment system (Figure 11.3) calculates replenishment based on actual sales. Thus, this not only replaces the initial stock figure but also builds on forward demand (Jackson & Shaw, 2001). It is programmed to look at weekly sales and multiply by a key number in order to ascertain the amount needed for replenishment. The key number is the standard-practice weeks cover that the retailer uses. This method is prone to sometimes over- or under-stocking due to key seasonal events or unpredictable

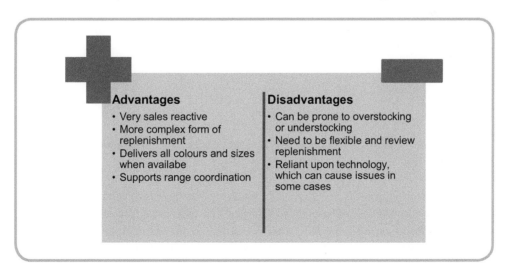

Figure 11.3 Advantages and disadvantages of a sales-reactive replenishment system

busy or quiet periods, so it is important to monitor the process carefully. Therefore, it is important to be flexible and review replenishment continuously for effective stock control. Merchandisers can alter the replenishment if there is a risk of over- or under-reacting to abnormal trading conditions.

Other considerations and influences that impact replenishment

There are many other elements that can impact whether a retailer needs to replenish more or less stock, or even not at all. The frequency of stock turn, which refers to the injection of new ranges, can remove regular stock replenishment. Some retailers choose not to replenish stock and just sell out of the product range entirely and move on to the next. This is seen more in trend-driven retailers as a strategy to encourage immediate sales with customers. This lack of replenishment takes away the issues found with regular stock deliveries but also means that the injection of new product ranges must be ready and available, particularly during unpredictable sales periods.

Regular marketing and sales promotions can change the pace of replenishment. A successful promotion that encourages additional and unexpected sales is great for business; however, it needs to be monitored in order to see the impact on stock levels and replenishment activities. The type of retailer can also impact on the style of replenishment needed or required. Value stores tend to carry more replenishment due to the nature of their strategy of having a high volume of sales. Luxury retailers, on the other hand, sell fewer items so may not replenish at all, an aspect that also promotes the exclusive nature of their brand identity.

A retail supplier's ability to resupply can also impact on the use of replenishment. If a product has been successful but there will be a delay in the resupply of the item, then replenishment is held back in order to help combat selling out of lines. Hence, replenishment is not a one-size-fits-all process; certain products need replenishment and some do not. Strategic stock management is vital to an effective business as well as a flexible approach that is reactive as well as proactive.

CHAPTER SUMMARY

This chapter has provided an outline of the last phase of the buying cycle, which focuses on distribution and allocation. As highlighted, it is important to carefully monitor allocation and distribution in order to ensure good customer service and a smooth customer experience. Previously, flagship stores have received full ranges, but the emergence of the internet has changed this, with retail websites and mobile commerce being prioritised due to their availability to all consumers and their lack of space constraints. DCs are used to manage allocations and to be able to logistically manage re-distributions if necessary, especially if mistakes may have been made or if products are selling better in one location than another, resulting in fragmented stock. Although buyers and merchandisers are supported by software and new technologies that track and monitor everything that is happening in terms of allocations and distributions, it remains vital for them to be actively involved. Even though technology can track products and provide algorithms, it cannot replace human intuition and experience. It is vital to emphasise here that the all phases of the buying cycle need to be carefully monitored through the critical path, in order to ensure that they run smoothly to avoid disappointments on the consumer side, which, in a worst-case scenario, can result in a loss of sales and profits. As such, buyers and merchandisers need to keep an eye on the critical path and develop strong relationships with their suppliers in order to avoid any hiccups in the allocation and distribution phases.

References

Castelli, C.M., & Brun, A. (2010). 'Alignment of retail channels in the fashion supply chain: An empirical study of Italian fashion retailers', *International Journal of Retail & Distribution Management*, 38(1): 24–44.

Clark, J. (2015). *Fashion Merchandising: Principles and Practices*. Basingstoke: Palgrave.

D'Avolio, E., Bandinelli, R., & Rinaldi, R. (2015). 'Improving new product development in the fashion industry through product lifecycle management: A descriptive analysis', *International Journal of Fashion Design, Technology and Education*, 8: 108–121.

Donofrio, T. (2009). 'Advanced planning and optimization, Part 3: Store clustering', 9 September, RIS, available at: https://risnews.com/advanced-planning-and-optimization-part-3-store-clustering.

Goworek, H., & McGoldrick, P. (2015). *Retail Marketing and Management: Principles and Practice*. Harlow: Pearson.

Granger, M.M. (2015). *The Fashion Industry and its Careers*. 3rd ed. New York, NY: Bloomsbury.

Jackson, T., & Shaw, D. (2001). *Mastering Fashion Buying and Merchandising Management*. London: Palgrave.

Koumbis, D. (2014). *Fashion Retailing: From Managing to Merchandising*. New York, NY: Bloomsbury.

Martino, G., Yuce, B., Iannone, R., & Packianather, M.S. (2016). 'Optimisation of the replenishment problem in the fashion retail industry using Tabu-Bees algorithm', *IFAC-PapersOnLine*, 49(12): 1685–1690.

PFL (the Planning Factory). (2019). 'A fresh look at store grading', n.d., available at: www.planfact.co.uk/a-fresh-look-at-store-grading/.

Sillitoe, B. (2019). 'Fashion retail's warehousing woes', 21 November, Drapers, available at: www.drapersonline.com/business-operations/fashion-retails-warehousing-woes/7038335. article.

Varley, R., & Clark, J. (2019). 'Fashion Merchandise Management', in Varley, R., Roncha, A., Radclyffe-Thomas, N., & Gee, L. (eds), *Fashion Management: A Strategic Approach*. New York, NY: Red Globe Press, pp. 155–174.

12 Retail sales

Introduction

Once the product range has launched on the shop floor and/or website, the buyer's and merchandiser's responsibilities are not over. The sales of the range must be monitored closely and the merchandiser must be proactive and reactive to the figures in order to maximise profits. This chapter will provide a detailed discussion of all the activities and analysis that (primarily) merchandisers conduct during the trading period, and their importance in buying and merchandising.

Learning outcomes

By the end of this chapter you will be able to:

- Explain the role and responsibilities of buyers and merchandisers during product trading;
- Explain how buyers and merchandisers monitor and react to product sales, and analyse the importance of this;

- Discuss the increasing importance of the open-to-buy (OTB) budget and how it is used by buyers and merchandisers;
- Discuss the nature, process, and purpose of re-forecasting sales;
- Explain how to calculate the sell-through rate of a product range and outline what it is used for;
- Identify when items should be marked down in price or put on promotion, and explain why the merchandiser does this.

Trading

Trading refers to the period of time that the product is available for sale to customers. Detailed planning defines the product itself, but it is trading that makes the product work to its best ability and fulfil its potential (Clark, 2015). There are many variables that can impact on trading conditions and change the original sales forecasts. Unplanned factors such as events or situations can occur, distracting customers from shopping or, alternatively, creating a demand for a certain product style. Unpredictable weather, either good or bad, can also cause trading challenges. If the weather is unseasonably hot or cold, it is likely that the products being retailed or promoted are not reflective of the weather outside, and so consumers will not want to buy them during the time that they were intended to be bought. Another challenge to trading is occurrences in the marketplace. If competitors launch promotions or events, or even new and innovative products, this can cause a distraction for consumers, and cause a loss in sales.

During the buying cycle, buyers and merchandisers spend a tremendous amount of time researching, reviewing, and planning product ranges so that they are the best and most profitable that they can be. Planning is a precise, accurate, and controlled set of activities. Trading, on the other hand, is exciting, fluid, and ever-changing (Clark, 2015). This means that buyers and merchandisers need to be reactive and proactive in order to ensure that the product ranges are still working to achieve what was intentionally planned, despite the challenging trading environment. Trading is about reviewing, adjusting, and developing actions from the original plan to maximise sales and profits. Reacting to the weekly or daily sales information is done continuously and is repeated for the duration of the season for every product. This needs to be done to ensure that gross profit is maximised and the merchandise plan is achieved. During the trading period, buyers and merchandisers monitor the sales figures alongside current social media interest, and review the forecasted sales and weeks cover in order to calculate if the products will meet their planned target and do as well as expected (Goworek & McGoldrick, 2015).

Armed with the early sales information, buyers and merchandisers will use it to inform decision-making. Indeed, even at the start of the trading period there will be some issues that need to be addressed by the buying and merchandising teams in order to maximise the potential of the range. The main aim of the trading period is that the product sells out at full price so that the planned margins can be achieved. There are some trading actions that the buying and merchandising team can use to support this process and make sure that the products reach their full potential and, therefore, maximise profits and minimise risk.

If products are selling as planned or doing better than expected, the actions that can be taken are:

- *Repeat orders or rebuys* – this involves placing an order for more of the product to be delivered as soon as possible. In some cases, this may need to be from a different supplier if, logistically or geographically (especially if in the Far East), it is not possible to order and get the product produced and delivered in time. For example, if the product range was originally produced in China, the long lead time for the delivery of the range will mean that the buyer may get a supplier from Turkey or Morocco to produce it as it can be delivered much quicker and maximise sales. The OTB budget is used for these types of orders;
- *Price review* – in some cases if products are selling too quickly, the recommended retail price (RRP) can be reviewed and increased to achieve a higher margin and slow down sales if needed. This, however, carries a lot of risk if customers notice it, and so brands/retailers must be very careful here in order to not diminish customers' trust of the brand;
- *Product transfer* – if the product is performing well in a specific set of locations, products can be transferred across from different stores and locations to make sure they are available in the most popular stores.

If products are not selling as well as planned, the actions that can be taken are:

- *Price review* – in some cases a small reduction in the RRP may be undertaken so that the product is perceived to be better value or more competitive in line with other retailers' products. This can improve sales; however, doing this needs careful consideration beforehand as it can impact on the expected margins planned for the product;
- *Promotion* – promotional campaigns, either in-store or online, can be used to drive attention to the product.

Buyers and merchandisers will also use this information in consideration of future orders or products still in production. Buyers and merchandisers will, wherever possible, try to cancel or restyle outstanding orders of poor sellers that are still due to be delivered into the business in order to make them more profitable (Jackson & Shaw, 2001).

Open-to-buy budget

Open to buy refers to the budget that is available to spend during the trading season on new orders or rebuys of bestsellers in the same or an additional colour. Merchandisers control the overall budget that is necessary to deliver the product assortment and ensure that there is a proportion allocated for in-season buying (OTB). The proportion allocated to the OTB budget is dependent on how much in-season reactive buying a retailer does. OTB provides buyers with the ability to be reactive during trading and, therefore, have more control over product options and ideally increase and maximise profits. For instance, if an unexpected, popular fad item takes the market by storm, buyers can quickly order it using the OTB budget, and thus capitalise on consumer demand and maximise profits. The increase in more fluid selling seasons and changing trends means that buyers are being much more reactive than ever to consumer demands and needs, and adding additional products in-store and online throughout the selling season. OTB is an important factor in catering for today's educated consumers who have increased expectations of retailers (Goworek & McGoldrick, 2015). Controlling the OTB is the responsibility of the merchandiser, who must ensure that the budget is split accordingly and appropriately. The following aspects need to be considered and reviewed in order to do this effectively:

- *Retail calendar* – merchandisers must review what time in the retail calendar the current trading season is in, and what other events or occasions may be coming up;
- *Trading conditions* – merchandisers must review how well the market is doing overall as it is important to understand their competitors' activities and successes as well as their own trading performance;
- *Levels of demand* – understanding what the target consumers want and need, then balancing that with time scales of orders and lead times.

However, in most super-fast-fashion, pureplay retailers, a smaller percentage of product assortments and ranges are planned ahead of the season and there is a much larger focus on reactive buying in-season using the OTB. Indeed, over the last decade the allocation of the OTB budget for fast fashion, and especially super-fast-fashion retailers, has increased significantly to reflect the shift to more demand-driven fashion sales. In some cases, such as with super-fast fashion pureplay retailers, the OTB can now make up to 60 per cent of the overall budget for the season, whereas in the past it would typically been around 20–30 per cent. This requires a more flexible approach to the control of OTB than there has traditionally been. Having a flexible and fluid approach to the use of OTB is certainly beneficial for these business types.

An OTB budget also gives buyers and merchandisers the opportunity to delay committing completely to product ranges or innovative products if there is any uncertainty. The use of the OTB budget means that buyers and merchandisers can wait and see the initial sales, and analyse consumer reaction to the products from social media channels, online, and in-store before ordering higher quantities of it. However, in order to be able to use the OTB budget effectively, there must be a strong and reliable buyer–supplier relationship in place and trust in the supplier to manufacture and deliver stock at a quick rate. This usually means that the manufacturers that supply the OTB orders are closer in location to the retailer so have much quicker lead times when transporting the finished orders. However, the consequence of a more immediate availability and speedy delivery is that the margin made on the items may be lower. Yet, because there is more certainty that demand will be strong for these items, the margin may be lower but the level of product sell-through at full price will be higher. Therefore, the level of markdown is lower and so the final margin will compensate for the higher cost price.

Re-forecasting sales

Prior to the range launch, merchandisers predict how successful it will be and how many sales it will make each week, during the process of sales forecasting. Once trading and actual sales are coming in, the merchandiser will then conduct the re-forecasting process. Hence, merchandisers will re-forecast their original sales forecast in order to create a more accurate sales forecast each week based on real data (sales figures) and actual consumer demand. This provides as accurate an indication of sell-through rate as possible and aids merchandisers in their decision-making about how to react to the sales. The variable and changing sales pattern of fashion products make it essential that re-forecasting occurs. There are planned and unplanned factors that will affect the original sales forecast (and subsequent re-forecasts), meaning that it is impossible to set a plan that is wholly accurate. Being reactive and proactive is vital to the success of fashion retailers today; buyers and merchandisers need to ensure that they take advantage of the opportunities and manage the liabilities.

Buyers and merchandisers will use the actual sales data in two main ways:

- Re-ordering of best sellers and purchase of new products using the trading performance of other products as an indication of demand;
- Markdowns of slow sellers to clear stock and reduce any concerns of overstocking. Using promotional markdowns and planned markdowns are some of the ways to increase sales and manage sales traffic as much as possible.

The WSSI (Weekly, Sales, Stock, and Intake; see Chapter 10) becomes a changing and flexible document once trading begins as the Actual Sales column becomes populated with data Merchandisers will compare this figure to the Forecast Sales information and use this to re-forecast accordingly. The Weeks Cover reflects a true indication of performance and can be used to aid decision-making for that particular week. In some cases, immediate action will need to ensue, whereas in others, further review or discussions with suppliers may need to happen. Thus, re-forecasting is concerned with being reactive and having a selection of actions that can support that process.

Figure 12.1 illustrates a basic WSSI with forecast sales and actual sales and the rationale for re-forecasting and actions considered.

Promotional activities

Promotions occur nearly all year round when trading in fashion retailing, some of which are very subtle and open to all customers, whereas others are much more personalised and targeted. Sales promotions are used as an incentive for customers to purchase immediately. They are a well-used tactic to get the customer to buy now, rather than tomorrow, next week, or next month.

Promotions can be price-reduction-related, such as a percentage off, or a 3-for-2 incentive, or they could just involve a campaign to draw attention to a particular product or style to gain more sales. Promotions often use key events and occasions in the retail calendar, such as Christmas partywear in December or active wear in January in order to appeal to consumers and show that retailers' items will meet their current needs. Social media is a key promotional tool, especially when combined with celebrity endorsement and influencer marketing to advertise products to widen the reach. Unlike celebrities who are established public figures through traditional media, social media influencers use the same channels for information exchange and relationship-building

Week	Opening stock	Intake	Forecast sales	Actual sales	Closing stock	Weeks cover	Sales analysis
1	26000	0	2166	2469	23531	10.5	Product launch very successful, increase in sales demand need to consider WC and rebuys where applicable
2	23531	0	1850	1979	21552	12	Performing better than forecast, issues with WC, discuss rebuys with suppliers and potentially review price points of bestsellers
3	21552	0	2300	6141	15411	3.5	Potential sell-out, Intake planned for week 4 will increase stock availability, rebuy order of best sellers to be delivered asap. Promotion considerations to maximise opportunity for more sales
4	17911	2500	2500	3325	14586	5	Intake increased stock levels, sales slowed slightly but still more than forecast, potential promotion planned for week 6, rebuy delivery of 3000 products for week 7 confirmed
5	14586	0	2400	3192	11394	4.5	Sales are consistent, still higher than forecast, original intake still planned for week 6 and rebuy deliver week 7 to increase stock levels
6	13894	2500	2633	4029	9865	3.5	Intake increased stock levels, reactive promotion of complimentary products launched to support outfit selling, Increased sales, potential sell-out due to new and planned promotions. Further discussions with suppliers for rebuy orders in week 9 and 10
7	12865	3000	4568	4500	8365	3	Planned holiday promotions begin – holiday outfit promotion plus celebrity social media promotion equals high sales as per previous week, rebuy delivery of 3000 products for week 9 confirmed
8	8365	0	3225	3500	4865	2	Planned May Day Bank Holiday promotion, rebuy delivery of 1500 products for week 10 confirmed
9	7865	3000	3960	4030	3835	2	Bank holiday, high sales as expected, deliver of rebuy balances WC
10	5335	1500	3850	3900	1435	1	Planned festival promotion and discount, 1500 intake to aid promotions and increased sales. WC is low although coming to end of selling time. Investigate stock transfer
11	4015	2580	2000	2560	1455	1.5	Planned promotions still running, stock transfer to relocate stock to popular stores for final promotion
12	1455	0	1158	1400	55	0	Bank holiday promotion, high sell-trough rate of product

Figure 12.1 An example of a basic WSSI with re-forecasting

as consumers. Thus, they are perceived to be 'regular people' or 'grassroots individuals' who happen to be online celebrities through their creation and posting of personalised content on social media (Lou & Yuan, 2019). This leads to consumers' higher acceptability levels and trust towards influencers' opinions (Xiao et al., 2018), and so collaborating with them is a very effective way for brands to promote their products. The rise in social media platforms also helps brands to build a fan base that can be used to form engagement and a dialogue concerning many things, but specifically regarding popular product options and styles. Using social media has, therefore, become a strategic tool for retailers and brands to encourage sales and drive customers to purchase promoted products. Furthermore, products are now often developed in reaction to products showcased on social media. Thus, social media has now become an effective tool for the merchandising team to enhance a product's performance, maximise opportunities, and minimise liabilities.

Markdown

Unfortunately, no matter how successful a buying and merchandising team are, there are always some products that do not sell. *Markdown* refers to a sale, a way for the retailer to promote a reduction in prices and reduce unwanted stock. It is important to remember that whilst it allows a retailer to decrease any overstocking, the markdown means that the business will make less profit overall, as reductions in the RRP impact on the planned gross margins for the products.

Markdowns can vary from 10–50 per cent; generally a higher markdown percentage is symbolic of poor sales performance. The WSSI helps merchandisers see the poor sellers and plan for the markdown. Although avoiding markdowns is much more favourable, they are often unavoidable as customers expect sales to happen, especially at key points in the year. It is the law of nature that markdowns will be required to manage stock levels within a fashion business; no buyer or merchandiser can predict with 100 per cent certainty every potential transaction within a season (Clark, 2015).

There are different two primary types of markdown: *permanent* and *point of sale promotion*. Each one has their merits and challenges for a merchandiser.

MARKDOWNS

Reducing products by 50 per cent means that retailers will need to sell over three times as many items in order to achieve the original overall profit planned.

1. *Permanent markdown* – this type of markdown means that the price is reduced permanently. Generally, this is a planned sale as part of the retail calendar, such as mid-season sales and end-of-season sales, such as Boxing Day sales. These prices are changed on the retailer's main electronic point of sale (ePoS) system and

automatically reduced at the till point. Whilst this type of sale is expected from the customer and can drive high volumes of attention and activity, it is not favoured by merchandisers when considering profits. In particular, the latter stage of the sale, the clearance markdown, is very costly for the retailer, with the power to wipe out any profits generated during the full-price selling season. Permanent markdown is, therefore, limited to main sale periods, or when a product is no longer in line with trends, requiring it to be withdrawn from a range (Clark, 2015).

2. *Point of sale promotion* – this type of markdown is a temporary promotion during a set period of time. It can be an unplanned and reactive strategy used to help improve the performance of slow sellers or increase sales on certain lines. These markdowns tend not to be programmed into the ePoS systems, and are changed by the salesperson in-store or via the customer using a discount code. An example of this type of markdown is 20 per cent off for a 24-hour period. The application of a PoS markdown can be used to tactically increase market share, overcome short-term stock issues, or increase cash profit (Clark, 2015) (Figure 12.2).

Markdowns and promotions are an effective tool for successful stock management and, if used strategically, they can enhance the performance of products and ranges (Clark, 2015). Trading is concerned with refinement and adjustment, and its effectiveness relies upon these activities (Clark, 2015).

Sell-through

Sell-through is an important statistic that can be used to see the products that are liabilities as well as the areas of opportunity. The term is seen as a percentage used as a measure of performance. Sell-through is the calculation of products sold against the products received, and allows retailers to see how well a product is performing. Thus, sell-through is used to determine the success of a product and is mostly used when products are at full price.

Minimise risk	Maximise profits
Rids retailers of the potential worst sellers	Reactive to consumer demand
Increases sell-through rate, although a reduced selling price will reduce margin achieved	Encourages immediate purchasing
Helps reduce weeks cover to a more manageable rate	Encourages best sellers' sales
Make way for next stock phase, eliminating overstocking	

Figure 12.2   How markdowns and promotions can minimise risk and maximise profits

SELL-THROUGH

Sell-through = Units Sold *divided by* Units Received (*multiply by* 100 to give you a percentage).

For example, if you sold 70 units, divided by 100 units received, the sell-through = 0.7

(*multiply by* 100 to give you a percentage) = 70 per cent.

Sell-through is 70 per cent

But what do these figures mean?

It is important to analyse the sell-through rate and understand what may have affected its performance. Figure 12.3 illustrates a breakdown of the different percentages and how they may be perceived. Although this is a typical illustration of sell-through, each retailer will have its own set of parameters to measure what is a good or bad sell-through rate.

A sell-through rate of 100 per cent clearly indicates that the product was forecast successfully, accurately priced, of high quality, and accurate in terms of fit, as well as appropriately matching customer demand. However, a 100 per cent sell-through rate poses the question: *could more products have been sold?*

To calculate this information in order to help with forward planning, how many weeks it took to achieve a 100 per cent sell-through rate will be analysed.

SELL-THROUGH CALCULATION

Multiply the average weekly sales in units by the desired selling period.

For example, if 12 units sold weekly: 12 *multiplied by* the desired selling period of 20 weeks = 240 units

Sell-through rate	
70% or below	This product needs improvement. Overall buy quantity too high, selling in the wrong store locations, priced too high, poor fit and quality
Around 80%	This product is considered good
Around 90%	This product is considered great
Around 100%	This is something all retailers want to achieve, however, was enough product purchased? could more have been sold?

Figure 12.3   Breakdown of sell-through figures

This formula can be used to calculate how many items should have been bought (in terms of quantity) to help plan for future product ranges or repeat orders. This figure is used in the post-mortem report and will inform future planning. Sell-through helps to show retailers at a glance what the bestselling products are, products that have a potential opportunity for increased sales, rebuys, and additional or similar products. It also highlights the poor-selling products, the liabilities, the products that need to be effectively managed with markdowns and promotions to ensure they reach the intended sales forecast and do not impact overall profits. Figure 12.4 illustrates a breakdown of products with sell-through rates and an analysis of the rates, with potential things to consider for future planning.

Returns

Having an online store now seems a compulsory outlet for all major brands and, for pure-play brands, the preferred way to sell. Consumers browse online stores without having the ability to try on products before making a purchase. Thus, online retailing channels limit the full evaluation of garment criteria (Reid et al., 2016). Thus, even with the increased technological advancements to improve product-fit awareness, unfortunately the lack of fitting rooms coupled with increased consumption rates of consumers leads to higher levels of returns. It has been highlighted that online returns expected to cost

Product	Units received	Units sold	Sell-through rate	Rate analysis
0000864721 Grey Maxi Dress	5790	5368	92.7%	Rate is considered very good, forecasting and volumes were calculated and reflected in the demand
000567238 Black Jersey Polo Neck	4570	3357	73.4%	Rate is considered good but needs improvement. Things to consider: • Quantity too high? • Selling in wrong store locations? • Launched too early/late? • Priced too high? • Is there a high returns rate?
000067352 Tweed Trousers	3490	2199	63%	Rate considered a poor seller and needs significant improvement Things to consider: • Quantity too high? • Selling in wrong store locations? • Launched too early/late? • Priced too high • Issues with quality and fit? • Is there a high returns rate?

Figure 12.4 **Sell-through example with rate analysis**

the fashion industry £5.6 billion over the next five years (Geogheagan, 2018). Customers could potentially change their minds once they see and feel the physical garment, as well as a multitude of other reasons for returns such as fit, quality, and over-ordering of multiple styles and sizes. A returns policy is a priority for all retailers and brands from a logistical and financial viewpoint. For multichannel retailers, when consumers buy online and return to a store, this causes a continuous imbalance in stock levels, which needs to be monitored and managed effectively. Therefore, retailers need an efficient reverse logistics supply chain, to allow returned products to flow backwards from the customer to a point where they can be resold or processed if faulty (Clark, 2015). Unwanted parcels put a £60-billion-a-year squeeze on stores as the average returned purchase in the UK passes through seven pairs of hands before it is listed for resale (Ram, 2016). Furthermore, when stock is returned, it can lose a percentage of its value due to customer damage. However, this dilution in stock value can be minimised by reducing the lead time for the return.

Moreover, returns cause challenging issues with stock management, as they can influence and misinterpret the understanding of how well products are performing. This is particularly challenging for buyers that work in-season and purchase large proportions of the product assortment when trading. Online fashion purchases often include multiple items of similar sizes, shapes, or colours, so-called 'intentional returns', when customers deliberately over-order, knowing that returns are free or cheap, in order to try the items on at home and ensure that they get the right item in terms of fit and style (Ram, 2016). Recently, retailers have also become victims of the concept of 'wardrobing', whereby a customer buys an item, gets a photo of them wearing it for social media (just in their house or garden), and then returns it. Some retailers have tried to combat this issue by including large tags on the front of items that, once removed, mean that the item can no longer be returned. Thus, the management of stock and analysis of sales is not always accurate as there is a constant threat that a percentage of the sold items will be returned. Merchandisers need to bear this in mind when reacting to sales. This creates concerns with the stock turnaround and availability of products for resale, an aspect that is particularly challenging for seasonal stock with short selling periods. Hence, returns have provided merchandisers with an additional stock element to control and react to as part of their job role. Returns that are no longer saleable will impact on the overall margin, therefore diminishing profits for the retailer. As a result, some retailers are starting to act against serial returners, blocking them from future purchases.

Flexible and agile trading

The activities that take place during trading are just as crucial to the product performance as the early stages in the buying cycle, despite taking less time overall. Being flexible and agile during the trading period will facilitate more effective stock management. In-season reactive buying enables stock to reach the target customer as intended and retailers to act upon the opportunities that present themselves during trading. Quick reactions to trends and product options that appear during the season ensure that there are no missed opportunities for a retailer. This analysis and reaction to sales and trends during the trading period is fast becoming an additional responsibility of the buying and merchandising teams. Thus, although accurate planning, precise and informed decision-making, and valuable research and analysis are crucial to the product-development process, the reactive actions of buyers and merchandisers during the trading season are just as valuable.

CHAPTER SUMMARY

This chapter has provided a detailed overview of the buyer's and merchandiser's roles and responsibilities when a product range is trading. The sales of the range must be monitored closely and the merchandiser must be proactive and reactive to the figures in order to maximise profits. Forecasted sales will be compared to actual sales figures and the sell-through rate of the range calculated. The merchandiser will then re-forecast the upcoming sales figures based on the information that has come in, with some items going on promotion or into markdown in order to increase the sell-through rate. Simultaneously, the merchandiser will replenish any bestsellers in order to capitalise on their success, and use the OTB budget to order any key items that are missing in the range, such as unexpected trends or fads, in order to maximise profits. It is key to highlight that although there are a variety of tools available (e.g. the WSSI) that make buyers' and merchandisers' jobs 'easier' in predicting sales, current consumer practices of ordering multiple sizes and styles with the intention of returning a majority of them makes it increasingly challenging for buyers and merchandisers to accurately predict 'actual' sales figures and identify potential bestsellers. As such, a buyer's and merchandiser's experience is vital in being able to react to changes as accurately as possible and be proactive in the trading period.

References

Clark, J. (2015). *Fashion Merchandising; Principles and Practices*. Basingstoke: Palgrave.

Geogheagan, J. (2018). 'Online returns to hit £5.6 billion', 14 December, Drapers, available at: www.drapersonline.com/7033625.article.

Goworek, H., & McGoldrick, P. (2015). *Retail Marketing and Management: Principles and Practice*. Harlow: Pearson.

Jackson, T., & Shaw, D. (2001). *Mastering Fashion Buying and Merchandising Management*. London: Palgrave.

Lou, C., & Yuan, S. (2019). 'Influencer marketing: How message value and credibility affect consumer trust of branded content on social media', *Journal of Interactive Advertising*, 19(1): 58–73.

Ram, A. (2016). 'UK retailers count the cost of returns', 27 January, *Financial Times*, available at: www.ft.com/content/52d26de8-c0e6-11e5-846f-79b0e3d20eaf.

Reid, L.F., Ross, H., & Vignali, G. (2016). 'An exploration of the relationship between product selection and engagement with "show rooming" and "web rooming" in the customers decision making process', *International Journal of Business and Globalisation*, 17(3): 364–383.

Xiao, M., Wang, R., & Chan-Olmsted, S. (2018). 'Factors affecting YouTube influencer marketing credibility: A heuristic-systematic model', *Journal of Media Business Studies*, 15(3): 188–213.

13 The impact of sustainability on fashion buying and merchandising

Introduction

With widespread media attention on the negative impact that the fashion industry is having on the environment in recent years, sustainability can no longer be ignored by retailers. Consumers are putting more pressure on fashion retailers to show how they are incorporating sustainability into their business model and have more transparent supply chains. As such, this chapter focuses on the impact of sustainability on the fashion industry and its importance in fashion buying and merchandising. An overview of fast fashion will be provided, highlighting the challenges that are faced in the industry before moving onto explaining how slow fashion emerged. The chapter will outline the definition and meaning of sustainability and why this needs to be considered in contemporary fashion retailing. The chapter will also discuss the impact that sustainability has had on the roles of fashion buyers and merchandisers.

Learning outcomes

By the end of this chapter you will be able to:

- Define and critically evaluate what sustainability entails;
- Discuss the key events that have resulted in sustainability being addressed and incorporated by the fashion industry;
- Examine key sustainability issues that impact on the role of the buyer;
- Examine key sustainability issues that impact on the role of the merchandiser.

From fast fashion to slow fashion

The contemporary fashion industry is global and has an impact on everyone. Whether people are directly or indirectly employed by the industry, such as those that produce or sell garments, those that are responsible for the make-up of models on the catwalk, or simply consumers of garments – it is an industry that concerns everyone. However, it is only in recent times that this ubiquitous industry has received more scrutiny. To provide an example, a buzz phrase of 2018, especially within the fashion sector, was 'microplastic fibres', which are tiny strands of fabrics released from synthetic fibres, such as acrylic, polyester, and nylon (Messinger, 2016; Blanchard, 2018). Although the microplastic issue is not new per se, with Browne et al. (2011) raising key concerns about plastic debris of all sizes increasingly accumulating on shorelines globally, it seems that the fashion industry and governmental organisations are only now slowly catching up on the issue. According to reports, microfibres account for 85 per cent of human-made debris found on our shorelines (Messinger, 2016). Simply washing a fleece jacket can account for 1.7 grams of microfibres, with a full load releasing up to 1,900 tiny strands that are too small to be caught in waste water facilities (Browne et al., 2011; Blanchard, 2018). Microplastics are not only released from virgin materials, but also recycled ones, which makes seemingly 'sustainable' solutions non-alternatives. T-shirts, for example, that are made from recycled plastics help to reduce large plastic waste items and reduce the use of oil needed to create virgin plastics, yet the newly spun fibre releases these tiny threads that are causing increasing environmental damage (Pirc et al., 2016). Companies of all sizes as well as governmental institutions are, therefore, investing in developing innovative solutions that provide a real alternative to synthetic fibres. For instance, some ground-breaking materials that can now be used to create garments were presented at the Sustainable Angle's Future Fabrics Expo, such as coffee grounds, orange, and apple peels (Sustainable Angle, 2018).

A further concern that has emerged with the development of online-only (pureplay) retailers is the 'death of the high street'. The internet has changed the way we shop. Whilst people may have gone to the high street only a couple of years ago to try on clothes, today the number of people shopping online is increasing each year as it not only saves time, but can also be less stressful and cheaper. Not having to pay for a brick-and-mortar store, as well as training sales assistants on the shop floor, implies reduced costs for retailers that can be translated into reduced garment prices. However, this can have devastating consequences, with over 5,855 stores closing their doors in 2017 in the UK alone, which results in job losses and seemingly deserted high streets (Butler, 2018). Shop closures can also impact on the supply chain – if companies can no longer attract customers and fail to make up their losses in online sales, it may lead to business insolvency and a total production stop affecting those individuals producing garments. This will be further investigated in this chapter.

Some of the negative reports dominating the media surrounding the fashion industry can be explained by understanding the underlying structures of the fashion industry, including what is meant by *fast* and *slow* fashion, as well as the issues and challenges associated with each of the different paradigms.

Fast fashion

We live in a world that is dominated by two polar opposite fashion paradigms: *fast fashion* and *slow fashion*. Fast fashion is often characterised as products and accessories that are cheap, mass-produced, fashionable, have a fast stock turnaround, and 'mimic current luxury fashion trends' (Joy et al., 2012, p. 273). As suggested by the name, fast fashion has, compared to slow fashion, increasingly shorter product life cycles whereby new clothing collections are introduced into the store on average every two to three weeks, which means approximately 20 fashion lines per annum (BSR, 2012), or even every week now in the case of some pureplay retailers such as Boohoo, Pretty Little Thing, Missguided, and ASOS.

Fast fashion	Slow fashion
• Cheap; • Mass-produced; • Fashionable; • Trend-influenced; • Fast turnover.	• Medium to high price; • Low to limited availability of items; • Less trend-influenced; • Slow turnover; • Empowers workers.

Gupta and Gentry (2018) have referred to fast fashion as a *retail strategy*, thereby highlighting the fact that fashion organisations/retailers have managed to adapt their supply chains in a way that allows them to produce on-trend garments in a quicker and more responsive manner than some of their counterparts. In order to do so, fast-fashion retailers have developed a careful 'net' of manufacturers in close proximity to their headquarters to produce more trend-led pieces, whilst also working together with factories further afield, such as Asia and the Middle East for more cost-effective basic/classic items (this is discussed in more detail in Chapter 8).

AGILITY

Drivers of an agile supply chain:

• Speed;
• Cost;
• Efficiency.

The agility of an organisation implies that it can respond quickly to changes in demand (volume and variety).

Understanding the shift of production patterns is vital in order to facilitate an *agile* supply chain and ensure that products are manufactured at a price and quality that is aligned with the company's strategy. To illustrate the complexities and impacts of fast fashion further within a *volatile market* environment, Zara is used as a case example.

VOLATILE MARKET

• Implies that preferences can change quickly;
• Companies need to be able to adapt quickly to changes in supply and demand.

CASE EXAMPLE: ZARA

A prime example of a fashion retailer that has pioneered the fast-fashion phenomenon since the 1980s (Reuters, 2018) is Zara. Zara was one of the first companies to perfect its supply chain to be able to create a five-week turnaround across its design-to-retail cycle, and thus provide customers with new fashion lines on a fortnightly basis (Petro, 2012). Zara has been able to achieve this by designing all of its products through its in-house teams (Ferdows et al., 2003). Further information on supply chain management and manufacturing can be found in Chapter 10.

Zara uses an agile supply chain. As a reminder, *agile* implies that an organisation is flexible and can adapt to change, which is vital in a volatile market environment such as the fashion industry (Christopher, 2000). In the case of Zara, 65 per cent of its production is based in close proximity to its headquarters. This implies that manufacturers are not only speaking in the same language, but are also located in the same time zone, which makes the communication process easier and faster. For example, fabric swatches and prototypes can be delivered fast and changes made fairly quickly as the (physical) distance between the manufacturer and organisation is short. This is especially important for buyers, who are responsible for selecting items for forthcoming collections, thereby also closely liaising with design teams. Thus, if design teams are located in-house, collaborations with buyers are often less 'challenging' as communication is quicker, as opposed to when design teams are outsourced.

The close proximity of manufacturers further implies that Zara guarantees that its products can be delivered within one working day to any of its stores globally, as all of its products are centrally distributed through its distribution facility in La Coruña, Spain (Weinswig, 2017). This impacts on the role of the merchandiser, who focuses on delivering the products to the end-consumer. If lead times can be guaranteed, advertising campaigns can be started in advance and thus increase awareness for the target market.

Zara has managed to successfully make its lead times shorter with 50 per cent of its product manufacturers being located in Spain, and the remaining manufacturers predominantly located in geographically close locations across Europe (e.g. Portugal) and Morocco, with some in Asia. Basic products are mainly produced in the latter area, as the designs generally do not change dramatically and a clear cost advantage exists (Ferdows et al., 2003). It can be concluded that Zara has managed to improve not only its design-to-retail cycle in the sense that communication flows quicker and response times are enhanced, but also its infrastructure enables Zara to design, source, make, and deliver new collections in a very short time frame.

However, Zara's former avant-garde position as a fast-fashion leader with short turnaround times is currently being challenged by *pureplay* retailers such as Missguided and Boohoo.

> **PUREPLAY**
>
> Company that invests its resources in only one line of business, e.g. online.
> Examples: Boohoo, ASOS, Amazon.

These new online-only businesses have moved the fashion industry into a new area, that of super-fast fashion. Missguided and Boohoo both have managed to establish a supply chain that allows for lead times to be shortened even further, and are thereby able to provide design-to-retail creations within an average of 1.5 weeks (FashionUnited, 2017). This links to a key challenge that will be discussed later in this chapter, concerning an increasing fashion appetite from the consumer side. Consumers are increasingly expecting fast fashion cycles as we have a growing demand for immediacy.

As discussed in Chapter 8, these super-fast-fashion retailers have tightly streamlined their supply chains as much as possible in order to minimise lead times and get the product from idea to online as quick as possible. In order to do so, they are using a multimodal sourcing strategy, whereby garments are produced both in low-cost countries off-shoring and those situated closer to the headquarters (near-shoring or even re-shoring). Furthermore, these pureplay super-fast-fashion retailers have very short lead times because they do not have to be distributed centrally to a multitude of stores, but rather can be stored in warehouses and sent out directly to the customers via their distribution centres. This has huge implications on the role of a merchandiser who is heavily involved in the store allocation process, as discussed in Chapter 11.

Whilst there are positive aspects associated with fast fashion, as consumers gain more choice and are able to make purchases more frequently, increased agility in the supply chain and the reduced cost of garments come at a price. Key questions that need to be raised here are: *What is the true cost of fast fashion? Why do we care about sustainability? And why is it an important issue for anyone looking to get into buying and merchandising?* These questions are addressed in the next section of this chapter.

Sustainability in the fashion industry

In order to address these questions it is vital to understand what sustainability entails. *Sustainability* is neither a new phenomenon, nor does it have a clear-cut definition (Epstein, 2008; Miller, 2013). However, one aspect of sustainability is agreed upon: it is seen as a positive construct, vital for future development within any society (Allen & Hoekstra, 1994; Athwal et al., 2019; Gigliotti et al., 2019). Sustainability is a fuzzy concept that is intuitively understood by people and organisations, yet it is hard to define. The most commonly cited definition of the term was brought forward by the Brundtland Commission, which states 'meeting the needs of the present without compromising the ability of future generations to meet their needs' (WCED, 1987). This report highlights the commitment to sustainability and the idea of having eco-friendly economic growth, which would have been an impossibility during the 1970s, as technology and innovation processes were not as advanced as they are today. *Eco-friendly economic growth* implies using advanced technologies, thereby reducing waste materials within the production process and overall carbon emissions – an aspect that can be seen as being of vital importance in regard to the sourcing of materials, and thus the role of the buyer. We will return to this in more detail later in the chapter.

SUSTAINABILITY

Considers three key areas: economic, environmental, and social sustainability. The more overlap between the three areas, the 'greater' level of sustainability achieved.

Although the Brundtland Report provides a valuable working definition of sustainable development, it has been described as limited (e.g. McClonskey, 1999; Robert et al., 2005), as it was written as part of a governmental report, and therefore predominantly centres 'only upon human needs […][and sees] economic growth [as a] necessar[y] part of development' (Diesendorf, 2000, p. 21). This implies that the natural environment dimension is not explicitly addressed in the report (Von Schomberg, 2002). A further key criticism of the Brundtland Commission's definition is the fact that it is ambiguous in nature, as forecasting what future generations need may be impossible with new technologies changing the norms of everyday life. Diesendorf (2000) builds upon the Brundtland Commission's definition by honing in on the environmental aspect: 'sustainable development comprises types of economic and social development which protect and enhance the natural environment and social equity' (p. 22). Whilst this interpretation is overarching in nature, the Brundtland Commission's understanding of the concept as a more political entity (and despite its limitations) has gained increasing importance and to date remains the most cited definition (Baumgartner, 2009; Nunan, 2011; IISD, 2019).

Following on from the Brundtland Report, the Earth Summit in 1992 in Rio de Janeiro saw environmental protection as a key issue that needed to be integrated on a global scale, through promoting sustainable development (Mitchell, 1995; Erskine & Collins, 1997). The introduction of Agenda 21 was a direct result of this summit and provides a blueprint towards sustainable development that was adopted by the world leaders attending the conference, on a voluntary, non-binding basis (FAO, 2007; UNEP, n.d.). 'Agenda 21 provides a comprehensive action programme to attain sustainable development and address both environmental and developmental issues […] at global, national, and local levels' (FAO, 2007).

The Triple Bottom Line (TBL), which is usually portrayed as a Venn diagram, sees the environmental, social, and economic areas overlap; with the overlapping area classified as sustainable. The TBL expands on the Brundtland Report's (WCED, 1987) definition of sustainability, by incorporating an environmental component to the predominantly political definition (Elkington, 2004). Using this approach implies that companies are not simply looking at financial aspects (Norman & MacDonald, 2004), but also focusing on environmental and social performance (Raar, 2002; Roper & Fill, 2012). The TBL is also often referred to as *profit, people, and planet.*

Although the TBL has been widely accepted and implemented by academics and practitioners alike (Holmberg, 1992; Reed, 1997; Elkington, 2004; Pava, 2007), it has been criticised for a lack of clarity and measurability of the individual components (Norman & MacDonald, 2004). Norman and MacDonald (2004) highlight that the TBL is a vague construct that in some instances is also interchangeably used with corporate social responsibility (CSR). The authors' main criticism is that there is a controversy 'in the promises suggested by the [TBL] rhetoric' (Norman & MacDonald, 2004, p. 244), which implies that it does not explicitly state how individual 'bottom lines' are measured and calculated (MacDonald & Norman, 2007). Pava (2007) responded to their article and emphasised that the TBL 'reporting is a metaphor to remind us that corporate performance is multi-dimensional' (p. 108). In other words, the author sees the term merely as an 'irony' (Pava, 2007, p. 108) that should encourage further investigations and provide an initial thought-provoking impulse that guides organisations and academics to think about sustainability and sustainable development.

Over the past decades, the fashion industry has witnessed a variety of movements that are fostered by increased awareness and education on sustainability. Media outlets have provided increasing coverage of fashion industry scandals, the reach of which has increased dramatically with social media platforms such as Twitter and Facebook. Issues reported are predominantly based on encounters between corporate power and non-governmental organisations (NGOs) (Skov, 2008). Examples of such encounters are the anti-sweatshop campaign that was launched against Nike and resulted in a global brand boycott in the 1990s. Since then Nike has come a long way and together with other sportswear brands such as Adidas and Reebok has made changes in its supply chain. Although some issues may still remain, the situation overall has improved (Birch, 2012). With consumers becoming increasingly aware and educated about social and environmental issues and able to gain information quickly and easily through the internet and social media campaigns, companies are forced to be more transparent and careful. Thus, fashion retailers are expected to not only check their supply chain regularly, but also take action on any issues if necessary in order to avoid scandals such as the more recent sweatshop allegations against Ivy Park sportswear (Oppenheim, 2016).

A brief snapshot of movements in the fashion industry is provided in Figure 13.1, which can be divided into social and environmental issues and mixed issues, which are seen to have led to the emergence of slow fashion.

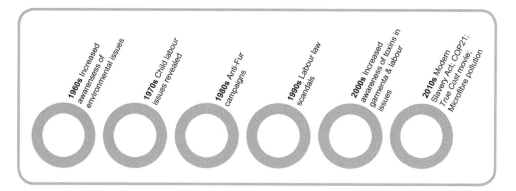

Figure 13.1   Movements leading to more conscious fashion

Slow fashion

As discussed, fast fashion and slow fashion can be seen as opposite ends of a spectrum; as such, slow fashion is neither mass-produced, nor does it have a fast stock turnover (Fletcher, 2008; Bourland, 2011). Organisations operating within the slow-fashion industry produce fewer collections than their fast-fashion counterparts, thereby actively seeking to move towards more seasonal distinctive collections (spring, summer, autumn, winter) (BSR, 2012). Although the term 'slow fashion' may be easily understood, there is a lot of debate within the academic literature about what it actually means, when it was established, whether it is a movement or developed into something more, and if it can actually exist or whether it is a plain idiosyncrasy. Some associate slow fashion with unfashionable items that are overpriced, whilst others refer to slow fashion as classic pieces that may still be 'relatively' cheap, depending on the price sensitivity of the consumer. Either way, the term 'slow fashion' is often interchangeably used with 'sustainable', 'eco-', 'ethical-', and 'green' fashion, thereby referring to fashion that has environmental and/or social aspects incorporated (Joergens, 2006; Henninger, 2015b; Henninger et al., 2016). Within the broader arch of 'slow fashion' there are key distinguishing points that are of interest.

Eco-fashion has previously had negative connotations, and was strongly associated with the hippie movement of the 1970s. Today eco-fashion is characterised by utilising bio and/or organic material; thus, 'eco-', 'bio-', 'environmentally friendly' and 'organic fashion' are often used interchangeably. The focus of here is on the environmental aspect of sustainability; whereby companies seek to reduce the negative impact that fashion items have on the natural environment (Niinimäki, 2010). *Ethical fashion* can be seen as an extension of eco-fashion in that it further considers social aspects as well as environmental considerations. As such, working conditions and well-being for both humans and animals are a key priority (Joergens, 2006). *Slow fashion* implies a change of the overall infrastructure in that operational processes are localised where possible and overall production reduced as garments are created in smaller batches. As such, it is often associated with higher costs as it provides a reflection of the true ecological and social costs (Fletcher, 2008). 'Sustainable fashion' is commonly used as an umbrella term; thus, for the purpose of this book, 'slow fashion' is used to refer to any type of fashion that features sustainability at its core.

Underpinning slow fashion is the promotion of ethical conduct, reduced fashion production, and purchasing quality over quantity when it comes to clothing (Fletcher, 2010; Ertekin & Atik, 2014). Companies committed to slow fashion actively empower their workers across the supply chain, as well as investing in innovative materials that have fewer negative impacts on the environment (Johnston, 2012). Slow fashion moves away from current industry practices of growth-based fashion, which requires a change in system thinking, infrastructure, and throughput of goods (Fletcher, 2010). Slow fashion is not simply just the opposite of fast fashion, but rather a philosophical approach to manufacturing garments (Clark, 2008; Henninger et al., 2016). Clark (2008) poses five ways that will promote a slow-fashion approach: (1) rethink the current hierarchical structures that exist between designer, producer, and consumer; (2) create timeless pieces that can be worn multiple times; (3) break the current associations of fashion with a specific image (e.g. luxury equals rich); (4) make fashion a choice rather than a mandate; (5) develop stronger relationships with workers and create a more collaborative approach.

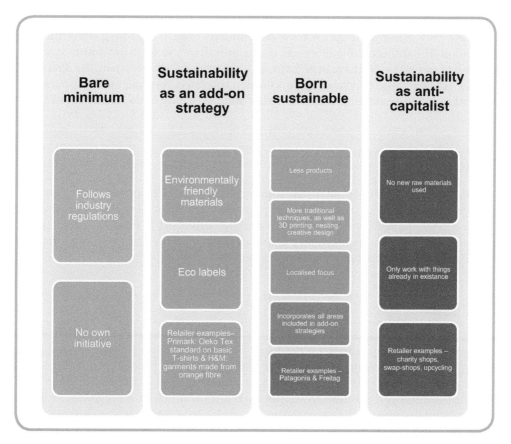

Figure 13.2   Interpretations of how companies can incorporate sustainability (Henninger 2015a)

Scandals and increased awareness have fostered some organisations to move away from the traditional interpretation of fast fashion (cheap, mass-produced) towards a slower fashion approach. Figure 13.2 provides a simplification of different approaches to incorporating sustainability in fashion organisations, ranging from only incorporating what is necessary and pushed upon the industry through regulations, to having an 'add-on strategy', to being 'born sustainable', and to seeing sustainability as 'anti-capitalist'.

Starting with the middle approaches first, the add-on strategies here imply that companies are actively trying to make changes that can lead to a more sustainable fashion industry. Despite the question of why companies have not acted faster and made changes that are seemingly obvious, it needs to be reinforced that the fashion industry is not only volatile, but also has complex supply chains. As such, making small changes, such as acquiring an eco label, can have huge implications on the supply chain, as checks need to be made in order to adhere to the acceptable quality level, and closer collaborations might be necessary in order to support suppliers in being able to fulfil and commit to these regulations. Add-on strategies are viable solutions for already established and, in particular, large retailers. Organisations that are currently set up have an opportunity to fully embed sustainability in the company's mission and vision and, as such, can be seen as being born sustainable. The bare-minimum approach and sustainability as anti-capitalist are two extreme positions. The *bare minimum* implies that the organisations are only making changes if these are enforced from a legal perspective through legislation. The anti-capitalist approach, on the other hand, seeks to not only reduce production of raw materials that can be harmful for the natural environment, but also reuse what is available, thereby changing how fashion is created. As such, fashion pieces may be unique due to availability of raw materials and the quality of the materials available.

Sustainable products

Due to the pressure to be more sustainable, buyers are having to consider new materials to incorporate into their ranges. Producing cotton uses a lot of water and pesticides, whereas synthetic materials such as polyester are derived from finite oil supplies and produce microplastics (as previously discussed). Therefore, alternative fabrics that are less harmful to the planet are now being explored.

What is a sustainable product?

Generally, eco-friendly fabrics are produced from crops that do not require pesticides or chemicals to be grown, use less water and energy to be produced and processed, and create less waste during production and processing and at the end of their lives. *Sustainable textiles* can also refer to man-made fabrics produced from renewable sources such as bamboo or wood. Some of the most popular eco-friendly fabric alternatives are listed below.

Lyocell

Lyocell was initially created in the 1990 and is produced from the wood pulp of trees. It is becoming a popular choice of sustainable fabric for fashion retailers due to its properties that not too dissimilar to those of viscose, and its affordability. Lyocell is fully biodegradable, so it will break down over time, and is created using a closed-loop process, which uses recycled water through solvent-spinning. Hence, Lyocell can be seen as a more sustainable and affordable alternative to the cotton or viscose often used to make shirts or blouses. High-street fashion retailer & Other Stories has incorporated Lyocell blouses into its latest product ranges, encapsulating its signature classic styling in a more sustainable way.

Organic cotton

Organic cotton is the most commonly used organic material for garments, mainly due to the fact that it has a lower environmental impact than regular cotton, as it uses fewer of the harmful chemicals and pesticides. It is also hypoallergenic. For these reasons, organic cotton is more expensive than regular cotton, and so buyers have to be prepared to pay higher costs, and often pass these on to the consumer. Yet, this has not put off even some value retailers such as Primark, whose sustainable cotton jeans are in the top five bestsellers of the whole business and cost the same as previously non-sustainable ranges, showing that they do not have to be more expensive (Whelan, 2019).

Vegan leather

Veganism has been a growing movement over the last decade, and, alongside the food industry, this trend has had a significant impact on the fashion industry. Vegan leather is an animal-friendly alternative to real leather and is often much more affordable. Vegan leather has become very popular in the last few years, helped by the strong advocacy of it by luxury designers such as Stella McCartney. Vegan leather bags and shoes are particularly popular. Indeed, even Dr Marten's iconic leather lace-up boots now provide a whole vegan range.

Recycled material

The majority of garments that are described as 'recycled' are recycled denim. Denim is particularly poor in terms of sustainability as it takes a lot of water to produce and creates a lot of pollution; therefore, by using recycled denim in the range, the buyer will reduce the amount of chemicals used, as well as the water consumption. As denim is such a durable material, and often a slightly 'distressed' feel is popular in terms of jeans, recycled denim is understandably an attractive option for fashion brands that wish to incorporate more sustainable lines. Levi's has done this successfully with its 'RE/DONE' line, and fast-fashion retailers such as ASOS have also incorporated many recycled denim items alongside their normal jeans ranges. Alternatively, some brands are being very innovative in their use of recycled materials. For example, the Adidas Parley range of trainers is created from ocean plastic waste, and Reformation has recycled fishing nets to create swimsuits, both of which deliver a strong message to consumers about the state of the planet.

Challenges in the fashion industry

Why do fashion companies engage with sustainability, apart from when it is necessary due to legislation? And how do they decide what needs to change? As is implicitly suggested, slow fashion can be produced in a variety of ways. Currently we are facing a key dilemma: with consumers becoming accustomed to fast stock turnovers, having been almost educated to pop into stores on a fortnightly basis and being able to expect new garments, accessories, and even make-up (BSR, 2012; Pasquinelli, 2012), reducing fashion cycles might be challenging and often economically not viable. Yet, key industry players including leading fast-fashion companies have highlighted that sustainability needs to be a top priority, as the current growth is seen to be 'unsustainable', with major social and environmental challenges.

Chapter 8 discussed how sourcing has shifted to countries that have low wages, which enables companies to cut costs. Aspects that are often not associated with these measures are social implications. Aside from debates that are currently in the media on what a living wage is, working conditions in developing countries are often not of the standard that would be expected in a developed country. This implies that workers not only have lower income than their counterparts in more developed parts of the world, but also work in conditions that can be rated as unsafe.

Is the obvious solution here to encourage buyers to only source garments that are made sustainably, and increase the price of the overall garments in order to overcome these social issues? Unfortunately, the answer is not as clear cut. Fashion supply chains are complex entities, with many workers relying on this income, even if the wages are low, as it is the best option available to them. From a consumer perspective, affordability is key; those who are living on the poverty line rely on fashion products to be affordable and fashionable. Without going into too much detail, being able to consume fashion and demonstrate what social grouping someone belongs to can be important for individuals, and as such, not being able to afford fashionable garments can have implications on well-being. Thus, fashion companies can be seen to walk a fine line between producing affordable garments that are not cutting corners and having negative ethical implications. Documentaries, such as the *True Cost* movie (2015), focus on some of the issues becoming more and more prominent in the fashion industry, thereby calling for action to be taken, such as the question of #WhoMadeMyClothes.

Yet, as a society, we are attracted by window displays, showcasing new trends and collaborations, as well as offers at a low price. It is increasingly common to go shopping on a regular basis and be up to date with trends. With T-shirts being sold for £2 or less on the high street, it is a bargain that many feel justifies purchasing in bulk. However, this mentality can have twofold environmental consequences: first, from a retailer's perspective, fast stock turnaround implies that any garments that are not sold within two weeks of being introduced into stores may need to be reduced in order to create room for new collections, thereby creating issues surrounding overstocking. Recent media reports have created a public outcry, scrutinising fashion companies for burning excess inventory that remained unsold. However, this is not just a high-street problem, but rather one across the industry, with renowned luxury fashion retailers having been named and shamed (e.g. Dalton, 2018; Siegle, 2018). Second, what is not as well known is the fact that fast fashion has been nicknamed 'throw-away fashion', as on the consumer side we are educated that garments are cheap and bargains can be made in store with 'sale season' being on all year round. The deflation of prices leads to consumers having an almost unrealistic idea in their mind of what it actually costs to make a fashionable item. Indeed, on average items are worn between three to seven times before being thrown away (Pithers, 2015; Šajn, 2019). It is generally accepted that garments are discarded relatively quickly, which leads to an increase in waste, particularly at landfills, as the average consumer bins 30kg of clothing and textiles per capita annually (EFF, 2008; WRAP, 2012).

According to Klepp (2001) there are five main reasons why products get discarded: (1) mass-produced garments are not always high-quality, and consumers may only get a few wears out of them before the product's overall performance fails, in terms of losing shape, being broken, or simply uncomfortable; (2) the twenty-first century has seen a rise of social media and with it peer pressure, and individuals feel they are unable to be seen wearing the same garment twice; (3) lifestyle changes can imply the 'need' to change wardrobes – examples here are starting a career path that expects a certain type of dress code, or changing body shape; (4) some items are simply bought as they were identified as cheap or part of an unwanted gift, and thus end up never being worn; (5) some items are associated with sentimental values, and remain in the possession of an individual even though they may not be worn.

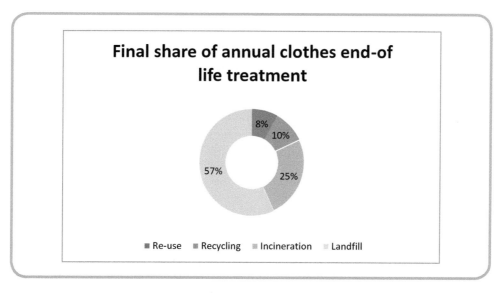

Figure 13.3   Final share of annual clothes end-of-life treatment

The Pulse Report (2017) identified that even though consumers may discard items by bringing them to charity shops, only 8 per cent get re-used, whilst 57 per cent of garments end up in landfill (Figure 13.3).

How can buyers and merchandisers be more sustainable?

Buyers could start by minimising the amount of harmful fabric used, and their creation of microplastics, replacing them with some of the materials discussed above to be more sustainable. Furthermore, in order to be more sustainable in terms of their product offering, buyers could stop using unsustainable materials such as coatings on jeans or real fur as part of their product range. However, buyers will need to be careful when eliminating certain types of products altogether that it does not negatively impact on their perceived brand positioning by consumers; for instance, they could be seen as 'less fashionable'. Buyers need to be aware of sustainable alternatives to materials and how they can incorporate them into their assortment. They also need to be more aware of their pricing, as eco-friendly products are not always more expensive. One of the perceived barriers for retailers of being more sustainable is often that it is too expensive and will have negative implications regarding the retailer's profit margin. However, in reality that is not always the case. Although some sustainable materials, such as organic cotton and bamboo, are more expensive than regular cotton, Lyocell products in particular are not more expensive than standard viscose products. Nevertheless, some brands are using the eco credentials to charge a premium price to customers and so have seen being more sustainable as an opportunity to maximise profits.

On the other hand, it is important to consider the implications of incorporating new materials into the product mix. Buyers will have to take the time to research the materials and potentially find a new supplier. With time being so precious due to the volatile nature of the fashion industry, this is adding a lot of extra pressure on them as it is unlikely that the other aspects of their role will be covered by someone else whilst they spend time researching alternatives. Moreover, if the buyer has to find a new supplier, then they will also need to build up their relationship with them, an aspect that is very important, as discussed in Chapter 8.

Other ways that buyers could be more sustainable would be to cut down on the amount of air miles that they do and the amount of water wastage that is produced in the buying cycle, especially in the sampling and fabric-testing stages. However, the nature of a garment means that there are often many processes involved in sampling and testing; thus, it will be hard for the buyer to be truly sustainable whilst doing their job effectively and ensuring quality control of items.

Whilst retailers are taking steps towards offering more sustainable products in their assortments, one of the biggest problems in fashion is its enormous contribution to landfill. The current mass production of garments is not sustainable. If there were fewer items produced then the current culture of throw-away fashion would be reduced and the material could be used for upcycling or recycling purposes. This implies that buyers/retailers need to consider the quick turnaround of new ranges and the number of new ranges/phases that they produce each year, as it is promoting a constant need for 'new-ness' on the part of the consumer, at huge cost to the environment.

Consumers now expect fast-fashion brands to drop new launches every month, even every week, rather than every season. Whilst there is such constant high demand for newness, a lot of it goes unworn. More than 50 per cent of fast-fashion items produced are disposed of by both consumer and retailer in under one year, leaving the UK with £34 billion worth of unworn clothes per year (Edited, 2018). Hence, the business model needs to change as whilst brands are producing far too many products, consumers will continue to buy far too much. So many garments are now being produced that charity shops and second-hand stores are completely overwhelmed and unable to sell it all. One way that brands could minimise this is through the implementation of new technology. Merchandisers could use new data and artificial intelligence to uncover how their products are performing in the market so that they can adjust their assortments, minimising the amount of product that they are delivering (Edited, 2018).

However, the solution is not that simple. If retailers reduce the quantities of items that they make available to sell then it may have a negative impact on their profit margins, making it an undesirable alternative for them to embrace. Despite the changes we have seen with retailers bringing in sustainable elements, the total amount of new product in the UK market is showing no signs of slowing down. Since 2014, retailers have not delivered fewer than 200,000 new styles a month (Edited, 2018). Hence, the number of 'new in' products greatly exceeds the number of products that are actually selling out, showing that the fashion industry has a long way to go before it will be anywhere near more sustainable.

CHAPTER SUMMARY

An increasing number of consumers have become more alert about the ethical and sustainability impacts and implications of their purchasing choices. It has been said that we are in an 'ethical era' where consumers will make more conscientious decisions based on the impact that their fashion products have (Joergens, 2006;

Shen et al., 2013). Ethical issues and sustainability issues must be addressed due to this growing pressure from consumers for more transparent supply chains. However, consumers may say one thing and do another, especially when they want to buy fashionable items at an affordable price. In times of economic uncertainty, consumer demand for cheap clothing remains high and the expectations are for immediacy or instant gratification in fashion-purchasing behaviour. The style and cost of the garment are often the decision-making factors, not its ethical credentials (Grose, 2012). Even if retailers use new materials and design garments to last longer, this will have a limited impact if consumers still discard these items prematurely based on trends.

Whilst there is still demand for newness, it is undeniable that the interest of consumers in sustainable fashion is growing and it is, therefore, something that brands can no longer afford to ignore. However, Henninger et al. (2016) point out that *sustainability and fashion* could imply an idiosyncrasy, as *fashion* suggests something that always changes, is trend-led, and thus may be discarded rather quickly. Contrarily, *sustainability* implies a long-term perspective, which further incorporates aspects of the social, environmental, and economic facets (Gardetti & Torres, 2014). This leaves us with the question: *is it possible for fast-fashion brands to actually be sustainable?*

References

Allen, T.F.H., & Hoekstra, T.W. (1994). 'Toward a Definition of Sustainability', in DeBano, L.F. & Covington, W.W. (eds), *Sustainable Ecological Systems: Implementing an Ecological Approach to Land Management*. Fort Collins, CO: Rocky Mountain Forest and Range Experiment Station, pp. 98–107.

Athwal, N., Wells, V., Carrigan, M., & Henninger, C.E. (2019). 'Sustainable luxury marketing: A synthesis and research agenda', *International Journal of Management Review*, 21(4): 405–426.

Baumgartner, R.J. (2009). 'Organizational culture and leadership: Preconditions for the development of a sustainable corporation', *Sustainable Development*, 17: 102–113.

Birch, S. (2012). 'How activism forced Nike to change its ethical game', 6 July, *The Guardian*, available at: www.theguardian.com/environment/green-living-blog/2012/jul/06/activism-nike.

Blanchard, T. (2018). 'Why microfibers are the new microbeads', 30 January, *Vogue*, available at: www.vogue.co.uk/article/why-microfibres-are-the-new-microbeads.

Bourland, J. (2011). 'What is slow fashion?', n.d., Slow Fashioned, available at: www.slowfashioned.com/archives/4909.

Browne, M.A., Crump, P., Niven, S.J., Teuten, E., Tonkin, A., Galloway, T., & Thompson, R. (2011). 'Accumulation of microplastic on shorelines worldwide', *Environmental Science & Technology*, 45(21): 9175–9179.

BSR (Business of a Better World). (2012). 'Sustainable fashion design: Oxymoron no more?' October, available at: www.bsr.org/reports/BSR_Sustainable_Fashion_Design.pdf.

Butler, S. (2018). '6,000 shops close in tough year for UK's high streets', 11 April, *The Guardian*, available at: www.theguardian.com/business/2018/apr/11/tough-year-high-street-internet-shopping-weak-pound.

Christopher, M. (2000). 'The agile supply chain: Competing in volatile markets', *Industrial Marketing Management*, 29(1): 37–44.

Clark, H. (2008). 'Slow + fashion – An oxymoron – Or a promise for the future…?', *Fashion Theory*, 12(4): 427–446.

Dalton, M. (2018). 'Why luxury brands burn their own goods', 6 September, *Wall Street Journal*, available at: www.wsj.com/articles/burning-luxury-goods-goes-out-of-style-at-burberry-1536238351.

Diesendorf, M. (2000). 'Sustainability and Sustainable Development, Chapter 2', in Dunphy, D., Benveniste, J., Griffiths, A., & Sutton, P. (eds), *Sustainability: The Corporate Challenge of the 21st Century*. Sydney: Allen & Unwin, pp. 19–37.

Edited. (2018). Where Do Trends Come From? Edited.com industry event.

EFF (Ethical Fashion Forum). (2008). 'Fast fashion, cheap fashion', n.d., available at: www.ethicalfashionforum.com/the-issues/fast-fashion-cheap-fashion.

Elkington, J. (2004). 'Enter the Triple Bottom Line, Chapter 1', in Henriques, A. & Richardson, J. (eds), *The Triple Bottom Line, Does It All Add Up?* London: Earthscan, pp. 1–16.

Epstein, M.J. (2008). *Making Sustainability Work: Best Practices in Managing and Measuring Corporate Social, Environmental and Economic Impacts (Business)*. San Francisco, CA: Berrett-Koehler.

Erskine, C.C., & Collins, L. (1997). 'Eco-labelling: Success or failure', *The Environmentalist*, 17: 125–133.

Ertekin, Z.O., & Atik, D. (2014). 'Sustainable markets: Motivating factors, barriers, and remedies for mobilization of slow fashion', *Journal of Macromarketing*, 35(1): 53–69.

FAO (Food and Agriculture Organization of the United Nations). (2007). 'Earth Summit and Agenda 21', n.d., available at: www.fao.org/sard/en/sard/2070/2071/.

FashionUnited. (2017). 'Boohoo, ASOS & Missguided pave the way for "ultrafast Fashion"', 24 May, available at: https://fashionunited.uk/news/fashion/boohoo-asos-missguided-pave-the-way-for-ultrafast-fashion/2017052424625.

Ferdows, K., Lewis, M., & Machuca, J.A.D. (2003). 'Zara', *Supply Chain Forum: An International Journal*, 4(2): 62–67.

Fletcher, K. (2008). *Sustainable Fashion and Textiles Design Journeys*. London: Earthscan.

Fletcher, K. (2010). 'Slow fashion: An invitation for systems change', *Fashion Practice: The Journal of Design, Creative Process and the Fashion*, 2(2): 259–266.

Gardetti, M.A., & Torres, A.L. (2014). *Sustainable Luxury: Managing Social and Environmental Performance in Iconic Brands*. Abingdon: Routledge.

Gigliotti, M., Schnidt-Traub, G., & Bastianoni, S. (2019). 'The sustainable development goals', *Encyclopedia of Ecology*, 4: 426–431.

Grose, V. (2012). *Fashion Merchandising*. New York, NY: Bloomsbury.

Gupta, S., & Gentry, J.W. (2018). 'Evaluating Fast Fashion', in Becker-Leifhold, C. & Heuer, M. (eds), *Eco Friendly and Fair: Fast Fashion and Consumer Behaviour*. Sheffield: Greenleaf, pp. 15–24.

Henninger, C.E. (2015a). *Corporate Identity in the Context of the UK's Green Slow-Fashion Industry and Micro-organisations*. PhD Thesis, University of Sheffield.

Henninger, C.E. (2015b). 'Traceability the new eco-label in the slow-fashion industry?– Consumer perceptions and micro-organisations responses', *Sustainability*, 7: 6011–6032.

Henninger, C.E., Alevizou, P.J., & Oates, C.J. (2016). 'What is sustainable fashion?', *Journal of Fashion Marketing & Management*, 20(4): 400–416.

Holmberg, J. (1992). *Making Development Sustainable: Redefining Institutions, Policy, and Economics*. Washington, DC: Island Press.

IISD (International Institute for Sustainable Development). (2019). 'What is sustainable development?' n.d., available at: www.iisd.org/sd/.

Joergens, C. (2006). 'Ethical fashion: Myth or future trend?', *Journal of Fashion Marketing and Management*, 10: 360–371.

Johnston, A. (2012). 'The first steps towards considerate design incorporating Cradle to Cradle principles', n.d., London College of Fashion, available at: http://

innovatingsustainablefashion.files.wordpress.com/2012/07/cradle-to-cradle_copenhagen_final_small.pdf.

Joy, A., Sherry, J.F., Venkatesh, A., Wand, J., & Chan, R. (2012). 'Fast fashion, sustainability, and the ethical appeal of luxury brands', *Fashion Theory*, 16(3): 273–296.

Klepp, I.G. (2001). 'Hvorfor går klær ut av bruk? Avhending sett i forhold til kvinners klesvaner. Why do clothes go out of use? Disposal in relation to women's dressing habits', n.d., SIFO, available at: www.hioa.no/extension/hioa/design/hioa/images/sifo/files/file48469_rapport2001-03web.pdf [Norwegian].

MacDonald, C., & Norman, W. (2007). 'Rescuing the baby from the triple-bottom-line bathwater: A reply to Pava', *Business Ethics Quarterly*, 17(1): 111–114.

McClonskey, M. (1999). 'The emperor has no clothes: The conundrum of sustainable development', *Duke Environmental Law & Policy Forum*, 9: 153–159.

Messinger, L. (2016). 'How your clothes are poisoning our oceans and food supply', 20 June, *The Guardian*, available at: www.theguardian.com/environment/2016/jun/20/microfibers-plastic-pollution-oceans-patagonia-synthetic-clothes-microbeads.

Miller, T.R. (2013). 'Constructing sustainability science: Emerging perspectives and research trajectories', *Sustainability Science*, 8(2): 279–293.

Mitchell, D. (1995). 'Learning the hard way: The EC and the eco-label', *European Environment*, 5: 165–170.

Niinimäki, K. (2010). 'Eco-clothing, consumer identity and ideology', *Sustainable Development*, 18(3): 150–162.

Norman, W., & MacDonald, C. (2004). 'Getting to the bottom of "Triple Bottom Line"', *Business Ethics Quarterly*, 14(2): 243–246.

Nunan, F. (2011). 'Does the Brundtland's sustainable development need a human dimension?', 14 November University of Birmingham: International Development Department Blog, available at: http://iddbirmingham.wordpress.com/2011/11/14/does-brundtland's-sustainable-development-need-a-human-dimension/.

Oppenheim, M. (2016). 'Beyonce's Ivy Park sportswear line denies claims its clothes were produced by "sweatshop workers paid £4.30 a day"', 18 May, *Independent*, available at: www.independent.co.uk/news/people/beyonces-ivy-park-sportswear-line-denies-claims-its-clothes-were-produced-by-sweatshop-workers-a7035926.html.

Pasquinelli, I. (2012). 'Could small be the new big for the fashion industry?', 3 April, *The Guardian*, available at: www.theguardian.com/sustainable-business/blog/fashion-industry-trends-innovation-small-business.

Pava, M.L. (2007). 'Response to "Getting to the bottom of 'Triple Bottom Line'"', *Business Ethics Quarterly*, 17(1): 105–110.

Petro, G. (2012). 'The future of fashion retailing: The Zara approach', 25 October, *Forbes*, available at: www.forbes.com/sites/gregpetro/2012/10/25/the-future-of-fashion-retailing-the-zara-approach-part-2-of-3/#1c1a31b67aa4.

Pirc, U., Vidmar, M., Mozer, A., & Krzan, A. (2016). 'Emissions of microplastic fibres from microfiber fleece during domestic washing', *Environmental Science and Pollution Research International*, 23(21): 22206–22211.

Pithers, E. (2015). 'Are you guilty of wearing things just once?' 14 June, *The Telegraph*, available at: www.telegraph.co.uk/fashion/style/are-you-guilty-of-wearing-things-once/.

Pulse Report. (2017). 'Pulse of the fashion industry', n.d., Global Fashion Agenda, available at: https://globalfashionagenda.com/wp-content/uploads/2017/05/Pulse-of-the-Fashion-Industry_2017.pdf.

Raar, J. (2002). 'Environmental initiatives: Towards triple-bottom line reporting', *Corporate Communications: An International Journal*, 7(3): 169–183.

Reed, D. (1997). *Structural Adjustment, the Environment and Sustainable Development.* London: Earthscan.

Reuters. (2018). 'Zara looks to technology to keep up with fast fashion', 15 June, Business of Fashion, available at: www.businessoffashion.com/articles/news-analysis/zara-looks-to-technology-to-keep-up-with-faster-fashion.

Robert, K.W., Parris, T.M., & Leiserowitz, A.A. (2005). 'What is sustainable development? Goals, indicators, values and practice', *Environment: Science and Policy for Sustainable Development*, 47(3): 8–21.

Roper, S., & Fill, C. (2012). *Corporate Reputation: Brand and Communication*. Harlow: Pearson Education.

Šajn, N. (2019). 'Environmental impact of the textile and clothing industry', January, European Parliament, available at: www.europarl.europa.eu/RegData/etudes/BRIE/2019/633143/EPRS_BRI(2019)633143_EN.pdf.

Shen, G., Richards, J., & Liu, F. (2013). 'Consumers' awareness of sustainable fashion', *Marketing Management Journal*, Fall: 134–147.

Siegle, L. (2018). 'Destroying unsold clothes is fashion's dirty secret. And we're complicit', 29 September, *Huffington Post*, available at: www.huffingtonpost.co.uk/entry/burberry-burn-clothes-fashion-industry-waste_n_5bad1ef2e4b09d41eb9f7bb0.

Skov, L. (2008). 'Creativity at work: Ethics and the fashion industry in West Europe', n.d., Creative Encounters, available at: www.researchnest.com/all_reports/13100175651ethics%20and%20the%20fashion%20industry%20in%20west%20europe.pdf.

Sustainable Angle. (2018). 'Future Fabrics Virtual Expo', n.d., available at: www.future-fabricsvirtualexpo.com.

The True Cost. (2015). Film. Directed by Andrew Morgan. Untold Creative/Life Is My Movie Entertainment, distributed by Life Is My Movie Entertainment/Bullfrog Films.

UNEP (UN Environmental Program) (n.d.). *The Trade and Environmental Effects of Ecolabels: Assessment and Response*, UNEP [online], retrieved from: www.uneptie.org/shared/docs/publications/Ecolabelpap141005f.pdf.

Von Schomberg, R. (2002). 'The objective of sustainable development: Are we coming closer?', n.d., European Commission Directorate General for Research, available at: ftp://ftp.cordis.europa.eu/pub/foresight/docs/fores_wp_0210.pdf.

WCED (World Commission on Environment and Development). (1987). *Our Common Future (The Brundtland Report)*. Oxford: Oxford University Press.

Weinswig, D. (2017). 'Retailers should think like Zara: What we learned at the August Magic Trade Show', 28 August, *Forbes*, available at: www.forbes.com/sites/deborahweinswig/2017/08/28/retailers-should-think-like-zara-what-we-learned-at-the-august-magic-trade-show/#105af1dd3e52.

Whelan, G. (2019). 'Primark still considering click and collect', 24 April, Drapers, available at: www.drapersonline.com/7035497.article.

WRAP (Waste & Resources Action Programme). (2012). 'Valuing our clothes: The true cost of how we design, use and dispose of clothing in the UK', n.d., available at: www.wrap.org.uk/sites/files/wrap/VoC%20FINAL%20online%202012%2007%2011.pdf.

14 The future of buying and merchandising

Introduction

This chapter will discuss what the future may be for fashion buying and merchandising. There are many challenges and opportunities that lie ahead for buyers and merchandisers, and whilst it is impossible to know exactly what is in store, there are certain trends and directions that are rising and will only grow in significance over the next decade or so. The predominant indicators for change are the emergence of more hybrid roles in buying and merchandising, technological developments, and sustainability. An overview of these three areas and how they will impact on the future of buying and merchandising will be provided in this chapter.

Learning outcomes

After reading this chapter you will be able to:

- Discuss the overall potential future direction of fashion buying and merchandising;
- Discuss the increasing trend towards hybrid roles in buying and merchandising;
- Explain how buying and merchandising has become a global role, and discuss the importance of cultural values and inclusivity in the role and responsibilities going forward;
- Discuss how technological developments could impact on the roles of buyers and merchandisers in the future;
- Discuss how sustainability could impact on the roles of buyers and merchandisers in the future.

Hybrid roles

The challenging retail climate, with ever-changing consumer demands and technological advancements, has dramatically changed the fashion buying and merchandising role since 2010. There has been a distinct move towards a more hybrid role than the traditional separate roles of buyers and merchandisers. The buyer of the future may well take on more of what was seen traditionally as the merchandiser's work (Jackson & Shaw, 2001) and vice versa, especially as there has been a move by most retailers to work as close to the season as possible in order to make the best product decisions. It will be interesting to see how this hybrid role develops in the future and what the key character-istics are in terms of skills, responsibilities, and experiences.

Technological skills and strong IT abilities will be essential for buyers and merchan-disers going forward. Their job roles will require them to be competent at using real-time data analytics systems and complex product lifecycle management systems as well as digital inventory, spreadsheet, and supply chain software. Thus, it is important that there is the professional development of buyers and merchandisers' IT skills from graduate level and throughout their career.

The development of social commerce, enabling social media platforms to now facil-itate purchases as well as content development and dialogue, has also demonstrated the need for close relationships to be formed between marketing, e-commerce, buying, and merchandising. Working in partnership will give a much stronger and bolder prod-uct and promotional strategy. Attention-grabbing content will be key, deployed on the right platform for each market, using persuasive calls-to action and, wherever possible, a seamless link to the checkout (BOF, 2019). Hence, in such a competitive industry, buyers and merchandisers must work much more closely with each other and other departments, particularly marketing, more than ever before in order to ensure that they accurately assess and meet consumer demand.

Globalisation and inclusivity

Over the last couple of decades, as a result of the challenges of growth stagnation in domestic markets, fashion retailers have looked to emerging markets for expansion and many have had significant successes in these countries (McCormick et al., 2014). Selling product ranges globally stretches and challenges the skillset of the buying and merchandising teams, as they need to ensure that the products ranges are culturally appropriate. Although retailing internationally exposes brands and products to new markets and consumers, this also means the buying and merchandising teams need to be aware of logistical, legal, and cultural challenges on top of the ones in their current and original markets. Furthermore, as fashion retailers test these growth markets, they will have to strengthen their brands and upgrade their operations to be able to create value (BOF, 2019).

Fashion buying and merchandising must also be more inclusive going forward in terms of the products and the ranges that they develop. Recently, there has been a cultural drive for inclusivity and diversity across fashion companies, not only in terms of leader-ship and visible positive action but also through communications and product offerings. This movement is gaining momentum, and thus making diversity the norm, rather than a special initiative, will ultimately have the biggest impact on corporate culture (BOF, 2019). Modest clothing, trans-gender-friendly and adaptive garments are soon going to be recognised as core product lines within the big fashion brands. Again, this will challenge the skill sets and knowledge of buyers, merchandisers, and garment technol-ogists. Therefore, it is crucial that any strategic direction within product development is supported with further staff development and training in order to ensure that they pos-sess the appropriate levels of expertise. Society certainly expects greater representation of difference, and there is also a strong economic case for diversity (BOF, 2019). This is highlighted through the rise of gender-neutral fashion, such as ASOS's Collusion range, and through the increased use of Black, Asian and minority ethnic models, transgender models, and models with disabilities to promote fashion brands and their products.

Furthermore, consumers themselves are now radically different to their counterparts from 15, ten, or even five years ago. Experience, ease, and emotion are rocketing their way to the top of shoppers' wish lists. Generation Z are now coming of age and are changing the market place and fashion industry as we know it. The whole concept of the Netflix generation is that they are used to getting what they want, when they want it, how they want, via whatever channel (Sunderland, 2019). Therefore, retailers need to become much more agile and shift their cultures in order to keep up with the opportunities.

Technology

Technology will continue to shape the roles and responsibilities of buyers and merchandisers, as it has done so incredibly dramatically over the last few decades. The design process is and will become further heavily dependent on digital technology. Body-scanning technology and 3D software applications are making it so that the range-planning and product-development processes are becoming increasingly done in 3D form rather than 2D sketches and CAD drawings. This may mean that in future there will be more accurate representations of garments much earlier on in the buying cycle, cutting down on lead times and fabric waste/air miles with fewer samples needed. The more accurate representations of garments in 3D form rather than 2D form will also help to improve communications between the buyer and the supplier, especially if there are language barriers, meaning there will be fewer errors and a stronger relationship developed between the two.

Technology has also enabled supply chains to become more customer-centric and allowed retailers to provide quicker responses to consumer demand than ever before. Consumers are demanding greater levels of personalisation in their consumption experience, resulting in companies having to re-assess their business models in order to become more responsive to consumer needs and demands (Roncha, 2019). This is changing the product-development process as well as the responsibilities of the buying and merchandising roles. Further digitisation of the supply chain could eventually lead to customised products being ordered through smartphones which are sent directly to a factory where a machine will cut the material to the correct shape and then a skilled seamstress will finish it (Twigg, 2017). Indeed, Christopher et al. (2004) predicted that the industry will soon have to embrace on-demand manufacturing in order to survive, which holds truer today than ever before. This is already starting to come to fruition, with major retailers investing in this technology. In April 2017, Amazon was awarded a patent for an on-demand manufacturing system that enables it to produce clothing very quickly, after the order has been made by the customer (Hounslea, 2017). Amazon acquires the fabric and has a 3D printer, cutting machine, and assembly line in place in order to make basic garments such as T-shirts, meaning that every step from manufacture to purchase, to delivery, can take place on one day (McGregor, 2019). Furthermore, the orders are made in batches based on customer order time and delivery location in order to save time on multiple deliveries (Hounslea, 2017; McGregor, 2019). For the buyer, this means they will need to negotiate with the supplier to get the fabric in advance but not have to wait for it to be manufactured, cutting down on lead times and potentially saving on waste. However, this type of operation may not be feasible for smaller companies to replicate.

Automation technology has seen the replacement of humans on the factory floor with robots, seeing a move away from the sourcing model of low-cost-labour countries with those that have these technologies in place and are closer to home geographically in order to minimise lead times (Twigg, 2017). Retailers are moving their sourcing closer to home in a process known as near-shoring or re-shoring in order to reap the benefits of speed-to-market and shorter lead times. Technology is innovating continuously and the sourcing model of chasing the cheapest wage that has dominated the fashion industry for so long may soon be overhauled due to technological advances in manufacturing along with customers' prioritisation of speed over cost. Consumers now want instant gratification and, in an industry dominated by social media influencers, speed-to-market and customisation have become more important to some fast-fashion retailers than cost alone (Twigg, 2017). The digitisation of the supply chain and the use of automation to create customised products is facilitating this for all sectors of the industry, from fast fashion to luxury (Twigg, 2017).

Sustainability

Some of the biggest challenges that are affecting, and will continue to affect, buyers and merchandisers in contemporary fashion retailing are sustainability and ethical issues. With corporate social responsibility (CSR) now high on the agenda for all fashion retailers, the pressure is often on buyers to ensure that the initiatives set at the top management level are carried out. This is often not easy. In fact, a lot of the time the top-line corporate message projected to stakeholders actually conflicts with the internal pressures that buyers and merchandisers are under, creating a juxtaposition. For instance, M&S has done a lot of work regarding sustainability and CSR over the last few years, such as introducing training and protection for workers in its suppliers' factories (Sutherland, 2018). However, it was uncovered that its buyers were not using those factories as the cost price of garment manufacture was a lot higher, which would negatively impact on its profit margins. This highlights the pressure that there is on buyers to perform well at their job and maximise profits for the retailer. In the end, M&S introduced a reward scheme where buyers were evaluated and rewarded based on the number of products bought from those factories (Sutherland, 2018), yet this was only after it had been reported in the media This highlights the important role of the media and sophistication of consumers, in that information can be broadcasted in real time and to a global audience on a 24/7 basis, making it essential for retailers to deliver on their promises.

A report from the Environmental Audit Committee Enquiry into Sustainable Fashion (Environmental Audit Committee, 2019) shows that the cheap prices that consumers are paying for fast-fashion items are coming at considerable cost to the environment and the exploitation of vulnerable factory workers. Slave labour, child labour, and poor working conditions are still very much in existence in the global supply chain, many years after the 2013 Rana Plaza factory collapse (see Chapter 8). Furthermore, the exploitation of workers is also apparent close to home, with a Channel 4 *Dispatches* programme (2017) showing that garment workers in Leicester, in the UK, were being paid less than the minimum wage. This shows that the exploitation of workers not only needs to be addressed in developing countries, but also in developed countries, such as the UK, especially with an increase in brands re-shoring now for faster lead times. Going forward, buyers will need to thoroughly vet factories and educate factory owners who are not treating workers fairly. Yet, this takes time, and in an already time-pressured role, buyers will need to be provided with this time, or maybe another role will need to be created in order to conduct it. Either way it is no longer an issue that can be swept under the carpet by any type of fashion retailer, from super-fast-fashion to luxury. The need and demand for a transparent supply chain is greater than ever; thus, retailers and brands need to be able to prove to their customers that they can trust them to sell them clothes that have not been involved in an exploitation of the workforce.

Fashion is now the second-biggest polluter in the world after the oil industry (Henninger et al., 2016, 2019; Hinsliff, 2019), and so something needs to be done to tackle this problem. Despite some modest progress made, fashion has not yet taken its environmental responsibilities seriously enough. Fashion players need to swap platitudes and promotional noise for meaningful action and regulatory compliance whilst facing up to consumer demand for transformational change (BOF, 2019). Buyers need to consider new materials to use in the production of garments, reducing their use of microplastics that are commonly found in materials such as polyester that are polluting the waterways. Lyocell and bamboo are two attractive alternatives to cotton and are much more environmentally friendly, yet still have challenges that need to be considered (e.g. use of chemicals in creating viscose). However, it will take time and effort for buyers to learn about these new sustainable materials, along with potentially more sampling and fabric testing in the first instance as they are different to fabrics that they have worked with before. There is also currently a gap between 'sustainable items' and 'fashionable items', which begs these questions: *why can sustainable items not also be fashionable? And why does this connotation exist?* Retailers should be able to use these more sustainable materials in their regular product range to make fashion items, and not just classics and basics. More investment in research and development of sustainable materials and their properties, as well as testing and sampling regarding making more complex garments out of them, needs to take place.

Furthermore, in order to be more sustainable, buyers need to look into producing items that are better-quality and that will last longer in order to stop the culture of disposable fast fashion. However, this has implications regarding the cost of garments and the retailer's profit margin. A survey conducted by trade show group ITE found that retailers estimated that they would have to increase their selling prices by an average of 19 per cent to make sustainable products but that their consumers would only be willing to pay 9 per cent more (Whelan, 2019). Thus, although fashion retailers are now starting to engage in more sustainable policies and ways of working, they will ultimately still prioritise profits over responsible retailing, which is not helped by the fact that consumers are often unwilling to choose a sustainable product over a cheaper product (Chapman, 2018).

Yet, designing garments to last longer is only one aspect of the problem, as this will have a limited impact if consumers still discard these items prematurely based on trends. Hence, the business model itself needs to change, which will not be an easy task, as behaviours need to change on both sides – industry and consumer. Fashion retailers are producing far too many products, encouraging customers to buy far too much. This implies that buyers/retailers need to consider the quick turnaround of new ranges and the amount of new ranges/phases that they produce each year, as this is promoting a constant need for 'newness' on the part of the consumer, at increasing cost to the environment. Buyers need to produce fewer garments in terms of quantities and reduce the number of product ranges, or product assortments within them, that they bring out. However, this will have a negative impact on profit margins and so is unlikely to happen.

Future retail models

Rental fashion and subscription models are changing the nature of ownership of fashion, yet these models have not become mainstream, with only a few companies having recorded popularity and large profit margins (e.g. Rent the Runway, Girl Meets Dress). The life span of fashion products is now being lengthened, as preowned, refurbished, repair, and rental business models continue to evolve and flourish. Consumers have demonstrated an appetite to shift away from traditional ownership to newer ways in which to access products in many different industries (BOF, 2019). This can be seen in the way that many people now listen to music (through streaming services rather than purchasing actual songs or CDs) and through the way that many people choose to rent a car as opposed to buying it outright. The application of the renting model to fashion is still in its infancy, but companies such as Rent the Runway and Hirestreet are gaining traction and increasing profits year-on-year so this may soon become much more mainstream. Nevertheless, whilst these ways are delivering a much-needed transparent, sustainable, and innovative way to shop, they will also challenge the buyer and merchandiser in terms of new responsibilities. Renting products will require a completely different sourcing strategy and will introduce new methods of stock management and product development. Furthermore, issues such as damaged goods and hygiene management will create new problems that buyers and merchandisers will need to consider.

CHAPTER SUMMARY

Eco-tech fashion will one day replace traditional fashion with the effective collaboration between the players of fashion at different levels, including the designers, manufacturers, technologists, corporates, retailers, and consumers (Agarwal, 2019). The impact of super-fast fashion and the speed at which technology is developing has witnessed a move towards more hybrid roles in buying and merchandising. Technology is continuing to transform the supply chain and buyers and merchandisers must be willing to adapt and learn how to use new platforms and software that will become integral to their job role.

The global fashion industry is extremely energy-consuming, polluting, and wasteful. By not engaging properly in a more sustainable buying cycle and product development, fashion retailers leave themselves at risk of a PR disaster such as the Rana Plaza scandal, and they may also get left behind by their competitors who are adopting more sustainable practices and appealing more to consumers are becoming increasingly aware of sustainability and the negative environmental impact of fast fashion, and therefore demanding change (Chapman, 2018).

References

Agarwal, V. (2019). 'Technology, Sustainability, and Consumer Expectation: New Ways of Thinking about Future Fashion', in Chakrabarti, A. (ed.), *Research into Design for a Connected World. Smart Innovation, Systems and Technologies*, vol. 134. Singapore: Springer, pp. 403–411.

BOF (Business of Fashion). (2019). *The State of Fashion 2019*, January, available at: www.mckinsey.com/industries/retail/our-insights/ten-trends-for-the-fashion-industry-to-watch-in-2019.

Chapman, M. (2018). 'Why sustainability is business critical', 2 November, Drapers, available at: www.drapersonline.com/7032668.article.

Christopher, M., Lowson, R., & Peck, H. (2004). 'Creating agile supply chains in the fashion industry', *International Journal of Retail & Distribution Management*, 32(8): 367–376.

Dispatches: Undercover – Britain's Cheap Clothes. (2017). TV documentary. Produced/directed by Kristin Hadland. Blakeway/Channel 4 News.

Environmental Audit Committee. (2019). 'Fixing fashion: Clothing consumption and sustainability', 19 February, UK House of Commons, available at: https://publications.parliament.uk/pa/cm201719/cmselect/cmenvaud/1952/1952.pdf.

Henninger, C.E., Alevizou, P.J., & Oates, C.J. (2016). 'What is sustainable fashion?', *Journal of Fashion Marketing & Management*, 20(4): 400–416.

Henninger, C.E., Bürklin, N., & Niinimäki, K. (2019). 'The clothes swapping phenomenon – When consumers become suppliers', *Journal of Fashion Marketing & Management*, 23(3): 327–344.

Hinsliff, G. (2019). 'Fast fashion is eating up the planet – and this feeble government enables it', 18 June, *The Guardian*, available at: www.theguardian.com/commentisfree/2019/jun/18/fast-fashion-environmental-audit-committee-polluting-industry.

Hounslea, T. (2017). 'Amazon trials private label lingerie brand in UK', 21 April, Drapers, available at: www.drapersonline.com/news/amazon-trials-private-label-lingerie-brand-in-uk/7020302.article.

Jackson, T., & Shaw, D. (2001). *Mastering Fashion Buying and Merchandising Management*. London: Palgrave.

McCormick, H., Cartwright, J., Perry, P., Barnes, L., Lynch, S., & Ball, G. (2014). 'Fashion retailing, past, present and future', *Textile Progress*, 46(3): 227–321.

McGregor, K. (2019). 'The high-tech new standard for sampling', 17 April, Drapers, available at: www.drapersonline.com/retail/the-high-tech-new-standard-for-sampling/7035281.article.

Roncha, A. (2019). 'Fashion Brand Management', in Varley, R., Roncha, A., Radclyffe-Thomas, N., & Gee, L. (eds), *Fashion Management: A Strategic Approach*. New York, NY: Red Globe Press, pp. 105–130.

Sunderland, E. (2019). 'Redefining retail: The high street in 2020 and beyond', 18 October, Drapers, available at: www.drapersonline.com/7037998.article.

Sutherland, E. (2018). 'If we can do it, everyone can: M&S's sustainable cotton mission', 3 July, Drapers, available at: www.drapersonline.com/business-operations/sustainable-fashion/if-we-can-do-it-everyone-can-mss-sustainable-cotton-mission/7031009.article.

Twigg, M. (2017). 'Is the old sourcing model dead?', 14 September, Business of Fashion, available at: www.businessoffashion.com/articles/global-currents/is-the-old-sourcing-model-dead.

Whelan, G. (2019). 'True sustainability not achievable until 2021', 1 August, Drapers, available at: www.drapersonline.com/7037003.article.

Index